Choosing Charters

Choosing Charters

Better Schools or More Segregation?

EDITED BY

Iris C. Rotberg
Joshua L. Glazer

TEACHERS COLLEGE PRESS

TEACHERS COLLEGE | COLUMBIA UNIVERSITY

NEW YORK AND LONDON

Published by Teachers College Press, 1234 Amsterdam Avenue, New York, NY 10027

Copyright © 2018 by Teachers College, Columbia University

Cover design by Jeremy Fink. Cover photo by Frankie's / Shutterstock.

Library of Congress Cataloging-in-Publication Data is available at loc.gov

Names: Rotberg, Iris C., editor. | Glazer, Joshua L., editor.
Title: Choosing charters : better schools or more segregation? / edited by
  Iris C. Rotberg, Joshua L. Glazer.
Description: New York, NY : Teachers College Press, [2018] | Includes
  bibliographical references and index. |
Identifiers: LCCN 2017055040 (print) | LCCN 2018002442 (ebook) | ISBN
  9780807776872 (ebook) | ISBN 9780807758991 (pbk.) | ISBN 9780807759004
  (case)
Subjects: LCSH: Charter schools—United States. | Segregation in
  education—United States. | Education, Urban—United States. | Educational
  change—United States.
Classification: LCC LB2806.36 (ebook) | LCC LB2806.36 .C6 2018 (print) | DDC
  371.05—dc23
LC record available at https://lccn.loc.gov/2017055040

ISBN 978-0-8077-5899-1 (paper)
ISBN 978-0-8077-5900-4 (hardcover)
ISBN 978-0-8077-7687-2 (ebook)

Printed on acid-free paper
Manufactured in the United States of America

25   24   23   22   21   20   19   18   8   7   6   5   4   3   2   1

For Maya, Sam, Eva, Madeline, Tess, Emma, Quinn, and Hayden,
who perhaps decades from now will know how this saga turns out.
—I.C.R.

For my parents, Mickey and Penina,
first teachers to whom I owe my love of education.
—J.L.G.

The best laid schemes o' Mice an' Men gang aft agley.

—Robert Burns

Contents

Acknowledgments

The focus of this book originated from extensive discussions over many years with colleagues and students. Their insights and firsthand experience with school choice inspired our interest in the field and informed our perspectives on the issues.

We are grateful to the book's authors, whose earlier publications played a major role in our choice of the book's themes and who generously gave their wisdom, their scholarship, and their time in writing the chapters and providing input on the overall framework of the book. Cynthia Orticio was an invaluable partner as we produced the manuscript. We are indebted to her for her expert management of the editorial process throughout the book's preparation and for her innumerable contributions that greatly enhanced the professionalism of the manuscript submitted to Teachers College Press.

The work of two doctoral students at The George Washington University made important contributions to the book. Tara Dunderdale conducted an extensive review of research on school choice in the United States and internationally for an earlier article, "Charter Schools and the Risk of Increased Segregation," by Iris Rotberg, which set the context for this book, and Breanna Higgins gathered research evidence and data that were particularly useful in addressing the issues in Chapter 4.

We are grateful to Brian Ellerbeck, executive acquisitions editor at Teachers College Press, for extending the invitation that led to the book, for his many perceptive comments as we developed the concept of the book, and for the expert and gracious support he and his colleagues provided in the production of the book.

Part I

THE CONTEXT

CHAPTER 1

Setting the Stage

Iris C. Rotberg and Joshua L. Glazer

> Speak the speech . . . trippingly on the tongue. Nor do not saw the air too much with your hands thus, but use all gently, for in the very torrent, tempest, . . . whirlwind of passion, you might acquire and beget a temperance that may give it smoothness. . . . Be not too tame neither, but let your own discretion be your tutor.
>
> —William Shakespeare, *Hamlet*

No issue in education better exemplifies the tensions in achieving a just education system than the struggle to integrate U.S. schools. The 60th anniversary of *Brown v. Board of Education* in 2014 was a reminder of the limited progress that has been made since the Brown decision ended *de jure* segregation. Although statements by political leaders honored the Brown decision, little was said about the role of federal and state policies in the expansion of charter schools and the impact of those policies on segregation.

Advocates have long held that charter schools coupled with the competitive pressures of the market would lead to the development of schools more focused on the needs of students, increased innovation, and greater efficiency. The extent to which this has happened is highly contested in the current research literature, as is the evidence on whether students who attend charter schools perform better than those in traditional public schools.

What does seem clear, however, is that the growth of charter schools has had social consequences that go beyond test scores. The expansion of charter schools since their beginning in 1992 has helped to transform the U.S. educational landscape. The extent of these changes has been remarkable. Beyond the more than 3 million students that currently learn in charter schools, the charter movement has given rise to new breeds of organizations, new forms of district management, new philanthropic priorities, and a new political discourse about education. Along with these changes has come a new set of questions that are of great importance for policymakers, researchers, and the public.

A primary concern, of course, is whether charter schools lead to better educational outcomes and, if so, for whom and under what conditions. But salient questions go beyond the effects on student learning outcomes. Other areas of concern include how charter schools (and school choice generally) shape the private and public goals of education, the impact on integration along racial, ethnic, and socioeconomic lines, the underrepresentation of students with disabilities and English-language learners, the role of religion in publicly funded schools, the prospect for increased racial and ethnic segregation in currently integrated school districts, the challenges faced by charter schools that have full responsibility for operating district schools, and other topics that lie at the intersection of education, politics, and social policy.

Moreover, it is argued that the growth of charter schools and charter school networks has increased the fragmentation of the education system and made it more difficult to integrate schools. Ironically, as some state leaders have attempted to bring educational and organizational coherence to state and local systems, the expansion of charter schools may be further splintering an already fractured system. This issue is often overlooked in the debate about the effectiveness of charter schools. The consequences are particularly apparent in high-poverty urban districts, which have experienced the greatest growth in charter schools.

This book brings together authors who represent different perspectives to assess the policy implications of the expansion of charter schools and charter school networks. The chapters analyze the link between charter schools and segregation and describe how segregation plays out in different situations and in different ways: by race, ethnicity, and income; by disability and language-minority status; by culture, language, and religion; by instructional programs designed specifically for low-income and minority students; and by the challenges faced by charter schools in guaranteeing students the civil rights and other legal protections required under federal laws. In addressing these issues, the book moves beyond the simplistic question of whether charter schools work to explore broader questions about the purposes of education and the role of public policy in shaping the educational agenda. The book was completed during the first year of the Trump administration, and many of the issues discussed are directly relevant to the administration's policies as well as to public policy more generally.

Part I sets the context for the book. Jeffrey Henig discusses the expansion of charter schools in the context of broader changes in education policy and argues that charter schools have thrived in part because they are aligned with these changes. James Harvey describes the impact of concentrated poverty and segregation on educational opportunities and questions whether the focus on charter schools provides an effective response to these underlying problems.

The book's second part, "Choices," focuses on the impact of the growth of charter schools and charter management organizations. Iris Rotberg introduces this section with an overview of how the expansion of charter schools in high-poverty urban districts exacerbates segregation, increases resource inequalities, and leads to different instructional methods in high-poverty schools as compared to schools attended by affluent students. Wagma Mommandi and Kevin Welner focus on the incentives that have led many charter schools to limit access and diversity, as well as on positive steps taken by others to encourage open access. Gordon Lafer describes the financial incentives that have encouraged some charter schools to rely on "blended learning" instructional methods and shows the implications of these methods for educational equity. Joshua Glazer, Diane Massell, and Matthew Malone report on a study of the Tennessee Achievement School District, which shows the challenges faced by charter school operators who have become responsible for the functions typically performed by school districts. Roslyn Mickelson, Jason Giersch, Amy Hawn Nelson, and Martha Bottia report on a study of Charlotte-Mecklenburg Schools, which concludes that the threat that middle-class white parents would leave the traditional public schools to enroll in charter schools has discouraged the adoption of desegregation plans. Adam Gamoran and Cristina M. Fernandez review the research literature and find that although the achievement effects of charter schools vary highly across the nation, the effects for some charter schools in high-poverty urban districts are more consistently positive. Brenda Shum describes the problems faced by charter schools in guaranteeing the civil rights and other legal protections afforded students under federal laws. Suzanne Eckes, Nina Buchanan, and Robert Fox discuss the constitutional issues that charter schools raise with respect to the separation of church and state and give examples of cases in which these issues have been considered. Jennifer Ayscue and Erica Frankenberg conclude Part II with an analysis of how school choice plans that incorporate diversity goals might further integration by breaking the link between school and neighborhood segregation.

Henry Levin leads off Part III, "Education in a Pluralistic Society," with an analysis of how the current shift from public to private purposes of education threatens to undermine the goal of democratic preparation. Janelle Scott analyzes the popular assertion that "education is the last remaining civil right to be secured and that charter schools and school choice policies are the most powerful manifestation of that right." The concluding chapter gives an overview of the main issues discussed in the book and describes the various forms that segregation takes, their compounding effects, and their educational and social consequences.

CHAPTER 2

Charter Schools in a Changing Political Landscape

Jeffrey R. Henig

"Would you tell me, please, which way I ought to go from here?"
"That depends a good deal on where you want to get to," said the Cat.
"I don't much care where—" said Alice.
"Then it doesn't matter which way you go," said the Cat.
"—so long as I get SOMEWHERE," Alice added as an explanation.
"Oh, you're sure to do that," said the Cat, "if you only walk long enough."

—Lewis Carroll, *Alice in Wonderland*

Things change.

When Minnesota enacted the nation's first charter school law in 1991, the conception of what charter schools stood for was fuzzy at the edges. At that time, it was reasonably accurate to talk about a dominant public school attendance zone–based system in which the normal expectation was that children would be assigned to a school based solely on where they lived. Charters were seen by early proponents as a way to loosen that tie between where one lived and where one's children went to school, to introduce more variety into the array of schools available to select from, to delegate a wider range of decisions to school- and community-based actors, to inject healthy competition into a system that was largely shielded, and to empower parents. A dominant image of charter schools at that time was of a small, stand-alone school launched by a group of dedicated educators and parents convinced that, freed from the homogenizing effects of top-down bureaucracy, they could develop new and exciting ways to develop young minds.

Today, of course, the charter phenomenon is widespread, institutionalized, and increasingly overseen by large for-profit or nonprofit networks that operate across multiple districts or states. In some local districts, the majority of public school students are now in charters, and the proportion of the nation's students in charters continues to rise (National Alliance for Public Charter Schools, 2016).[1] In some instances, charters have been incorporated into portfolio models, where districts or states manage a diverse array of schools, and a small but growing number of places have single-enrollment systems where parents can apply to both charter and district schools with a single form (Bulkley, Henig, & Levin, 2010; Hill, Campbell, & Gross, 2013; Marsh, Strunk, & Bush, 2013; Tully, 2017). Charter proponents are a distinguishable interest group active in state and local politics, in some instances able to mobilize substantial numbers of charter parents to exert pressure on policymakers (Shapiro, 2014).

During the same time that Minnesota and a pioneering cluster of additional states began to enact charter school legislation, the broader landscape of education politics and policy also was shifting in ways that were not yet fully recognized or understood. Some of these centered on education governance institutions, particularly those that related to the distribution of power and activity within our federal system. Localism—long a defining element of the American public education system—was beginning to lose some of its hold. States, traditionally content to leave the nuts and bolts of both funding and steering schooling to local districts, were taking a greater interest, shouldering more of the costs and more aggressively requiring districts to meet specified standards. Some of the changes related to policy and values priorities. After decades of deference toward state rights, the federal government was tentatively expanding its involvement. The focus of debate was shifting from inputs and equity to accountability for outcomes. Some changes related to the mix of involved actors. A private sector of education service providers was expanding, and general-purpose politicians, such as mayors and governors, were becoming more involved in schooling decisions previously delegated to education specialists. Yet much of this was still inchoate and had the appearance of constituting incremental change.

This chapter traces the evolution of the political landscape for the charter school experiment. Although it is not possible to do so with precision, the chapter attempts to distinguish changes that emerge from the charter phenomenon from those that are rooted in other, broader sources of social change. While charters have indisputably been important, I suggest that much of the impetus has also involved broader and somewhat independent shifts and that charters have thrived in part because they aligned with these broader forces. This discussion suggests some possible implications for what we can anticipate in the era of the Every Student Succeeds Act (ESSA) and President Trump.

THE LANDSCAPE OF EDUCATION GOVERNANCE, POLITICS, AND POLICY CIRCA 1990

The three decades from 1960 to 1990 were hardly placid when it came to American public education. The 1960s were marked by the passage of the Elementary and Secondary Education Act—which substantially increased the flow of funds from Washington and, over time, provided leverage by which Congress could steer state and local actions—and by tremendous turmoil as the federal government began to more aggressively pursue the local desegregation agenda that had been announced but only sporadically implemented by the *Brown v. Board* decision. The 1970s were marked by an expansion of the desegregation agenda into states and communities that had not previously operated dual school systems, by the ascension of blacks to leadership positions in school boards and superintendent positions in a number of large central-city school systems, and by the emergence of a handful of Southern "education governors" who emphasized improving schools as a tool for economic development. The 1980s saw the release of *A Nation at Risk* and other business and civic-led commission reports challenging Americans' complacency about the quality of U.S. public schools, the emergence of an emphasis on excellence and measureable outcomes in place of the previous emphasis on equity and resources, and the development of a standards-oriented school reform partnership among the White House, governors, and business leaders culminating in a coalition of governors at the Charlottesville Education Summit in 1989.

Despite these efforts, by the end of the 1980s a number of reformers had concluded that none of these changes had gained much traction. These dissatisfied reformers called for upping the ante by either replacing the hortatory, voluntary promotion of standards with strong accountability regimes or substantially increasing the pressures of supply and demand. Chubb and Moe, in *Politics, Markets, and America's Schools*, for example, offered a theoretical argument for why all reform efforts would fail unless we moved away from democratic control, which they characterized as the source of bureaucratic rigidity and mediocre educational performance, to a program of government-funded "scholarships" that families could use in private schools (Chubb & Moe, 1990).

Helping to promote this emerging set of dynamics was a coterie of political actors relatively new to education politics. "The forces that galvanized economic concerns and dissatisfaction with schooling into an action agenda were neither professional educators nor the general public, but rather 'spokesmen in the business community, media, and government'" (Murphy, 1990, p. 19; also see Fuhrman, 1987). While they might not have induced the broad impact they hoped for, they did manage to throw shadows on the traditional notion that locally controlled schools were a core and distinct strength of the American system. Importantly, these new actors were less wedded to the habits and ingrained practices of local districts than the school boards, professional educators, and even parents who had dominated education politics previously.

ENTER CHARTERS

In 1991, Minnesota became the first state to pass enabling legislation for charter schools. Although not entirely detached from national dynamics and policy entrepreneurs,[2] this original effort was hatched by local actors responding to that state's context, culture, and traditions, animated by a pragmatic desire for a less rigid, bureaucratic, one-size-fits-all vision of public education, and committed to a vision of collaborative school-based decisionmaking in which both teachers and parents played critical roles.[3]

But the national context quickly grabbed hold. Frustrated with the perceived failure of more conventional reform approaches, those who supported a more radical market-oriented restructuring of the system fastened on charters as a testing ground for their ideas about how parent choice and interschool competition would work in the field. President Reagan had twice tried to get Congress to establish a federal school voucher, and between 1981 and 1996 school voucher referenda had been proposed (and defeated) in five states and Washington, DC. Charters did not raise the same concerns as vouchers did about dismantling public education or government entanglements with religious schools. Because popular support for the traditional model of public school system was resilient, even those who preferred vouchers saw a tactical advantage in switching their emphasis to charters in order to assuage fears that choice would favor the already advantaged by "creaming" off white, affluent families.

In states that passed charter laws, proponents struck a set of political bargains: accepting laws that established lottery-based admission to oversubscribed schools (so charters could not enforce their own selection criteria), prohibiting charters from charging tuition beyond the public funding that accompanied the student (so that schools could not use the tuition add-on as a way to exclude poorer families), and agreeing that charter students would take state-mandated achievement tests (so responsible officials would know whether charters were delivering on their promise of improving educational outcomes).

But the economic theories that made market advocates believe choice would improve education also made them deeply wary that public bureaucracies would do everything in their power to maintain a dominant role. They assumed that teachers, elected school boards, and others with vested interest in the existing system would battle to protect it by blocking charters or making it more difficult for charters to compete.

Accordingly, organizations that supported charters as a form of market-based accountability fought for state policies that placed fewer obstacles in the way of opening charter schools and lightened the oversight and regulatory pressure that government could apply. The result was the institution of formal provisions that multiplied the number and types of charter authorizers, allowed certain nonprofit groups or institutions of higher education to issue charters, gave applicants opportunities to appeal to the state if initially turned down at the local level, and granted longer periods between charter renewals.

Many school boards, public school teachers, and liberals also saw charters as a first step down a journey toward vouchers and more complete privatization, and their political strategies were based on that belief. They mobilized to fight charter laws and, when they failed to accomplish that, to have caps placed on the number of charters and limits placed on the amount and type of funding they could receive. Yet, broader shifts already underway meant that these traditionally powerful groups no longer held center stage. Governors, state legislatures, business leaders, public interest groups, and education reformers looking for a way to break out of the tinkering mode were a more receptive audience, even if they did not share the market advocates' unabashed enthusiasm for the restorative powers of simple supply and demand.

Democrats, importantly, were divided on charter schools. While some hoped to cram the charter genie back into the bottle, others returned to the vision of the Minnesota founders and sought to reclaim the argument that charters represented sensible governmental flexibility, decentralization, and a pragmatic strategy for diversifying schooling options. So-called New Democrats, including then President Bill Clinton, embraced charters while rejecting both vouchers and the premise that market forces were reliable alternatives to good government. They argued that charters could be a valuable tool in the government's arsenal for improving education. But they also noted that public officials would need to ensure they were self-consciously designed, effectively managed, and rigorously held accountable.

MATURATION OF THE CHARTER SECTOR

One of the most memorable, if not successful, slogans in automobile advertising was the 1988 commercial touting the new and purportedly hipper "not your father's Oldsmobile." The charter sector, similarly, is different today than it was in the decade of its origin. In this section I review some major changes in the spread, scale, and form of charters, with special attention to changes in the constellation of animating ideas, supporting constituencies, and governance attributes. Had charter schools developed according to the dictates of standard market models, these changes would have reflected the pull and tug of parental demand. While there is no straightforward way to disentangle all of the factors that account for how charters have evolved, I'll suggest that parent demand played less of a role than supply-side factors, which need to be understood in reference to politics and government.

Spread

Both supporters and critics of charters have emphasized the impressively fast and broad expansion of the charter sector. Supporters emphasize this as a measure of the popularity of the concept; critics see it as a reflection of political maneuvering by a tight group of funders and advocates promoting a broad privatization agenda.

It's useful to distinguish the several levels at which this expansion occurred. The first is the cross-state dissemination of charter school laws. Minnesota passed the first law in 1991, and California followed in 1992; by 1995, 19 states had charters, and by 1999, 36. Analysts have attempted to account for the pattern of adoption with some limited success (Holyoke, Henig, Brown, & Lacireno-Paquet, 2009; Shober, Manna, & Witte, 2006; Wong & Langevin, 2007). While efforts to statistically model the process have been disappointing, some general patterns seem to

Figure 2.1. Charter schools (bars, with scale of 0 to 8,000) and students (line, with scale of 0 to 3.5 million), 1996–2016.

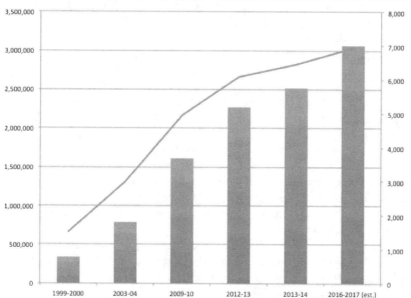

apply. First, neither the speed of adoption nor the favorability that the legislation shows toward charters is determined solely by need, region, culture, or the tendency to imitate neighboring states. Second, political factors—including governance structure, party, ideology, and interest group alignments—play important roles. Third, state-specific factors, including the presence and skills of legislative proponents and the history and perceptions of past reform efforts, seem important, as does some degree of idiosyncrasy. Some of the states that embraced charters most enthusiastically are traditionally conservative market-oriented places like Arizona, but charters are widespread also in states like Michigan with a strong union history and California with a generally liberal political culture. Some of the laggards in charter adoption are states like Alabama and West Virginia that have generally been slow to invest in public education and have poor test scores to show for it, but some, like Kentucky, have been leaders in other aspects of education reform or, like Vermont, generally perform well on the National Assessment of Educational Progress exams.

Growth in the Number of Schools and Students

Figure 2.1 illustrates a second dimension of expansion: the growing number of both charter students and charter schools in the United States for the 20-year period of 1996 to 2016. Within states, the number of schools is somewhat related to how long the charter legislation has been in effect, but longevity is not the sole driver of growth. Arizona and Michigan passed their laws in 1993 and have high numbers of charters (547 and 301, respectively), while New Mexico and Massachusetts, which launched charters the same year, have just 99 and 81, respectively. Kansas, which enacted charter school legislation in 1994, had only 10 charter schools statewide as of 2016–2017.

More than longevity per se, growth in the number of schools is a factor of growth within a small proportion of the states that allow it. For example, in 2016–2017, more than two-thirds of the over 3 million students enrolled in charter schools nationwide were accounted for by the top 10 states.[4] Some of this might reflect state-specific family demand for choice, but it's more likely influenced by the relative conduciveness of the policy environment. Some states, such as Arizona and Michigan, simply make it easier to open charters. Others have been more careful in phasing in charters; Massachusetts is a prime example. Policy conduciveness is partly a question of whether state law makes it easy or hard to form charters (e.g., by multiplying the number and type of authorizing bodies or conversely setting a formal limit on the number allowed) and whether it is aggressive in oversight and intervention.

Whether charters proliferate in a particular state is also a question of whether state funding is sufficient to convince charters that running a school is economically viable. Most states provide somewhat less public funding for charters than they do for their traditional public schools, but that gap is much smaller for some (e.g., Indiana, New Mexico, California, Texas) than others (e.g., Louisiana, District of Columbia, New Jersey, New York, Missouri) (Batdorff, Maloney, May, Doyle, & Hassel, 2010). Some states have large gaps but still provide quite substantial per-pupil funding for charters (e.g., District of Columbia, New Jersey), while others (e.g., North Carolina, Texas) have small gaps because they relatively underfund both charters and traditional schools.

Concentration in Particular Districts

Since the early years of the charter movement, there has been considerable ambiguity around the question of what proportion of public schools should or would be charters. For the first two decades, this ambiguity was more a theoretical problem than a real one because the concentration of charters everywhere was too small to represent either a pressing threat or a prod to systemic change. By the 2015–2016 school year, however, 190 districts had a market share at or above 10%; 44 at or above 20%; 17 at or above 30%; 6 at or above 40%; and 3 (New Orleans, Detroit, Flint) above 50% (National Alliance for Public Charter Schools, 2016). This concentration represents a third way that charters' maturation has led to expansion.

Theories of market behavior might provide a partial explanation for this tendency of charter schools to cluster in some districts. For example, locating near other charter schools might save money on marketing if the overall concentration serves to increase visibility, or concentration might give them more clout as a lobbying force advocating around shared interests, such as free or low-cost access to underutilized district school buildings. But market conditions don't suffice to explain the concentration of charters in particular places. Also important were deliberate efforts by some within the charter community to strategically maximize impact by concentrating on expansion within a smaller number of localities where prospects for success were high. The Walton Family Foundation (2017), for example, is explicit in targeting its giving geographically.

Scale

Related to its spread, but distinct in some important ways, are the changes in the scale of provision within the charter sector. The early evolution of the charter school phenomenon was tied to the image of small schools and the intimacy and responsiveness they were expected to provide. Along with dissemination of the charter school model has come expansion in scale. This change in scale is expressed first as growth in the average enrollment of individual schools; many charters initially served a grade level or two and then added additional grades. In 2003–2004, for example, 71% of charter schools had fewer than 300 students; 10 years later, in the 2013–2014 school year, 52% did. Over that same 10-year period, the percentage of charter schools with 500 or more students increased from 13% to 24% (National Center for Education Statistics, 2017).

But the more meaningful shift in scale has to do with the development of charter school networks. A substantial number and growing proportion of charter schools are associated with management organizations that run multiple schools in networks. These networks may be for-profit or nonprofit and may be loosely or tightly controlled. By convention, for-profit management organizations typically are referred to as education management organizations (EMOs), while those that are nonprofit are referred to as charter management organizations (CMOs)—although some authors discuss all as CMOs.

As of the 2011–2012 school year, about 36% of charter schools and about 44% of charter school students were in schools run by EMOs or CMOs (Miron & Gulosino, 2013). EMOs and CMOs together accounted for 16% of newly opened charter schools in 2010 and 39% in 2014, with the percentage accounted for by stand-alone charters dropping from 83% to 61% (Mead, Mitchel, & Rotherham, 2015).[5]

Even more than with geographic concentration, concentration within networks has the potential to provide certain economies of scale. But some indications suggest that the relative growth of networks might also reflect the preference of intermediaries such as funders, authorizers, and local districts. Some major funders of charter networks emphasize their goal of quickly expanding, and network leaders have expressed frustration at being pushed to open new schools at a faster pace than they would like. "If we had opened one school a year, many foundations would not have paid any attention to us," one CMO leader put it. "Funders and other organizations think it's great if you have a high-performing school but want to see if you can do it again" (Lake, Dusseault, Bowen, Demeritt, & Hill, 2010, p. 36). It also appears that both charter authorizers and school districts that employ a portfolio model (more on this later) may prefer working with networks because of their established reputation, perceived reliability, and the fact that they typically have philanthropic support that augments their capacity.

Institutionalization: Portfolio Models and Contracting Regimes

In place of a direct relationship between individual schools and parents, the charter movement has moved toward a stable and institutionalized relationship between charters (often drawn from large networks) and central districts or, in a few cases, states. The term generally applied to these relationships is "portfolio management models" (PMMs).

In PMMs, the central office overseeing public schools shifts away from a top-down posture of regulatory oversight of a system of similarly configured, geographically assigned schools and instead takes on the role of managing school supply. Key elements of the shift include establishing a performance-based accountability system within which a diverse set of schools operate with substantial autonomy; closing or otherwise intervening when schools fail to meet outcome objectives; systematically recruiting, developing, and contracting for new providers; and cultivating public school choice (Bulkley, 2010; Bulkley & Henig, 2015). The PMM concept effectively situates the central district office as a key gatekeeper, mediating between local needs and demands on the one hand and external pressure and resources on the other.

Since PMMs establish a contracting relationship with districts, it is in large measure the district to which they must "sell" themselves and to which they must respond. Although there is a chance that districts will opt not to renew their relationship with specific charters, the relationship is more stable, rule-bound, and predictable than that characterizing raw market relationships where firms sell to disparate individual consumers. To the extent that districts embed charters as part of their operation, they may become dependent on charters for the capacity they provide.

The point is not that PMMs are alien to real-world markets; they resemble various forms of public–private partnerships, such as private vendors that occupy public buildings to provide a service, such as food sales or wireless service or gas at highway rest areas. What's important to understand, however, is that the market relationships are embedded in governance systems and mediated between providers and government rather than in an idealized consumer provider model. That means that change over time will not depend only on how charters meet parents' perceived needs, but also on intricate relationships among politicians, interest groups, public bureaucracies, and voters.

CONCURRENT CHANGES IN THE EDUCATION LANDSCAPE: GOVERNANCE, POLITICS, AND POLICY

The growth and maturation of the charter sector is one important component of changes in the nation's education landscape, but it is by no means the only important change. The past 25 years have witnessed several other broad shifts that are conceptually distinct from charters. It's almost inarguable that these shifts affect one another—sometimes complementing, sometimes competing, and sometimes generating unanticipated interaction effects—but the ways that they do so have not been well explored. In this section I briefly summarize some of the important concurrent changes in the broader education landscape, including the growing role of the federal government, high-stakes accountability, the growth of the private education sector, and the expanding role of general-purpose rather than education-specific government and political actors.

Many of these broader changes have been supported by the same groups that have promoted charter schools and share some core principles. In conventional discourse, the ideas are often linked by the term "school reform." Some opponents link them as elements in a "privatization" movement, and some scholars have used terms like "market-oriented" or "incentivist" to characterize an underlying rationale and supportive constituency (Burch, 2009; Lubienski, Scott, & DeBray, 2014; Ravitch, 2013). But historical concurrence might not be the same as linked fates; in some instances, the theoretical rationales differ between charters and these other phenomena, and in some instances the political alignments may be tactical and historically contingent rather than natural and permanent.

The Growing Role of the Federal Government

The initial impetus toward charters and choice was led by states and came amidst the general centralization of authority within states at the expense of traditional deference to localism. In many instances, state legislatures pursued charters (or occasionally vouchers) out of mistrust of local districts and a sense that the reform impulse needed to be embedded elsewhere. While the federal government played a supportive role, centralization did not flower until the No Child Left Behind (NCLB) legislation of 2001 and the subsequent supercharging of the federal role via Race to the Top and the aggressive use of waivers under President Obama (Hess & Eden, 2017; McGuinn, 2006, 2014; McGuinn & Manna, 2012).

The relationship between the charters movement and this growing federal role is complex. Although they occurred more or less simultaneously and shared some political sponsors, the core ideas behind choice and centralization are not complementary. The central values emphasized by charter proponents included decentralization (from districts to schools), responsiveness to locally variant needs and desires, and resistance to bureaucracy and hierarchical chains of command. For many Republican proponents of choice, the alliance with the White House was opportunistic and contingent, predicated on the president's support of charters rather than a natural alignment between a stronger federal government role and their goal of charter growth.[6] For many Democrats, the alliance also was tactical, rooted in both a desire to forestall more dramatic forms of marketization (via vouchers) and in a battle inside the party on adopting a more attenuated commitment to public employee unions. Such opportunistic and tactical alliances of otherwise strange bedfellows make for a shaky foundation. Latent cleavages between charter proponents and proponents of a strong national government leadership role began to reveal themselves in the run-up to the passage of ESSA and have the potential to unwind further depending on developments under President Trump (Henig, Houston, & Lyon, 2017).

High-Stakes Accountability

Just as centralization predated charter schools but then accelerated subsequently, so too did accountability. The state-led standards moment, which flowered in the 1980s, precipitated the shift in attention from inputs to outcomes and initiated the development of testing and data systems to monitor district performance. In 1991, when the charter movement was born, this accountability impulse remained relatively weak, and the data systems to bring it to fruition were not yet in place. The 1980s accountability movement also focused more on students—and whether their test scores would allow them to graduate from high school—than it did on teachers, districts, or states.

NCLB escalated the accountability movement and gave the federal government more leverage over states, districts, and schools. It also contributed to the development of longitudinal student-level data systems that made it possible to isolate—albeit with questionable reliability and precision—the independent impact of teachers. Under President Obama and Department of Education Secretary Duncan, this technical possibility graduated to a federal priority to prod states and districts to hold teachers accountable for student educational outcomes.

Here, again, there was a tactical and contingent alliance. Charter proponents accepted accountability as a price of admission in the 1990s, and many believed that outcome data would dramatically support their cause. Over time, it became clear that test score data failed to show the consistent superiority of charters. While some charters and charter networks performed well, there was minimal and contested evidence of a large and consistent charter sector advantage and consistent evidence that some charter schools—like some traditional public schools—were failing and dysfunctional (Henig, 2008). In the face of this evidence, the alliance between true market-oriented supporters and those animated by a vision of a well-regulated charter system began to fray. Some charter proponents (e.g., the National Association of Charter School Authorizers and the Thomas B. Fordham Foundation) recognize that choice and competition are not sufficient—and can be damaging—unless combined with clear regulation and authorizer expertise and capacity. Others (e.g., Betsy DeVos) take the position that overregulation is the greater threat and favor a charter sector that is more akin to the voucher ideal, recognizing that some bad schools will emerge but confident that parent exit will suffice to put them out of business.

Growth of the Private Education Sector

Some private investors and for-profit companies have long dreamed that they could carve off for themselves a substantial piece of the K–12 $600 billion public education investment. In 1991, as Minnesota was launching the charter school movement, for-profit school firms such as Education Alternatives Inc. and Edison Schools Inc. (now EdisonLearning) were beginning to come to the fore. That year, Chris Whittle, who would soon launch Edison Schools, was proclaiming that within 15 years he would start 1,000 schools, educating as many as 2 million students (Kleinfield, 1991). Five years after the first charter school legislation was enacted, *Education Week* was proclaiming that "Wall Street is discovering the business of education." In mid-February 1996, Lehman Brothers hosted its "first annual" education conference, bringing together "some of the hottest companies in school management, software, child care, postsecondary education, and corporate training face to face with investment bankers and fund managers looking for opportunities to profit from what Lehman Brothers and others describe as a $619 billion education market in the United States" (Walsh, 1996, para. 4).

Political resistance and market realities have made this expansion of private involvement slower and less complete than some boosters predicted, but as others have detailed, the march toward a greater role for private providers has been steady (Abrams, 2016; Burch, 2009; Ravitch, 2013). Education technology firms pulled in $1.25 billion in venture investments in 2013, and a successor to the Lehman Brothers conference attracted over 2,000 attendees and nearly 300 presenting companies in 2014 (Fang, 2014).

While early narratives discussed a Walmart-like franchise in which for-profit providers would offer full-service schools, the shape of privatization differed from this image in at least three ways. First, rather than full-service provision, the real growth has been in the provision of a wide array of supplemental services, including management and budgeting, curriculum, test design and analysis, and professional development. Second, in some areas—notably charter school management, teacher training, and teacher and principal certification—nonprofit providers have rivaled or eclipsed for-profit companies.[7] Third, rather than competing in a market comprising providers and families, private providers—not just charters but also publishers, testing companies, providers of supplemental education services, and professional development firms—are more often in partnership or contracting relationships with schools, districts, or states (Bulkley & Burch, 2011; Burch, 2009).

This expansion of private-sector involvement was helped along by two other shifts in the education landscape: growing centralization and the accountability movement. As Burch observed, some of the impetus grew out of NCLB's predecessors: the Improving America's Schools Act (1994) and Goals 2000, both of which prodded states in the development and use of data for accountability purposes, opening up a niche for private firms with greater technical capacity and the ability to leverage investment in one state's systems to offer similar services to other states. NCLB took this to a higher level.

Especially in some places, and especially early on, charters offered an important market for the entry of private providers. For example, Rocketship, a nonprofit charter network that emphasizes personalized instruction via technology, used software from Dreambox Learning to provide students one-on-one math instruction for 2 hours per day. Dreambox is a for-profit company with $18 million in venture capital support (Simon, 2012). Charters could do this in part because they are less constrained than elected school boards by the pressure to contract with groups with local roots and by political sensitivity around the notion of working with companies that "profit off kids."

Growing Role of General-Purpose Governance

A final broad shift in the American educational landscape is the growing role of general-purpose government as distinct from school-specific governance institutions such as local school districts and state boards of education. This shift is manifested at all levels of our federal system, as seen in the growing movement toward mayoral control of schools, the assertion for formal and informal authority by governors, and the greater visibility of education in national presidential campaigns and agendas.

General-purpose officials feel less allegiance to traditional education institutions, interest groups, and ideas, and they have played a role in the speedy embrace of charters (Henig, 2013, chap. 4). The roots of this broad governance shift predated the emergence of charters; for example, states began providing governors a stronger role in the selection of state boards of education in the middle of the 20th century and stronger roles in appointing chief state school officers in the mid-1970s. But the most visible element in the shift away from school-specific governance institutions has been the contemporary move to mayoral control, which was kicked off in Boston in 1992 and in Chicago in 1995.

The charter movement has strategically sought to take advantage of its readier access to general-purpose governance venues. From the beginning, charter advocates sought laws that embedded chartering authority in institutions outside local districts. In places like New York City and Washington, DC, charter proponents have allied with those pushing for mayoral control specifically because they expected them to be more accommodating to their interests. Foundations that have supported the expansion of charter schools have also systematically targeted cities with mayoral control of schools (Reckhow, 2012).

IMPLICATIONS AND PROJECTIONS

The rapid expansion, evolution, and institutionalization of charter schools occurred against a broader landscape of education politics and policy that was shifting concurrently and just as dramatically. These two dynamics certainly were related, but the interrelationship is complex. The rhetoric supporting charters and the broader array of reforms was largely cut from the same cloth—including elements of market choice and competition and outcome orientation combined with a fundamental critique of traditional local districts, bureaucratization, and unions. This rhetoric, though, papered over some important differences in animating values and ideas: Charters as constructed in the United States are less a manifestation of free markets than of public–private partnerships, quasi-markets in which governance institutions, government capacity, and politically shaped policies play at least as great a role as do interactions between school providers and families.

The political constituencies backing the charter and overall education reform movements also substantially overlapped. They included free market advocates, private education service providers, foundations, so-called New Democrats, some civil rights organizations, elements of the business community, many charter school families, and deep-pocketed individual donors. While this movement could hold together when framed in opposition to a resistant status quo, its constituent groups held quite different visions of the alternative they favored—different in the commitment to funding, to democratically controlled institutions, and to emphasizing public versus private aspects of education. There are good reasons to believe that the charter movement's successes and supporters at times have lent legitimacy and political tailwinds to other changes in the education landscape, such as partial displacement of local control, high-stakes teacher and school accountability, and the growing role of general-purpose institutions and politicians. But the causal direction also seems at times to run in the other direction, with strong White House leadership, pressure of accountability, private-sector involvement, and the growing influence of general-purpose arenas making for a more hospitable environment for the growth of charter schools. Charters have thrived in part because they aligned with these broader forces.

What lessons can we draw from this complicated interplay, and what might it imply in terms of likely developments in the era of ESSA and President Trump? The big lesson, in my view, is not particularly new and is not specific to charter schools. It is rather an affirmation of the difficulty of disentangling correlation from causation, proclaimed rationale from motivating strategy, and general tendency from historical contingency when assessing complex phenomena still in the process of unfolding. Policy initiatives that coincide are not necessarily linked. When they are promoted using similar arguments, that might not be because they share the same underlying theory. When constituencies join hands, their grip may be loose and provisional.

Deciphering what this might mean for the future of charters is made especially difficult by the unusual degree of uncertainty that currently marks the political landscape. Some broad shifts reviewed in this chapter likely will continue to unfold, but others are subject to reversal. Consider the issue of centralization within our federal system. The passage of ESSA signaled that, as the Obama administration was coming to a close, Congress wanted to apply the brakes to the centralization of education policy, and candidate Trump's strong rejection of the Common

Core and strong affirmation of state rights and local control seemed to signal the same. Yet President Trump's bold statements about how his administration will lead a systemic, choice-oriented redesign of K–12 education leaves it unclear whether we are entering a period of decentralization or simply one in which central authority is pushed in a different direction. The crystal ball is similarly cloudy when it comes to accountability. If states are freed from the Bush/Obama visions of accountability, does that mean that outcome-based accountability will wane as a driving force, or will fiscally pressed states lean even harder on test-based accountability as a tool for doing more with less? On the face of it, the Trump/DeVos team seems a likely ally for a much more expansive private-sector role, especially when it comes to higher education. But political resistance to for-profit education remains potent at the local level, and if we are genuinely heading toward a return to greater local discretion, that may prove an important obstacle. Both ESSA and the Trump approach seem to reinforce the shift from education-specific to general-purpose governance and politics, marking the strong role of Congress and the president while leaving at the margins education professionals and the governance institutions in which they have been most influential.

The unstable and uncertain landscape does not tell us what *will* happen to the charter phenomenon, so much as it hints at the tactical complexities faced both by charter proponents and those who continue to see charters as a threat to their vision of public education. In this context, I expect that the strange bedfellow nature of the school choice coalition—the coalition that has incorporated supporters of vouchers and of charters; supporters of both loosely and carefully regulated charters; and supporters of pragmatic and incremental expansion of choice and those who see choice as a vehicle for radical and rapid systemic change—will be truly tested. Those favoring a more market-driven vision of charters will be tempted by the new landscape to push hard to reinvigorate a movement that they feel has become too institutionalized and tamed by partnership with government. Those favoring a more pragmatic, incremental, and carefully regulated expansion of chartering may look to lie low and do their best to keep charters outside the treacherous currents of ideology and partisanship, possibly even expanding their alliances with traditional public schools as an anchor. Given that the election of Trump had little if anything to do with the issue of K–12 schooling, if the market advocates win out, it will be evidence that the broader landscape has pulled the choice movement in its wake. If the pragmatic, low-visibility strategy prevails, it might suggest that the contemporary charter phenomenon is sufficiently mature, sheltered, protected, and distinct that it can set its own course even on a wind-swept plain.

NOTES

1. There is at least some indication that the rate of growth may be leveling off (Lake, 2017).

2. Although his precise role is the subject of contention, Albert Shanker, then president of the American Federation of Teachers, visited the state in October 1988 and shared some of his own ideas about the potential for charters to lead to a more innovative and teacher-responsive model for schools. See Kahlenberg (2007) and, for a contrasting view, Peterson (2010).

3. This section draws on some of my previous writing (e.g., Henig, 2013, 2017).

4. This is the author's calculation based on "Estimated Charter Public School Enrollment, 2016–17" (National Alliance for Public Charter Schools, 2017).

5. EMOs accounted for 4% in 2010 and 15% in 2014; CMOs accounted for 12% in 2010 and 24% in 2014.

6. On opportunistic federalism, see Conlan (2006).

7. For a discussion of the conditions under which nonprofits have advantages over for-profits, see Muldoon (2013).

REFERENCES

Abrams, S. E. (2016). *Education and the commercial mindset.* Cambridge, MA: Harvard University Press.

Batdorff, M., Maloney, L., May, J., Doyle, D., & Hassel, B. C. (2010). *Charter school funding: Inequity persists.* Retrieved from cms.bsu.edu/-/media/WWW/DepartmentalContent/Teachers/PDFs/charterschfunding051710.pdf

Bulkley, K. E. (2010). Introduction: Portfolio management models in urban school reform. In K. E. Bulkley, J. R. Henig, & H. M. Levin (Eds.), *Between public and private: Politics, governance, and the new portfolio models for urban school reform* (pp. 3–26). Cambridge, MA: Harvard Education Press.

Bulkley, K. E., & Burch, P. (2011). The changing nature of private engagement in public education. *Peabody Journal of Education, 86*(3), 236–251.

Bulkley, K. E., & Henig, J. R. (2015). Local politics and portfolio management models: National reform ideas and local control. *Peabody Journal of Education, 90*(1), 53–83.

Bulkley, K. E., Henig, J. R., & Levin, H. M. (Eds.). (2010). *Between public and private: Politics, governance, and the new portfolio models for urban school reform.* Cambridge, MA: Harvard Education Press.

Burch, P. (2009). *Hidden markets: The new education privatization.* New York, NY: Routledge.

Chubb, J. E., & Moe, T. M. (1990). *Politics, markets, and America's schools.* Washington, DC: Brookings Institution Press.

Conlan, T. (2006). From cooperative to opportunistic federalism: Reflections on the half-century anniversary of the Commission on Intergovernmental Relations. *Public Administration Review, 66*(5), 663–676. doi:10.1111/j.1540-6210.2006.00631.x

Fang, L. (2014, September 25). Venture capitalists are poised to "disrupt" everything about the education market. *The Nation.* Retrieved from www.thenation.com/article/venture-capitalists-are-poised-disrupt-everything-about-education-market/#

Fuhrman, S. H. (1987). Education policy: A new context for governance. *Publius, 17*(3), 131–143.

Henig, J. R. (2008). *Spin cycle: How research is used in policy debates: The case of charter schools.* New York, NY: Russell Sage Foundation/Century Foundation.

Henig, J. R. (2010). Portfolio management models and the political economy of contracting regimes. In K. E. Bulkley, J. R. Henig, & H. M. Levin (Eds.), *Between public and private:*

Politics, governance, and the new portfolio models for urban school reform (pp. 27–52). Cambridge, MA: Harvard Education Press.

Henig, J. R. (2013). *The end of exceptionalism in American education: The changing politics of school reform.* Cambridge, MA: Harvard Education Press.

Henig, J. R. (2017, January). Charter schools and democratic accountability. *The State Education Standard, 17,* 26–29.

Henig, J. R., Houston, D. M., & Lyon, M. A. (2017). From NCLB to ESSA: Lessons learned or politics reaffirmed? In F. M. Hess & M. Eden (Eds.), *The Every Student Succeeds Act: What it means for schools, systems, and states* (pp. 29–42). Cambridge, MA: Harvard Education Press.

Hess, F. M., & Eden, M. (Eds.). (2017). *The Every Student Succeeds Act: What it means for schools, systems, and states.* Cambridge, MA: Harvard Education Press.

Hill, P. T., Campbell, C., & Gross, B. (2013). *Strife and progress: Portfolio strategies for managing urban schools.* Washington, DC: Brookings Institution Press.

Holyoke, T. T., Henig, J. R., Brown, H., & Lacireno-Paquet, N. (2009). Policy dynamics and the evolution of state charter school laws. *Policy Sciences, 42*(1), 33–55.

Kahlenberg, R. (2007). *Tough liberal: Albert Shanker and the battles over schools, unions, race, and democracy.* New York, NY: Columbia University Press.

Kleinfield, N. R. (1991, May 19). What is Chris Whittle teaching our children? *New York Times.* Retrieved from goo.gl/qI1TkJ

Lake, R. (2017, February 17). *Is charter school growth flat-lining?* [Blog post]. Retrieved from www.crpe.org/thelens/charter-school-growth-flat-lining

Lake, R. J., Dusseault, B., Bowen, M., Demeritt, A., & Hill, P. (2010). *The national study of charter management organization (CMO) effectiveness: Report on interim findings.* Seattle, WA: Center on Reinventing Public Education. Retrieved from www.crpe.org/sites/default/files/pub_ncsrp_cmo_jun10_2_0.pdf

Lubienski, C., Scott, J. T., & DeBray, E. (2014). The politics of research production, promotion, and utilization in educational policy. *Educational Policy, 28,* 131–144.

Marsh, J. A., Strunk, K. O., & Bush, S. (2013). Portfolio district reform meets school turnaround: Early implementation findings from the Los Angeles Public School Choice Initiative. *Journal of Educational Administration, 51*(4), 498–527.

McGuinn, P. (2006). *No Child Left Behind and the transformation of federal education policy 1965–2005.* Lawrence, KS: University Press of Kansas.

McGuinn, P. (2014). Presidential policymaking: Race to the Top, executive power, and the Obama education agenda. *The Forum, 12*(1), 61–79.

McGuinn, P. J., & Manna, P. (Eds.). (2012). *Education governance for the twenty-first century: Overcoming the structural barriers to school reform.* Washington, DC: Brookings Institution Press.

Mead, S., Mitchel, A. L., & Rotherham, A. J. (2015). *The state of the charter school movement.* Retrieved from goo.gl/aPKqSb

Miron, G., & Gulosino, C. (2013). *Profiles of for-profit and nonprofit education management organizations: Fourteenth edition—2011–2012.* Boulder, CO: National Education Policy Center. Retrieved from nepc.colorado.edu/publication/EMO-profiles-11-12

Muldoon, M. (2013). The costs and benefits of nonprofit and for-profit status. In F. M. Hess & M. B. Horn (Eds.), *Private enterprise and public education.* New York, NY: Teachers College Press.

Murphy, J. (1990). The educational reform movement of the 1980s: A comprehensive analysis. In J. Murphy (Ed.), *The educational reform movement of the 1980s: Perspectives and cases* (pp. 3–55). Berkeley, CA: McCutchan.

National Alliance for Public Charter Schools. (2016). *A growing movement: America's largest charter public school communities and their impact on student outcomes*, 11th annual edition. Washington, DC: Author.

National Alliance for Public Charter Schools. (2017). *Estimated charter public school enrollment, 2016–17*. Washington, DC: Author. Retrieved from www.publiccharters.org/wp-content/uploads/2017/01/EER_Report_V5.pdf

National Center for Education Statistics. (2017, March). *Public charter school enrollment.* Retrieved from nces.ed.gov/programs/coe/indicator_cgb.asp

Peterson, P. (2010, July 21). No, Al Shanker did not invent the charter school. *Education Next.* Retrieved from educationnext.org/no-al-shanker-did-not-invent-the-charter-school

Ravitch, D. (2013). *Reign of error: The hoax of the privatization movement and the danger to America's public schools.* New York, NY: Alfred A. Knopf.

Reckhow, S. E. (2012). *Follow the money: How foundation dollars change public school politics.* New York, NY: Oxford University Press.

Shapiro, E. (2014, March 5). City's charter movement gets the Albany day it wanted. *Politico New York.* Retrieved from goo.gl/21mHtD

Shober, A. F., Manna, P., & Witte, J. F. (2006). Flexibility meets accountability: State charter school laws and their influence on the formation of charter schools in the United States. *Policy Studies Journal, 34*(4), 263–287.

Simon, S. (2012). Private firms eyeing profits from U.S. public schools. *Reuters.* Retrieved from www.reuters.com/article/usa-education-investment-idUSL2E8J15FR20120802

Tully, S. (2017, March 7). Applications double for Boston charter schools under new enrollment system. *Education Week.* Retrieved from goo.gl/FoIfTv

Walsh, M. (1996, February 21). Brokers pitch education as hot investment. *Education Week.* Retrieved from www.edweek.org/ew/articles/1996/02/21/22biz.h15.html

Walton Family Foundation. (2017). *Investing in cities: K-12 education.* Retrieved from www.waltonfamilyfoundation.org/our-impact/k12-education/investing-in-cities

Wong, K. K., & Langevin, W. E. (2007). Policy expansion of school choice in the American states. *Peabody Journal of Education, 82*(2–3), 440–472.

CHAPTER 3

Charter Schools in the Context of Poverty, Changing Demographics, and Segregation

James Harvey

The human understanding, when it has once adopted an opinion . . . draws all things else to support and agree with it. And though there be a greater number and weight of instances to be found on the other side, yet these it either neglects or despises, or else by some distinction sets aside and rejects . . .

—Sir Francis Bacon, *Novum Organum Scientiarum*

Is it possible that the conditions of poverty under which some children live so diminish their life prospects that schools face major obstacles in responding to their educational needs? In the face of what has become a large and growing body of evidence documenting enormous out-of-school challenges facing many students, that troubling question presents itself to any objective observer. In some communities, said Anthony Bryk following 15 years of research on school improvement in Chicago, the "density of problems walking through the front door is so palpable every day, it virtually consumes all your time and energy and detracts from efforts to improve teaching and learning" (Viadero, 2010).

In these circumstances, it is reasonable to examine the potential that charter schools offer as a response. Do they, as charter advocates claim, represent a viable response to the needs of students? Or, as critics contend, are charters a bromide, one that leaves unattended the underlying issues interfering with students' academic growth?

On one level, lack of attention to out-of-school issues is understandable given the policy context in which education has been framed in recent decades. Since *A Nation at Risk* was published (National Commission on Excellence in Education, 1983), public policy for education has focused relentlessly on schools, teachers, and administrators as the key problems and the principal actors in improving student performance. Only limited, intermittent, and poorly funded attention has been paid to the communities in which schools function. But emerging and persuasive evidence points not only to the powerful influence of out-of-school factors on student performance but also to dramatic levels of inequality and rates of student poverty in the United States. The public school population has become poorer and more diverse while many students and schools have grown increasingly isolated by race and income (Jargowsky, 2015; Reardon, 2011; Rothstein, 2015). Recent reports, for example, indicate that many schools today are more segregated than they were in the 1960s (Rothstein, 2013) and that more than 1 million students annually are homeless during at least some portion of the school year (U.S. Department of Education, 2016).

Moving forward, the questions become: How can public policy be reshaped to address these issues? What is the role of the schools in responding to these developments? Is there any reason to believe that charter schools are better equipped to deal with these challenges than traditional public schools?

This chapter is divided into five parts. The first reviews the research on the relationship between poverty and student achievement. The second outlines the growth of student poverty in the United States in recent decades and the growing diversity of the student population. The third examines the challenges of segregation. Next, the chapter turns to the phenomenon of concentrated poverty and how concentrated poverty differs between students of color and white students. The fifth part examines the extent to which charter schools are likely to provide effective responses to the conditions described here and offers some observations and recommendations for moving forward.

RELATIONSHIP BETWEEN POVERTY AND STUDENT ACHIEVEMENT

Poverty, when inserted into the school reform debate, is not "just an excuse," the claim of several observers, including Downey (2016), Thernstrom and Thernstrom (2003), and Rhee (2012). On the contrary, according to an analysis by the Organization for Economic Co-operation and Development (OECD) of the results of its Program for International Student Achievement (PISA):

> On average among OECD nations, the combined socioeconomic status of families and schools accounts for about 60% of the variation in tested achievement. In Finland, the combined measure accounts for some 30% of variation in tested achievement, while in the United States it accounts for about 80% (OECD, 2009). In short, socioeconomic status is the majority factor explaining student achievement in all countries; in the United States, it is an overwhelming factor. (Harvey, 2014, pp. 37–38)

The OECD findings are among the latest in half a century of research dating back to the "Coleman Report" in 1966 that documents the powerful relationship between poverty and achievement. The consensus by scholars on both the left and the right is that schools account for somewhere between 20% and 30% of observed differences in average student achievement (Berliner, 2006; Coleman, 1966; Goldhaber, 2002; Hanushek, Kain, & Rivkin, 1998; Ladd, 2012; Miller, 2003). Other research indicates that the verbal development of preschool children in families on public assistance lags far behind language development in their more prosperous peers (Hart & Risley, 1995), and that exposure to prolonged trauma in childhood produces "toxic stress" that damages the developing brain (National Scientific Council on the Developing Child, 2012).

Demography is not destiny. It is easy to find individuals who have heroically escaped the pull of childhood poverty—and schools that beat the odds for the most disadvantaged children. But 50 years of research is consistent and powerful: On average, poverty and its accomplices—joblessness, parental absence, household violence, adult substance abuse, poor nutrition, lack of medical and dental care, homelessness and evictions, and the shame and humiliation of perceived family failure—are powerful influences on student achievement and life outcomes.

STUDENT POVERTY

What do we know of the extent of childhood poverty in the United States? How widespread is it? Is the situation improving or deteriorating? Although no databases are entirely satisfactory, a number of sources exist to explore these questions. These include estimates of families living in poverty according to the federal government's official definition of poverty, counts of children participating in free and reduced-price meal programs, and several different series on wages and household income from the Bureau of the Census in the Department of Commerce and the Bureau of Labor Statistics in the Department of Labor.

Studies of child-poverty rates in the world's most advanced economies show that the United States has among the highest rates of relative poverty, defined as "the proportion of each nation's children living in households where disposable income is less than 50% of the national median (after taking taxes and benefits into account and adjusting for family size and composition)" (Harvey, 2014; UNICEF, 2013, p. 9).

More than 50% of students in American public schools are low income, as defined by eligibility for free and reduced-price meals (Southern Education Foundation [SEF], 2015). In some states, according to SEF calculations, more than 60% of enrolled students are low income (SEF, 2013). As a very rough proxy of concentrated poverty, the SEF 2013 analysis found that close to 60% of U.S. public school students enrolled in city schools are eligible for free and reduced-price meals, with astonishingly high rates in city schools in some states—83% in Mississippi, 78% in New Jersey, 75% in Pennsylvania, and 73% in New York (SEF, 2013, p. 4).

Table 3.1 outlines the share of children under the age of 18, by race and ethnicity, who live in families below the federal poverty level, as defined by the U.S. Office of Management and Budget. Large numbers of children in each of these

Table 3.1. Children in Poverty by Race and Ethnicity, 2015

Race/ethnicity	Number	Percentage
American Indian	233,000	34%
Asian/Pacific Islander	455,000	13%
Black or African American	3,719,000	36%
Hispanic or Latino	5,446,000	31%
Non-Hispanic white	4,645,000	12%
Two or more races	941,000	21%
Total	15,000,000	21%

Source: Kids Count Data Center, 2016.

groups are in families recognized to be living below the official poverty line. While the proportion for non-Hispanic white students is relatively low at 12%, the raw number of such students exceeds 4.6 million. For American Indian, Hispanic/ Latino, and black or African American children, the numbers amount to millions of students and the proportions approach and exceed one-third.

Diversity. Not only are schools challenged by the presence of low-income students and their needs, they are also enrolling a much more diverse student body than a generation or two ago. It no longer makes sense to speak of "minority" students in today's schools; no racial or ethnic group makes up a majority. As shown in Figure 3.1,[1] demographic changes in the last two generations have been dramatic. In 1970, close to 90% of students in the United States were white; by 2015, the figure was less than 50%. The growth in students of color—African American, Hispanic, Asian/Pacific Islander, Native American and Alaska Native, and children of two or more races—made up the difference. If policymakers want to know the demographic shape of the United States in the future, they need only look inside American classrooms. The nation's demographic future is sitting in them.

CHALLENGE OF SEGREGATION AND ISOLATION BY RACE AND POVERTY

Meanwhile, it seems clear that since the turn of the century, many schools have become more segregated, many students have become more isolated by race and poverty, and schools that are isolated by race and poverty offer fewer opportunities for students to experience a rich curriculum (Duncombe & Cassidy, 2016; U.S. Government Accountability Office [GAO], 2016). According to the GAO's April 2016 report:

- The percentage of schools that were both high poverty and high minority enrollment (i.e., with 75% of enrollment made up of black or

Figure 3.1. Public elementary and secondary school enrollment by race/ethnicity, selected years, fall 1970 to fall 2015 (2015 figures projected).

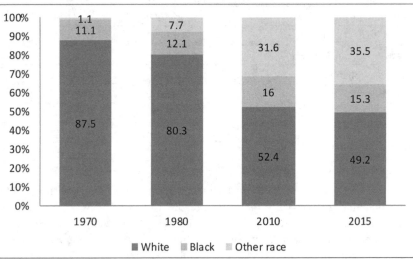

Source: National Center for Education Statistics, 2015.

Hispanic students and also eligible for free and reduced-price lunches) increased from 9% in 2000–2001 to 16% in 2013–2014 (GAO, 2016, p. 11). Not surprisingly, the proportion of students enrolled in racially or economically isolated schools increased from 10% to 17% over that period (GAO, 2016, p. 13). These increases reflect a growth in poverty and near-poverty (Rothstein, 2013).

- Meanwhile, although 72% of low-poverty schools offered Advanced Placement courses, just 48% of racially and economically isolated schools did so. This pattern did not hold for gifted and talented programs, offered by 55% of low-poverty schools but 59% of racially and economically isolated schools (GAO, 2016, p. 21).

Paul A. Jargowsky (2014; see also Jargowsky, 2013), director of Rutgers University's Center for Urban Research and Education, asked why so many communities are isolated in this way. His response was that they have been built that way. Patterns of gentrification and exclusionary zoning have exacerbated neighborhood segregation, encouraged unbridled suburban development, and created a "durable architecture of segregation." Rothstein (2015) made a similar point. Segregated neighborhoods produce segregated schools, he pointed out, and they are a "constitutional insult." Rothstein argued that "de facto" segregation in the North was not an accident but the consequence of federal, state, and local practices that included exclusionary zoning, "redlining" that denied housing to minorities in many communities, denial of mortgages, and even federal loan guarantees to builders on the explicit condition of prohibiting sales to African American buyers.

Not surprisingly, the achievement gap has grown apace (Reardon, 2011). It appears, said Reardon, that the "achievement gap between children from high- and low-income families is roughly 30 to 40 percent larger among children born in 2001 than among those born twenty-five years earlier" (p. 4). The achievement gap appears to be income related. What Reardon found "striking" is that although for cohorts born in the 1940s to the 1960s, the black–white achievement gap was substantially larger than the 90/10 achievement gap, the opposite was true for co- horts born in the 1970s and later (p. 12).[2] Among cohorts currently in school, he reported, "the 90/10 income gap at kindergarten entry was two to three times larger than the black-white gap at the same time."

CONCENTRATED POVERTY

Jargowsky (2014) analyzed census tracts considered to be neighborhoods of con- centrated poverty because 40% or more of the families within them met the federal poverty level. In these communities, fewer than half of the men were employed and half of the children were in single-parent households (primarily female- headed). Jargowsky reported:

- Concentrated poverty doubled between 1970 and 1990, declined amid economic growth in the 1990s, and increased by 57% between 2000 and 2013 when the number of high-poverty census tracts reached record levels.
- By 2012, about 7% of whites (of all ages) were living in areas of concentrated poverty, compared to 16% of Hispanics and 24% of black Americans.
- In almost all metropolitan areas, a few communities bear the entire burden of concentrated poverty, while suburbs use exclusionary zoning to wall out the poor.

In later analyses, Jargowsky (2015) disaggregated concentrated poverty in the 25 largest metropolitan areas by race and ethnicity. As Figure 3.2 illustrates, the proportion of white Americans living in concentrated poverty in large metropol- itan areas is always and in every area substantially lower than the proportion for African Americans or Hispanics. Large metropolitan areas include surrounding suburbs, frequently entire counties. Among the nine metropolitan areas displayed in Figure 3.2, Philadelphia and Phoenix stand out for the large proportion of the Hispanic population living in conditions of concentrated poverty (54% and 34%, respectively). In each of the other seven metropolitan areas, the proportion of Af- rican Americans living in concentrated poverty greatly exceeds the comparable proportions for Hispanic and white Americans. In some cities, including Chicago, St. Louis, Tampa, and Baltimore, African American residents are 10 to 15 times more likely than white residents to live amidst concentrated poverty.

Figure 3.2. Concentration of poverty by race and ethnicity, selected large metropolitan areas, 2009–2013

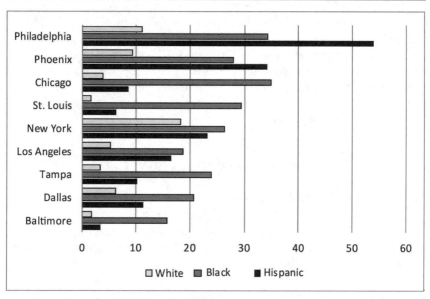

Source: Jargowsky, 2015, Appendix B, Table 6.

The official statistics on poverty, and even Jargowsky's troubling data, obscure an even more disturbing and shocking reality. Hidden from view in the United States, there exists poverty of a kind that is so extreme one would expect to find it in a developing nation—families with almost nothing to eat, sometimes living at subsistence levels by selling blood plasma to blood banks. Shaefer and Edin (2016) documented the existence of nearly 1.5 million families living on $2.00 per person per day. These families include nearly 3 million children.

OBSERVATIONS AND RECOMMENDATIONS

This chapter began by asking two major questions: First, is it possible that the conditions of poverty under which some children live so diminish their life prospects that schools face major obstacles in responding to their educational needs? Second, do charter schools represent a viable response to the needs of these children? The answer to the first question is clearly yes. The conditions in which many children in the United States live are a moral rebuke to the nation. The answer to the second question is no. The problem is not one of "fixing" schools by creating novel administrative arrangements for them; it is one of addressing poverty and disinvestment in the neighborhoods in which these schools are located. Reformers who insist that poverty is just an excuse have developed a remarkable capacity to ignore all of the unpleasant facts outlined above.

This concluding section argues that schools by themselves are a necessary but insufficient response to the challenges described here. Schools, however organized, administered, or chartered, cannot address these issues by themselves because they have neither the funds, the staff, nor the technical competence to do so.

Troubling Reality of Charter Schools

Perhaps the safest thing to say about the research on charter schools is that there is little agreement on their effectiveness. Moreover, much of the research, both that supporting charters and attacking them, is advocacy based. While the evidence is mixed, it appears that most charter schools are neither better nor worse than traditional public schools. Students in 17% of charter schools outperformed their peers in traditional public schools in one of the first large-scale assessments of charters, while students in 37% of charters performed significantly worse, and outcomes were little different from traditional public schools in the remaining 46% of charters (Center for Research on Education Outcomes [CREDO], 2009). In 2015, CREDO issued a more encouraging report on urban charter schools in 41 regions, concluding that, even with local variation, more than twice as many urban regions demonstrated their charter schools outperformed their district school counterparts (CREDO, 2015). Epistemological warfare around those findings has raged ever since; arguments about how we know what we know and the accuracy of our yardsticks have dominated the debate (Gabor, 2015; Hoxby, 2009; Maul, 2015).

This discussion has revolved around student outcome data. In these debates, only rarely do issues of the effects of charter schools on the larger school system surface and, by and large, it is only the critics of charter schools who point out the obvious: Charter schools do not reduce the effects of concentrated poverty; they often exacerbate them by increasing segregation (Ladd, Clotfeller, & Holbein, 2015). Moreover, in many charter schools, students with disabilities and English-language learners are underrepresented and suspension rates are high (Boundy, 2012; Decker, Snyder, & Darville, 2015; Sattin-Bajaj & Suarez-Orozco, 2012).

Even if these problems could be resolved, it seems clear that charters, far from being an adequate response to the challenges outlined in this chapter, paper over the problems by distracting attention from significant issues. While masquerading as a civil rights response to students' educational needs, charter advocates ignore and downplay the underlying issues interfering with students' academic growth.

The effects are pernicious: Some charter schools restrict enrollment or expel students who do not meet their requirements, leaving traditional public schools with fewer resources to cover overhead and the costs of educating students that the charter schools reject (American Civil Liberties Union of Southern California, 2016). And they have created a situation in some urban communities in which taxpayers are now assuming a burden once assumed by parents of children in private and parochial schools (Lustig, 2016). In fundamental ways in some cities, the proportion of children attending charter schools is now so large that the very nature of public education has changed in poorly understood ways into systems encouraging rote and narrow learning of basics at the expense of a rich curriculum and preparation for work and for active participation in a democracy.

Structures of Opportunity

Against the backdrop of the challenges outlined in this chapter, the concept of "structures of opportunity" offers a way to think about moving forward. The concept is taken from a recent Educational Testing Service (ETS) research program, The Opportunity Project, but it readily accommodates two other recent, significant calls for rethinking how American society responds to educational needs in the 21st century—the Broader, Bolder Approach to Education and the Harvard Education Redesign Lab. ETS's Opportunity Project argued:

> Some [children] are born to privilege . . . ; others are born to struggling families who face daily challenges to provide for them. . . . These different starting points place children on distinctly different trajectories of growth, leading to the accelerated accumulation of advantage or disadvantage and, ultimately, to vastly different adult outcomes. (Kirsch, Braun, Lennon, & Sands, 2016, p. 1)

The gist of the ETS message is that opportunity for some young people is characterized by advantage added to advantage, while for others disadvantage added to disadvantage is the norm. Children in advantaged communities can expect to enjoy the benefits of a solid family income, excellent schools, extended learning opportunities in summer camps, and even foreign travel. Children in struggling families experience life on poverty or below-poverty income and underfunded schools, while summers are spent trying to find something to do in abandoned communities, and many are unaware of the larger world outside their immediate neighborhood. Kirsch and his colleagues pointed to gates and barriers to progress for the disadvantaged as early as the prenatal period and throughout the school years, and they called for a national conversation to develop a path forward.

Two very similar approaches from the Broader, Bolder Approach to Education and the Harvard Education Redesign Lab point a way ahead.

The Broader, Bolder Approach to Education.[3] In 2009, dismayed at the misplaced emphasis on competition and accountability that lay at the heart of the school reform movement, a group of analysts and researchers proposed a "Broader, Bolder Approach to Education" (Economic Policy Institute, 2009). This agenda was relaunched in 2016 with a policy framework emphasizing the need to address out-of-school barriers to success (enriched early childhood programs, enhanced after-school and summer opportunities, improved health care, and improved nutrition); narrowing school opportunity gaps (equitable funding, supports-based accountability, enhanced teacher and principal quality, and strengthened accountability systems for charter schools); and focused attention to strengthening communities (addressing issues of segregation and concentrated poverty and grounding reform in community input).

The Harvard Education Redesign Lab. Citing a "persistent and iron law of correlation between socioeconomic status and educational achievement," Paul Reville, director of the Education Redesign Lab at the Harvard Graduate School of Education and a former secretary of education in Massachusetts, believes that schools are overwhelmed "with students too traumatized to learn" (Reville, 2016). His lab is working with six communities from California to Massachusetts to put all the resources in these communities behind school improvement. Like ETS's Opportunity Project and the Broader, Bolder Approach to Education, the Education Redesign Lab emphasizes customized and student-centered learning, the "braiding" of health and social services into the supports children need to thrive, and expanded learning opportunities that provide a full complement of after-school, summer, and work-based opportunities.

These three efforts are similar. Whether any of the three is adequate or not, it is clear that each of them responds to many of the issues outlined in this chapter in ways that charter schools do not.

Community Redesign

Laudable though they be, only the Broader, Bolder Approach to Education touches on a central problem identified by Jargowsky as a "durable architecture of segregation." One should not be surprised that schools are segregated when the communities in which they are found have themselves been deliberately segregated.

"The fundamental question is not how to fix failing schools," said Jargowsky (2014), "but how to fix the metropolitan development paradigm that creates high-poverty neighborhoods and failing schools in the first place." This is a very tall order. Housing built 50 years ago under restrictive covenants and with government encouragement of redlining and discrimination still exists. An adequate response is likely to take decades.

Undoing the damage that has been done will require both ceasing practices that create housing developments emblematic of the architecture of segregation and then consciously setting out to undo that architecture. The results might take decades to see, but they will be well worth the wait.

Theory Blindness

The epigraph at the outset of this chapter drew on the observation of Sir Francis Bacon, a 17th-century English philosopher and scientist, that once individuals reach an opinion they are likely to stick to it through thick and thin, regardless of any evidence to the contrary. Kahneman (2011) referred to this phenomenon as theory blindness: "We can be blind to the obvious, and we are also blind to our blindness" (p. 24). It is not unreasonable to conclude that much of the reform advocates' commitment to charters (and vouchers) is based on devotion to free market and privatization principles that are clung to through thick and thin, all other evidence, in Bacon's terms, neglected or despised and set aside and rejected.

It is time advocates on both sides of the charter question begin to examine their own biases and blind spots. It is surely the case that charters have something to contribute to the reform mix and that, properly accountable, they can be part of a renewal of public education. But it is also surely the case that they are a narrow, technocratic, and inadequate response to a profound and painful human tragedy in the United States. The original sin of American racism, embedded in the text of the Constitution of the United States, still rears its head today. Entire communities remain isolated by race, class, lack of opportunity, and the absence of hope, a situation aided, abetted, and promoted, even if subconsciously, by leaders and policymakers of all persuasions, at all levels, public and private.

The difficult work of examining and exploring these blind spots needs to be taken up. Perhaps, then, American society can heal its wounds, make peace with its past, and renew itself and its schools.

NOTES

1. Figure 3.1 reports on student enrollment by race/ethnicity from 1970 to 2015 in three categories: white, black, and "other race." The term "other race" dates back to 1970. That was the term in use at the time, when the category accounted for only 1.1% of enrollment and additional breakdowns were unavailable. To produce comparable "other race" data in succeeding years, Figure 3.1 sums data for the following ethnic groups: Hispanic, Asian/Pacific Islander, American Indian/Alaska Native, and two or more races.

2. The 90/10 achievement gap is an income-related achievement gap that compares the assessed performance of children in families at the 90th percentile of the family income distribution (about $168,000 in 2008) with performance of children at the 10th percentile (about $17,800 in 2008).

3. The author of this chapter signed the Broader, Bolder Approach to Education's original 2009 statement of purpose and serves as an advisory board member to the effort relaunched in 2016.

REFERENCES

American Civil Liberties Union of Southern California. (2016). *Unequal access: How some California charter schools illegally restrict enrollment.* Los Angeles, CA: Author.

Bacon, F. (1620). *Novum organum scientiarium (The new organon or true directions concerning the interpretation of nature).* In J. Spedding, R. L. Ellis, & D. D. Heath (Trans.), *The works* (Vol. 8). Boston, MA: Taggard and Thompson.

Berliner, D. C. (2006). Our impoverished view of educational reform. *Teachers College Record*, *108*(6), 949–995.

Boundy, K. B. (2012). Charter schools and students with disabilities: Preliminary analysis of the legal issues and areas of concern. Boston, MA: Center for Law and Education. Retrieved from tinyurl.com/gonto2h

Center for Research on Education Outcomes. (2009). *Multiple choice: Charter school performance in 16 states*. Stanford, CA: Author.

Center for Research on Education Outcomes. (2015). *Urban charter school study: Report on 41 regions*. Stanford, CA: Author.

Coleman, J. S. (1966). *Equality of educational opportunity*. Washington, DC: Department of Health, Education and Welfare.

Decker, G., Snyder, S., & Darville, S. (2015, February 23). Suspensions at city charter school far outpace those at district schools, data show. *Chalkbeat* [Blog post]. Retrieved from tinyurl.com/zxgmrh3

Downey, M. (2016, January 4). Are we using poverty as an excuse for school failure? *Atlanta Journal Constitution*. Retrieved from tinyurl.com/zy28zyn

Duncombe, C., & Cassidy, M. (2016, November 4). *Increasingly separate and unequal in U.S. and Virginia schools* [Blog post]. Retrieved from tinyurl.com/jz85q6l

Economic Policy Institute. (2009). *A broader, bolder approach to education*. Washington, DC: Author. Retrieved from tinyurl.com/hovysx2

Gabor, A. (2015, April 28). *New CREDO study, new credibility problems: From New Orleans to Boston* [Blog post]. Retrieved from tinyurl.com/zvb2h3p

Goldhaber, D. (2002, March). The mystery of good teaching. *Education Next*. Retrieved from educationnext.org/the-mystery-of-good-teaching

Hanushek, E. A., Kain, J. F., & Rivkin, S. (1998). *Teachers, schools, and academic achievement* [Working Paper No. 6691]. Cambridge, MA: National Bureau of Economic Research.

Hart, B., & Risley, T. R. (1995). *Meaningful differences in the everyday experience of young American children*. Baltimore, MD: Paul H. Brookes.

Harvey, J. (2014). *School performance within the economic and cultural contexts of nine nations: An exploratory study of education indicators*. Unpublished doctoral dissertation, Seattle University, Seattle, WA.

Hoxby, C. M. (2009). *A statistical mistake in the Credo study of charter schools*. Retrieved from tinyurl.com/jjb3l5p

Jargowsky, P. A. (2013). *Concentration of poverty in the new millennium: Changes in the prevalence, composition, and location of high poverty neighborhoods*. Washington, DC: The Century Foundation. Retrieved from tinyurl.com/yaps9vww

Jargowsky, P. A. (2014, Fall). A durable architecture of segregation [Report on a July 2014 meeting of the National Superintendents Roundtable]. *Roundtable News*, *3*. Retrieved from www.superintendentsforum.org/wp-content/uploads/2016/03/2014.12-Fall-Poverty-copy.pdf

Jargowsky, P. A. (2015). *Architecture of segregation: Civil unrest, the concentration of poverty, and public policy*. New York, NY: Century Foundation.

Kahneman, D. (2011). *Thinking, fast and slow*. New York, NY: Farrar, Straus and Giroux.

Kids Count Data Center. (2016). *Children in poverty by race and ethnicity*. Retrieved from tinyurl.com/jypz6nv

Kirsch, I., Braun, H., Lennon, M. L., & Sands, A. (2016). *Choosing our future: A story of opportunity in America*. Princeton, NJ: Educational Testing Service.

Ladd, H. F. (2012). *Education and poverty: Confronting the evidence.* Durham, NC: Duke University Sanford School of Public Policy.

Ladd, H. F., Clotfelter, C. T., & Holbein, J. B. (2015). *The growing segmentation of the charter school sector in North Carolina* [Working Paper 133]. Washington, DC: National Center for Analysis of Longitudinal Data in Education Research.

Lustig, M. (2016, March 2). *Rethinking equity in Pennsylvania: The Philadelphia case* [Student paper]. Graduate School of Education and Human Development, The George Washington University, Washington, DC.

Maul, A. (2015). *Review of urban charter school study, 2015.* Boulder, CO: National Education Policy Center. Retrieved from tinyurl.com/hvg8r5v

Miller, K. (2003). *School, teacher, and leadership impacts on student achievement* [McREL Policy Brief]. Denver, CO: McREL International.

National Center for Education Statistics. (2015). *Digest of education statistics 2013.* Washington, DC: Author.

National Commission on Excellence in Education. (2003). *A nation at risk.* Washington, DC: U.S. Department of Education.

National Scientific Council on the Developing Child. (2012). *Establishing a level foundation for life: Mental health begins in early childhood* [Working Paper 6]. Cambridge, MA: Center on the Developing Child, Harvard University. Retrieved from developingchild. harvard.edu/index.php/resources/reports_and_working_papers/working_papers/ wp6

Reardon, S. F. (2011). The widening academic achievement gap between the rich and the poor: New evidence and possible explanations. In R. Murnane & G. Duncan (Eds.), *Whither opportunity? Rising inequality and the uncertain life chances of low-income children* (pp. 91–116). New York, NY: Russell Sage Foundation Press.

Reville, P. (2016, July 16). *Poverty matters: Making the case for a system overhaul* [PowerPoint slides]. Presented at the National Superintendents Roundtable, San Francisco, CA. Retrieved from tinyurl.com/z5zdxb6

Rhee, M. (2012, September 5). Poverty must be tackled but never used as an excuse. *Huffington Post.* Retrieved from tinyurl.com/hpkkpj9/

Rothstein, R. (2013). *For public schools, segregation then, segregation since: Education and the unfinished march.* Washington, DC: Economic Policy Institute.

Rothstein, R. (2015). The racial achievement gap, segregated schools, and segregated neighborhoods—a constitutional insult. *Race and Social Problems, 7*(1), 21–30.

Sattin-Bajaj, C., & Suarez-Orozco, M. (2012). *English language learner students and charter students in New York state: Challenges and opportunities.* Report from the NY Governor's Leadership Team for High Quality Charter Public Schools. Albany, NY: New York State Department of Education.

Shaefer, H. K., & Edin, K. J. (2016, December 7). What is the evidence of worsening conditions among America's poorest families with children? $2 a day [Blog post]. Retrieved from tinyurl.com/z4p87bu

Southern Education Foundation. (2013). *A new majority: Low income students now a majority in the nation's public schools.* Atlanta, GA: Author.

Southern Education Foundation. (2015). *A new majority: Low income students in the South and nation.* Atlanta, GA: Author.

Thernstrom, A., & Thernstrom, S. (2003). *No excuses: Closing the racial achievement gap.* New York, NY: Simon & Schuster.

UNICEF. (2013). *Child well-being in rich countries: A comparative overview* [Innocenti Report Card 11]. Florence, Italy: UNICEF Office of Research.

U.S. Department of Education. (2016). *Total number of homeless students enrolled in LEAs, with or without McKinney-Vento subgrants. Total: 2013–14.* Retrieved from tinyurl.com/gqb7qtk

U.S. Government Accountability Office. (2016). *Better use of information could help agencies identify disparities and address racial discrimination.* Washington, DC: Author. Retrieved from www.gao.gov/assets/680/676745.pdf

Viadero, D. (2010, January 27). Scholars identify 5 keys to urban school success. *Education Week.* Retrieved from tinyurl.com/hvc3u2s

Part II

CHOICES

CHAPTER 4

A School System Increasingly Separated

Iris C. Rotberg

When we trace the rhetoric of choice across the decades, we see that it has migrated from describing an obstructionist power held by white, middle-class families to a supposedly curative one increasingly offered to poor families of color. Rarely in American history have public goods moved from doing service for the elite and powerful to being tools for disadvantaged communities. When the rhetoric suggests that choice has become such a tool, we should pay close and skeptical attention.

—A. T. Erickson,
"The Rhetoric of Choice, Segregation, Desegregation, and Charter Schools"

School choice options in the United States have expanded rapidly in recent years. The expansion has occurred for charter schools as well as for voucher and tax benefit programs.

The first charter school in the United States opened in 1992 (Jacobs, 2015; Minnesota Legislative Reference Library, 2016). By 2015, 42 states and the District of Columbia had passed charter school legislation (Zgainer & Kerwin, 2015) and 6,900 charter schools were in operation, serving 3.1 million students (National Alliance for Public Charter Schools, 2017), or about 6% of the U.S. student population in public elementary and secondary schools. The most dramatic increases have occurred in urban districts with high concentrations of low-income and minority students (National Center for Education Statistics [NCES], 2016).

As charter schools have proliferated, other forms of school choice have also expanded. In 2000, only five states had voucher programs, serving about 70,000 students; by 2017, 15 states and the District of Columbia had voucher programs, serving about 170,000 students (EdChoice, 2017). In 2001, only five states had tax benefit programs for elementary and secondary education; by 2017, 20 states had tax benefit programs (EdChoice, 2017).

This chapter focuses on the implications of the expansion of charter schools and charter management organizations. The expansion continues despite research evidence showing that charter schools generally increase segregation (Ladd, Clotfelter, & Holbein, 2015; Mathis & Welner, 2016; Miron, Urschel, Mathis, & Tornquist, 2010; Rotberg, 2014). High-poverty urban districts have experienced a significant portion of the expansion as charter schools have become responsible for educating large numbers of the districts' students. As a result, these districts are undergoing major structural and programmatic changes that are having significant consequences for equity and integration.

The first section of this chapter describes the changes occurring in high-poverty urban districts. The sections that follow show why these changes matter. Section 2 describes how the expansion of charter schools and charter management organizations has magnified resource constraints and inequalities in districts already struggling with declining budgets and high needs. Section 3 describes the proliferation of education programs that are virtually unique to these districts, thereby creating a form of segregation in which many high-poverty, minority students attend schools that are considerably different from those attended by the rest of the student population. Section 4 considers the implications of these findings in a broader educational and social context.

CREATING A NEW LEVEL OF
INEQUALITY IN HIGH-POVERTY SCHOOL DISTRICTS

Urban school districts that serve high proportions of low-income and minority students have become increasingly different from traditional districts that serve the rest of the student population.

Traditional districts are familiar to anyone who attended U.S. public schools. They combine mostly comprehensive schools with some choice and specialized schools. The inequities are well known. These inequities begin with the stark contrast among districts in the income and wealth of the families they serve and are then reflected in the inequities of the education systems. Resources are unequal; some schools are segregated; some are tracked; some have discriminatory discipline practices. Affluent communities tend to have schools with more qualified teachers, more varied and advanced curricula, better infrastructure, and more amenities (Adamson & Darling-Hammond, 2011). But the basic management structure of traditional public school districts does not differ based on the demographics of students enrolled in them.

It is understandable given these inequities that an alternative to traditional districts might seem attractive. However, the inequities between high-poverty and more affluent districts have not been mitigated by a transition to charter schools. Instead, the opposite has occurred. The transition has exacerbated those inequities as districts with concentrated poverty are being transformed into districts that now include competing management systems operating within the same district:

for-profit and nonprofit charter management organizations, each running multiple schools; freestanding charter schools; and schools—traditional and, in some cases, charter—run by the district. These management systems compete for students and financial resources, and each has its own management structure.

Table 4.1 describes the demographic characteristics of districts with charter school enrollment shares of 30% or higher (National Alliance for Public Charter Schools, 2016). The table shows the major role that charter schools play in many districts throughout the country—typically urban districts with high proportions of low-income and minority students. In New Orleans, for example, 92% of public school students are enrolled in charter schools; in Detroit, 53%; in Flint, 53%; in the District of Columbia, 45%; in Gary, 43%; in Kansas City, 40%; in Camden, 34%; and in Philadelphia, 32%. In many other districts, charter school enrollment is 20% to 30% of total school enrollment.

An increasing number of charter school students attend schools run by charter management organizations. In 2002, 91,000 students were served by charter management organizations; by 2012, that number had increased to 900,000 students (Miron & Gulosino, 2013). Table 4.2 shows the number of competing charter management organizations operating in school districts with charter school enrollment shares of 30% or higher (Miron & Gulosino, 2013). Table 4.3 gives the same information for school districts with the highest charter school enrollments (Miron & Gulosino, 2013).

Added to the variety are foundations, which contribute to some charter schools and not to others, and venture capital firms and hedge funds, which select charter schools for investment based on potential profitability (Baker & Miron, 2015; Hess & Henig, 2015). During the Bush and Obama administrations, the federal government played a major role in the expansion of charter schools by awarding grants to state departments of education and charter management organizations and by giving financial incentives to states to reduce or eliminate caps on the number of charter schools (Howell, 2015; U.S. Department of Education, 2016). The current Trump administration proposals give even greater priority to school choice in the form of charter schools, vouchers, and tax benefits.

The trends described, in combination, have resulted in two very different school systems—one for low-income, minority students in high-poverty districts and the other for everyone else. But some states have gone even further and created what are called "achievement" districts that group schools with low test scores into one district, regardless of the geographical proximity of the schools (Glazer, Massell, & Malone, 2018). These districts have been established in Louisiana, Mississippi, Nevada, North Carolina, and Tennessee (Dreilinger, 2016; Glazer & Egan, 2016; Hinchcliffe, 2016; Mississippi Legislature, 2016; Nevada Department of Education, n.d.). Charter schools and charter management organizations assume much of the responsibility, formerly held by districts, for operating schools. Because of the strong correlation between poverty and low achievement, high-poverty and minority students are further segregated by being assigned to separate, unique districts.

Table 4.1. Demographic Characteristics of Districts with Charter School Enrollment Shares of 30% or Higher

School district, state	Charter school enrollment share[a]	Locale[b]	Poverty rate, school-aged population	Percentage African American	Percentage Hispanic	Source[c]
New Orleans Public School System, LA	92%	City: large	62%	76%	5%	Cowen, 2012–13
Detroit City School District, MI	53%	City: large	74%	83%	13%	NCTQ, 2013–14
School District of the City of Flint, MI	53%	City: midsize	70%	78%	3%	CEP
District of Columbia Public Schools, DC	45%	City: large	78%	64%	18%	District
Gary Community School Corporation, IN	43%	City: small	80%	93%	2%	Niche
Kansas City Public Schools, MO	40%	City: large	99%	58%	28%	NCTQ
Camden City School District, NJ	34%	City: small	95%	48%	50%	District
Philadelphia City School District, PA	32%	City: large	83%	53%	19%	NCTQ
Indianapolis Public Schools, IN	31%	City: large	72%	50%	23%	NCTQ
Dayton City School District, OH	31%	City: midsize	74%	67%	2%	State
Cleveland Municipal School District, OH	31%	City: large	83%	66%	15%	NCTQ

School district, state	Charter school enrollment share[a]	Locale[b]	Poverty rate, school-aged population	Percentage African American	Percentage Hispanic	Source[c]
Grand Rapids Public Schools, MI	31%	City: midsize	83%	32%	36%	District
Victor Valley Union High School District, CA	31%	City: midsize	79%	19%	57%	Ed-data
San Antonio Independent School District, TX	30%	City: large	93%	6%	91%	NCTQ
Natomas Unified School District, CA	30%	City: large	51%	18%	31%	Ed-data
Newark City School District, NJ	30%	City: large	75%	46%	45%	NCTQ
St. Louis Public Schools, MO	30%	City: large	85%	83%	3%	NCTQ

a. Source: National Alliance for Public Charter Schools, 2016.

b. Source: NCES district locale label.

c. Source codes: *Blackerby*, www.blackerbyassoc.com/HeadStart/RSD.CA2.pdf; *CEP*, www.cep-dc.org; *Cowen*, www.coweninstitute.com/wp-content/uploads/2013/07/2013_SPENO_Final2.pdf; *Ed-data*, www.ed-data.org/district; *HAR*, www.har.com/school_district/manor-isd_227907; *NAF*, New America Foundation, febp.newamerica.net; NCTQ, nctq.org; *Niche*, k12.niche.com; *Startclass*, public-schools.startclass.com/l/3161/Gilbert-High-School; *State*, www.dps.k12.oh.us/content/documents/DPS-Fast-Facts02-24-2016RC.pdf. *District data* were obtained from the following URLs: dcps.dc.gov/page/dcps-glance-enrollment; www.grps.org/images/quicklinks/District_Improvement_Plan.pdf; www.google.com/url?sa=t&rct=j&q=&esrc=s&source=web&cd=1&ved=0ahUKEwi-49C2jIDPAhXKVz4KHYbXB6EQFggeMAA&url=http%3A%2F%2Fwww.state.nj.us%2Feducation%2Fsboe%2Fmeetings%2F2014%2FJanuary%2Fpublic%2FPowerpoint_Camden.ppt&usg=AFQjCNGUg-bvMEz3cfERD_fF-0hTFbD45Q.

Table 4.2. Number of Charter Management Organizations and Freestanding Schools in Districts with Charter School Enrollment Shares of 30% or Higher

School district, state	Charter school enrollment share[a]	Total charter management organizations[b]	Schools run by charter management organizations[b]
New Orleans Public School System, LA	92%	9	30
Detroit City School District, MI	53%	20	66
School District of the City of Flint, MI	53%	5	5
District of Columbia Public Schools	45%	13	47
Gary Community School Corporation, IN	43%	5	6
Kansas City Public Schools, MO	40%	3	8
Camden City School District, NJ[c]	34%	3	7
Philadelphia City School District, PA	32%	7	29
Indianapolis Public Schools, IN	31%	9	14
Dayton City School District, OH	31%	7	19
Cleveland Municipal School District, OH	31%	8	43
Grand Rapids Public Schools, MI	31%	6	13
Victor Valley Union High School District, CA	31%	0	0
San Antonio Independent School District, TX	30%	14	39
Natomas Unified School District, CA	30%	0	0
Newark City School District, NJ	30%	2	2
Saint Louis Public Schools, MO	30%	4	11

a. Source: National Alliance for Public Charter Schools, 2016.
b. Includes for-profit and nonprofit. Source: Miron & Gulosino, 2013.
c. Source: camdenenrollment.org

Table 4.3. Number of Charter Management Organizations in Districts with the Highest Charter School Enrollments

School district, state	Charter school enrollment share[a]	Total charter management organizations[b]	Schools run by charter management organizations[b]
Los Angeles Unified School District, CA	24%	14	94
New York City Department of Education, NY	9%	18	69
Philadelphia City School District, PA	32%	7	19
Chicago Public Schools, IL	15%	19	84
Miami-Dade County Public Schools, FL	16%	4	34
Houston Independent School District, TX	22%	15	73
Detroit City School District, MI	53%	20	66
Broward County Public Schools, FL[c]	16%	3	31
New Orleans Public School System, LA	92%	9	30
District of Columbia Public Schools, DC	45%	13	47

a. Source: National Alliance for Public Charter Schools, 2016.
b. Includes for-profit and nonprofit. Source: Miron & Gulosino, 2013.
c. Source: browardschools.com.

COMPETING FOR SCARCE RESOURCES

High-poverty urban districts face increased fiscal constraints as traditional schools, charter management organizations, and freestanding charter schools compete for scarce resources in a zero-sum game in which total education resources are declining (Cohen, 2016a; Cook, 2016a).

Increased fiscal constraints are to be expected in this environment. It is more expensive to run multiple school systems than a single system. Charter schools require extra facilities. Charter school management organizations and freestanding charter schools also come with their own management structures and administrative costs over and above those of the school district. A significant portion of the costs is paid for with public funds (Baker, 2016; Bifulco & Reback, 2014; Cook, 2016b).

Philadelphia is an example of a district in which the competition for scarce resources has been particularly severe. The district has had large budget cuts and longstanding school finance inequities. Added to its existing problems, Philadelphia is now faced with fiscal deficits associated with charter schools. The district loses the per-pupil expenditure for each student who attends a charter school, but the expenses of the traditional schools are not reduced by a commensurate amount. A class of 25 instead of 30 students, for example, still needs a teacher, and the district still needs to operate the school and to fund central services that apply to all students, whether in traditional or charter schools. Further, English-language learners and students with disabilities, especially those with more severe disabilities, are underrepresented in many charter schools and, as a result, traditional schools have proportionately more students who require additional resources for their education. The problems are compounded by student enrollment rates that are fluid and unpredictable. Charter schools open and close—sometimes midyear. Some are undersubscribed; others have waiting lists. Despite lotteries, charter schools, as compared to traditional schools, have more control over which students will enroll and which students will remain in the school. Students leave charter schools and return to traditional schools at various times during the school year. It is virtually impossible to estimate enrollment counts for any given school and make realistic resource allocation projections (Baker, 2016; Council for Exceptional Children, 2012; Dudley-Marling & Baker, 2012; Lustig, 2016; Sattin-Bajaj & Suarez-Orozco, 2012).

Urban districts in Michigan are another example. A study of districts in financial trouble found that very high and sustained levels of charter school enrollment are associated with steep declines in fiscal resources available to traditional schools, in part linked to an increasing proportion of special education students in these schools. These fiscal declines have been compounded by general enrollment declines, an oversupply of schools in the districts, and cost differentials that are not accounted for in allocating funds. The result is "a fierce downward spiral in the state's urban districts" (Arsen, DeLuca, Ni, & Bates, 2015, p. 26). The students in these districts are predominantly low-income and African American.

Charter schools have also added to fiscal problems in other high-poverty urban districts throughout the country, including Albany, Boston, Buffalo, Chicago, Los Angeles, and Newark (Baker, 2016; Bifulco & Reback, 2014; Boston Municipal Research Bureau, 2016; Butkovitz, 2014; Farrie & Johnson, 2015; Lawyers' Committee for Civil Rights and Economic Justice, 2016a; Sanchez & Belsha, 2015; Stokes, 2016). Traditional schools lose funds to charter schools in different ways and in different amounts depending on states' school finance policies, districts' management practices, the economic strength of state and local economies, enrollment and dropout trends, and a number of other factors. But regardless of exactly how the competition plays out, increasing numbers of school districts report budget constraints associated with the proliferation of charter schools (Gurley, 2016).

Charter schools too face budget constraints. In some states and districts, they receive lower per-pupil expenditures than traditional schools, or facilities are not supported (Center for Education Reform, 2012). In addition to these differences in public funding, the resources available to charter schools from all sources vary, even within the same district, depending on decisions by education management organizations, donors, and investors. Some charter schools, therefore, have considerably more resources than traditional schools or other charter schools in the same district, while others are underfunded (Chandler, 2015).

The competition for resources among multiple schools and multiple school management systems, whether traditional or charter, has created school finance inequities over and above the longstanding inequities that already existed among schools. The burden created by this competition falls primarily on districts with large proportions of low-income and minority students.

SEPARATE SCHOOL SYSTEMS, SEPARATE EDUCATION PROGRAMS

As the multiplicity of school management systems has become the norm in many high-poverty communities, education programs virtually unique to these communities have proliferated. Decisions about programmatic approaches have come to depend on the preferences of education management organizations and freestanding charter schools. The private sector, therefore, now plays a major role in formulating education policies for many of the schools attended by low-income and minority students. Although charter schools and their management organizations receive significant public funding, their policies are set by private boards of directors (typically not representative of the communities served by the schools), rather than by elected school boards—a stark contrast to other school districts throughout the country (Education Commission of the States, 2014; Education Encyclopedia, n.d.; Green, Baker, & Oluwole, 2013; Raise Your Hand for Illinois Public Education, n.d.).

Some charter schools have education programs similar to those found in public or private schools more generally, or programs that could readily be applied in these settings. In addition, a small but rapidly growing group of charter management organizations relies on online learning, either full- or part-time. These online programs, typically less costly than regular programs, serve a significant number of low-income and minority students in some districts (Lafer, 2014). Research evidence gives little cause for optimism that students in these programs are receiving an education equal to that of students in regular classrooms (Woodworth et al., 2015).

The instructional models that are the most distinct—and controversial—are the "no-excuses" models, which began in high-poverty communities in the 1990s and are now widespread in many communities. The term "no-excuses" is a label applied to different education programs that combine a strong emphasis on structured teaching methods and testing with highly prescriptive and controlled behavior requirements and strict disciplinary practices (Goodman, 2013). As reported by Hernandez (2016), the focus on student behavior in the two no-excuses charter management organizations she studied is reinforced by marketing materials that emphasize discipline, control, and character development. The marketing materials "negatively depict the communities and families" served (Hernandez, 2016, p. 56) or portray students as coming to school with "character dispositions that require rehabilitation" (Hernandez, 2016, p. 58).

A number of education management organizations are generally acknowledged to use no-excuses models. Complete lists are difficult to compile because not all schools that use no-excuses models identify themselves by that term. And, like U.S. education more generally, the approaches vary both among and within models—some harsher, some gentler. The schools' per-pupil expenditures are also highly variable, with some schools receiving substantial additional funding from private sources. Special education students and English-language learners are underrepresented in many of these schools. Parents and students in some no-excuses schools are required to sign a contract committing to specific academic and behavioral requirements. The students who are expelled, suspended, or "counseled out" return to traditional schools (Bean, 2010).

Although schools with an emphasis on structured teaching methods, testing, and disciplined classrooms can be found in both low-income and affluent communities, the stringent behavioral and school discipline policies central to many no-excuses models are rarely found outside high-poverty communities (Losen, Keith, Hodson, & Martinez, 2016). Based on website information from major charter management organizations—for example, Democracy Prep Public Schools, Knowledge Is Power Program (KIPP), Success Academy Charter Schools, and Yes Prep Public Schools—the large majority of students enrolled in no-excuses schools are low-income (percentages typically in the 70s to high 80s) and minority (typically over 90%).

Like traditional schools, charter schools have been strongly influenced by test-based accountability requirements and have responded by narrowing the curriculum to leave more time for teaching the tested material. No-excuses schools are designed to do well in this environment because they specialize in instructional and behavioral strategies that are highly focused on the tested material; it is not surprising, therefore, that some of these schools score higher on standardized tests than comparison groups (Gamoran & Fernandez, 2018).

However, the incentive to teach to the test makes it difficult to interpret the results (Koretz, 2009), a problem that has been apparent since the early days of test-based accountability. We do not know the extent to which test scores result from extensive test preparation, whether students also have access to a broad-based education, and whether the test score gains generalize either to other tests of the same material or to broader measures of achievement. Policymakers do not have the information needed to identify the factors that contributed to test score gains, or the "costs" associated with them.

They also do not have the information to assess whether the samples being compared are comparable. Although that issue arises for all comparisons, it is much more difficult to ensure that samples are comparable when charter schools are involved because they have more leverage than traditional schools in determining which students will enroll, whether special education students and English-language learners will be discouraged from enrolling, and which students will be encouraged to leave. It is not unusual for enrollment to decline significantly by the later grades. These factors, in combination, suggest that many studies compare very different samples of students (Welner, 2013).

So, the debate about the interpretation of test scores continues. Given the prevalence of no-excuses models in high-poverty communities, however, we do know that many low-income, minority students have become segregated by education program as well as by the lack of racial and ethnic diversity within the schools they attend.

IN PERSPECTIVE

The controversy over school choice reflects a tension between competing values in U.S. society. For some, school choice is a basic parental right that proponents believe will strengthen children's educational experience. Fiscal policy, they argue, should be designed to give families wide leverage in selecting their children's schools by facilitating the expansion of charter schools, vouchers, or tax benefits. Others, while acknowledging the appeal of school choice, question whether current policies are the best way to strengthen education given their social costs in terms of the adverse effects on the public education system and on the diverse student population it serves. A large body of research evidence is available to assess the benefits and costs of both positions. But conclusions about which approach is optimum are also based on value judgments that extend well beyond education, and what research can tell us, to more general beliefs about the role of government and what it should encourage and fund.

Proponents of expanding school choice have based their support of charter schools on two main assumptions: first, that schools would become more effective if they were no longer constrained by the district bureaucracy and, second, that the introduction of charter schools would create a market economy in which schools would compete, strong schools would thrive, and weak schools, if they did not improve, would drop out (Loeb, Valant, & Kasman, 2011).

The actual results have been quite different. They show wide variation in the academic outcomes of charter schools—some higher, some lower, and many the same as traditional public schools (Center for Research on Education Outcomes, 2009, 2013; Loveless, 2013). As might be expected, the quality of schools varies substantially within each category.

The multiple competing systems have led to greater inequalities, not to stronger schools. Districts now face increased financial constraints linked to multiple management systems. As a result, traditional schools are weakened. Charter schools too have financial shortfalls, covered by donors and investors for some schools, but not for others. Inequities compound within and between districts; high-poverty districts face the greatest hardships.

Moreover, the fact that charter schools have more control than traditional schools over student recruitment, enrollment, and retention might serve as an incentive for parents to choose charter schools if they believe these practices lead to a safer learning environment for their children (Lamberti, n.d.). However, the competition between one set of schools that can shape its student body and another responsible for serving all students comes at a cost as traditional schools are weakened by budget losses at the same time they are responsible for educating increasing proportions of students with the greatest needs. The risk is that the rhetoric of public school failure will become a self-fulfilling prophecy if traditional schools actually do fail because they are so weakened by budget losses and increased demands that they can no longer afford to educate their students. Based on the experience to date, it is not at all certain that charter schools will then be willing and able to assume all the responsibilities currently held by traditional schools (Glazer et al., 2018).

The preponderance of research evidence also shows that charter schools have led to increased segregation by race, ethnicity, income, disability status, and English language proficiency (Baker, 2016; Ladd et al., 2015; Malkus, 2016; Orfield & Ee, 2017; Whitehurst, Reeves, & Rodrigue, 2016). Among the factors contributing to this outcome are family and school preferences, competitive advantages for some families over others in the application process, lack of transportation, differences among schools in the availability of special services, school location that favors one population over another, and targeting of specific racial or ethnic groups either directly or through the types of programs offered (Hechinger, 2011; Rotberg, 2014). The small proportion of settings where charter schools do not increase segregation is typically found in programs specifically designed to achieve that goal (Hechinger, 2011; Kahlenberg & Potter, 2012; Orfield & Frankenberg, 2013). Moreover, the competitive pressures in districts with multiple management systems have encouraged the widespread use of no-excuses models. These schools, rarely found outside high-poverty school districts, are designed specifically for children in communities with concentrated poverty.

The repercussions of charter schools have led to lawsuits and civil rights complaints on district budget shortfalls, inequitable charter school funding, school discipline, increased segregation, and underrepresentation of special education students and English-language learners (Albright, 2014; Boundy, 2012; Bryant, 2016; Cohen, 2016b; Green et al., 2013; Lawyers' Committee for Civil Rights and Economic Justice, 2016b; Leung & Alejandre, 2016; Loudenback, 2016; Prothero, 2015, 2016; Public Counsel, 2015; Raghavendran, 2016; Southern Poverty Law Center, 2016). The National Association for the Advancement of Colored People (NAACP, 2016) and the Movement for Black Lives (2016) issued statements calling for a moratorium on the expansion of privately managed charter schools. Among the reasons given by the NAACP were lack of public representation, increased segregation, and punitive disciplinary policies. The Movement for Black Lives asked for a moratorium on school closures and increased funding for community schools that offer health and social services. However, the issue of charter schools remains highly controversial. Like the population more generally, the African American community is divided about the merits of charter schools, with some emphasizing their social costs and others arguing that they produce options that would not otherwise be available (Movement for Black Lives, 2016; NAACP, 2016; Scott, 2013; Zernike, 2016).

As charter schools have proliferated in cities, they have also increased in suburban districts, rural districts, and towns. The demand, however, remains relatively low. Some districts, for example, have opposed opening charter schools, in part based on a concern that charter schools draw resources from district budgets. The opposition also reflects the fear that charter schools in currently diverse districts will increase segregation by enrolling a student body that is not representative of the larger community—a quite likely outcome given the experience to date in many diverse communities, where charter schools are separated by race, ethnicity, and income (Albright, 2014; Hawes & Parker, 2015; Henig, 2013a, 2013b; Institute on Metropolitan Opportunity, 2013; Ladd et al., 2015; McCoy, 2016; Nevarez & Wyloge, 2016).

Generally, charter school enrollment in nonurban, low-poverty districts remains quite scattered. For example, all of the districts with charter school enrollment shares of 30% or more are urban districts (Table 4.1). The districts with multiple competing management systems remain largely a high-poverty, urban phenomenon.

Peter Schrag (2010) wrote:

> American schools have been charged with creating unity out of a nation of immigrants from a hundred different cultures and languages and thus to perfect democracy; to mitigate, if not eliminate, economic and social inequity; . . . and now, of course, to educate children from that great diversity of backgrounds—all of them—to a high degree of technical and academic competence. (p. 355)

Meeting these goals, however, depends on whether education and social policies are working in the same direction. In the years since *Brown v. Board of Education*, civil rights legislation and legal decisions have helped to increase the access of minority groups to integrated communities and schools, to higher education, and to full participation in the labor market and in political and civic life. The United States has changed enormously—and for the better—in the past 60 years. But high poverty rates, segregated housing and schools, low-paying jobs, and discrimination continue to constrain the progress of many. Although research shows that the black–white achievement gap has narrowed when family income is controlled, the achievement gap based on income has widened (Reardon, 2011).

For the past 15 years, federal education policies have focused on expanding charter schools and making accountability standards more rigorous, apparently in the hope that the policies might mitigate the effects of poverty and segregation that contribute to low achievement (Berliner, 2013; Ferguson, Bovaird, & Mueller, 2007; Poverty & Race Research Action Council, 2015). Not surprisingly, neither policy has been effective in addressing these fundamental problems; however, they have had the unintended consequence of exacerbating segregation of low-income, minority students and the type of education programs available to them. This chapter is intended as a cautionary note. In an attempt to reduce the achievement gap, it is important that we do not implement policies that risk further separating the educational experiences of students in high-poverty communities from those of their more affluent peers.

REFERENCES

Adamson, F., & Darling-Hammond, L. (2011, December). *Addressing the inequitable distribution of teachers: What will it take to get qualified, effective teachers in all communities* [Research brief]. Stanford, CA: Stanford Center for Opportunity Policy in Education. Retrieved from edpolicy.stanford.edu/sites/default/files/publications/addressing-inequitable-distribution-teachers-what-it-will-take-get-qualified-effective-teachers-all-_1.pdf

Albright, M. (2014, December 3). ACLU: Delaware charter schools causing resegregation. *USA Today*. Retrieved from www.usatoday.com/story/news/nation/2014/12/03/complaint-delaware-charter-schools-segregation-discrimination/19841227

Arsen, D., DeLuca, T. A., Ni, Y., & Bates, M. (2015, November). *Which districts get into financial trouble and why: Michigan's story* [Working Paper #51]. East Lansing, MI: Education Policy Center. Retrieved from www.education.msu.edu/epc/library/papers/documents/WP51-Which-Districts-Get-Into-Financial-Trouble-Arsen.pdf

Baker, B. D. (2016, November 30). *Exploring the consequences of charter school expansion in U.S. cities.* Washington, DC: Economic Policy Institute. Retrieved from www.epi.org/publication/exploring-the-consequences-of-charter-school-expansion-in-u-s-cities/

Baker, B., & Miron, G. (2015, December). *The business of charter schooling: Understanding the policies that charter operators use for financial benefit.* Boulder, CO: National Education Policy Center.

Bean, M. (2010). The no-excuses charter school movement. *Dewey to Delpit* [Blog]. Retrieved from edcommentary.blogspot.com/p/no-excuses-charter-movement.html

Berliner, D. C. (2013). Effects of inequality and poverty vs. teachers and schooling on America's youth. *Teachers College Record, 115*, 203–209.

Betts, J. R., & Tang, Y. E. (2011, October). *The effect of charter schools on student achievement: A meta-analysis of the literature.* Seattle, WA: National Charter School Research Project.

Bifulco, R., & Reback, R. (2014). Fiscal impacts of charter schools: Lessons from New York. *Education Finance and Policy, 9*, 86–107.

Boston Municipal Research Bureau. (2016, April 3). *The true cost of Boston's charter schools* [Special report]. Retrieved from bmrb.org/wp-content/uploads/2016/04/SR16-2Charter.pdf

Boundy, K. B. (2012). *Charter schools and students with disabilities: Preliminary analysis of the legal issues and areas of concern.* Boston, MA: Center for Law and Education. Retrieved from tinyurl.com/gonto2h

Bryant, J. (2016). A new lawsuit challenges the legality of "no excuse" charter schools. *The Progressive.* Retrieved from www.progressive.org/pss/new-lawsit-challenges-legality-no-excuse-charter-schools

Butkovitz, A. (2014, October). *The impact of charter schools on the finances of the School District of Philadelphia.* Philadelphia, PA: Office of the Controller. Retrieved from www.philadelphiacontroller.org/publications/CharterSchool_FinancialImpact_October2014.pdf

Center for Education Reform. (2012). *Just the FAQS—charter schools.* Retrieved from www.edreform.com/2012/03/just-the-faqs-charter-schools

Center for Research on Education Outcomes. (2009). *Multiple choice: Charter school performance in 16 states.* Stanford, CA: Author. Retrieved from credo.stanford.edu/reports/MULTIPLE_CHOICE_CREDO.pdf

Center for Research on Education Outcomes. (2013). *National charter school study.* Stanford, CA: Author. Retrieved from credo.stanford.edu/documents/NCSS%202013%20Final%20Draft.pdf

Chandler, M. A. (2015, August 26). Some D.C. charter schools get millions in donations; some almost nothing. *Washington Post.* Retrieved from www.washingtonpost.com/local/education/some-charter-schools-get-millions-in-donations-others-almost-nothing/2015/08/22/b1fdaef0-4804-11e5-8e7d-9c033e6745d8_story.html?utm_term=.8cd0109417ff

Cohen, R. M. (2016a, June 6). Charter and traditional schools fight over money. *The American Prospect.* Retrieved from prospect.org/article/charter-and-traditional-public-schools-fight-over-money

Cohen, R. M. (2016b, January 26). School desegregation lawsuit threatens charters. *American Prospect.* Retrieved from prospect.org/article/school-desegregation-lawsuit-threatens-charters

Cook, J. B. (2016a). *The impact of charter schools on district school budgets* [Working Paper No. 229]. New York, NY: National Center for the Study of Privatization of Education. Retrieved from ncspe.tc.columbia.edu/working-papers/OP229.pdf

Cook, J. B. (2016b, May 14). *The effect of charter competition on unionized district revenues* [Working Paper]. Retrieved from ncspe.tc.columbia.edu/working-papers/OP229.pdf

Council for Exceptional Children. (2012, April). *Improving special education in charter schools* [Issue brief]. Retrieved from www.cec.sped.org/~/media/Files/Policy/ESEA/Recommendations/Improving%20Education%20in%20Charter%20Schools.pdf

Dreilinger, D. (2016, July 14). New Orleans' Katrina state takeover to end, Legislature decides. *NOLA.com.* Retrieved from www.nola.com/education/index.ssf/2016/05/new_orleans_schools_reunify.html

Dudley-Marling, C., & Baker, D. (2012). The effects of market-based reforms on students with disabilities. *Disabilities Studies Quarterly, 32*(2). Retrieved from dsq-sds.org/article/view/3187/3072

EdChoice. (2017). *School choice: School choice in America.* Retrieved February 14, 2017, from www.edchoice.org/school-choice/school-choice-in-america

Education Commission of the States. (2014). *How does education in my state compare?* Retrieved from www.ecs.org/clearinghouse/01/15/79/11579.pdf

Education Encyclopedia. (n.d.). *School boards—selection and education of mem-*

bers. Retrieved from education.stateuniversity.com/pages/2390/School-Boards-SELECTION-EDUCATION-MEMBERS.html

Erickson, A. T. (2013). The rhetoric of choice, segregation, desegregation, and charter schools. In M. B. Katz & M. Rose (Eds.), *Public education under siege* (pp. 122–130). Philadelphia, PA: University of Pennsylvania Press.

Farrie, D., & Johnson, M. (2015, November). *Newark Public Schools: Budget impacts of underfunding and rapid charter growth.* Newark, NJ: Education Law Center. Retrieved from www.edlawcenter.org/assets/files/pdfs/publications/NPS%20Budget%20Impacts%20of%20Underfunding%20and%20Rapid%20Charter%20Growth.pdf

Ferguson, H. B., Bovaird, M. P. H., & Mueller, M. P. (2007). The impact of poverty on educational outcomes for children. *Pediatrics and Child Health, 12*(8), 701–706.

Gamoran, A., & Fernandez, C. M. (2018). Do charter schools strengthen education in high-poverty urban districts? In I. C. Rotberg & J. L. Glazer (Eds.), *Choosing charters: Better schools or more segregation?* (pp. 133–152). New York, NY: Teachers College Press.

Glazer, J. L., & Egan, C. (2016, April). *The Tennessee Achievement School District: Race, history, and the dilemma of public engagement* [Working Paper]. Graduate School of Education & Human Development, The George Washington University, Washington, DC.

Glazer, J., Massell, D., & Malone, M. (2018). Charter schooling in a state-run turnaround district: Lessons from the Tennessee Achievement School District. In I. C. Rotberg & J. L. Glazer (Eds.), *Choosing charters: Better schools or more segregation?* (pp. 95–115). New York, NY: Teachers College Press.

Goodman, J. F. (2013). Charter management organizations and the regulated environment: Is it worth the price? *Educational Researcher, 42*(2), 89–96.

Green, P. C., III, Baker, B. D., & Oluwole, J. O. (2013). Having it both ways: How charter schools try to obtain funding of public schools and the autonomy of private schools. *Emory Law Journal, 63*(2), 303–337.

Gurley, G. (2016, April 7). The great diversion: Charter schools may or may not improve student outcomes—but they divert funds away from other public schools. *The American Prospect.* Retrieved from prospect.org/article/great-diversion-0

Hawes, J. B., & Parker, A. (2015, February 7). Schools still separate and unequal. Locals, records detail the path to integration of Charleston's libraries. *The Post and Courier.* Retrieved from www.postandcourier.com/archives/schools-still-separate-and-unequal-locals-records-detail-the-path/article_9e4605dd-436b-56c9-b310-30d9e124f2e6.html

Hechinger, J. (2011, December 22). Segregated charter schools evoke separate but equal era in U.S. *Bloomberg Business.* Retrieved from www.bloomberg.com/news/articles/2011-12-22/segregated-charter-schools-evoke-separate-but-equal-era-in-u-s-education

Henig, J. R. (2013a). Charter inroads in affluent communities: Hype or turning point? In R. Lake (Ed.), *Hopes, fears, & reality: A balanced look at American charter schools in 2012* (pp. 1–20). Seattle, WA: Center on Reinventing Public Education.

Henig, J. (2013b, May 1). *Charters branch out: Do moves into affluent areas signal an important trend?* Seattle, WA: Center on Reinventing Public Education. Retrieved from www.crpe.org/updates/charters-branch-out-do-moves-affluent-areas-signal-important-trend

Hernandez, L. E. (2016). Race and racelessness in CMO marketing: Exploring charter management organizations' racial construction and its implications. *Peabody Journal of Education, 91*(1), 47–63.

Hess, F. M., & Henig, J. R. (Eds.). (2015). *The new education philanthropy: Politics, policy, and reform*. Cambridge, MA: Harvard Education Press.

Hinchcliffe, K. (2016, August 4). 5 things to know about NC's new Achievement School District. *WRAL News*. Retrieved from www.wral.com/5-things-to-know-about-nc-s-new-achievement-school-district/15899993/

Howell, W. G. (2015). Results of President Obama's race to the top. *Education Next, 15*(4). Retrieved from educationnext.org/results-president-obama-race-to-the-top-reform

Institute on Metropolitan Opportunity. (2013, October). *Charter schools in the Twin Cities: 2013 update*. Minneapolis, MN: University of Minnesota Law School. Retrieved from www.law.umn.edu/sites/law.umn.edu/files/newsfiles/579fd7a6/Charter-School-Update-2013-final.pdf

Jacobs, P. (2015, June 20). Here's how America's first-ever charter school got off the ground. *Business Insider*. Retrieved from www.businessinsider.com/inside-the-first-charter-school-in-america-city-academy-2015-6

Kahlenberg, R. D., & Potter, H. (2012). *Diverse charter schools: Can racial and socioeconomic integration promote better outcomes for students?* Washington, DC: Poverty & Race Research Action Council and The Century Foundation.

Koretz, D. (2009). *Measuring up: What educational testing really tells us*. Cambridge, MA: Harvard University Press.

Ladd, H. F., Clotfelter, C. T., & Holbein, J. B. (2015). *The growing segmentation of the charter school sector in North Carolina* [Working Paper 133]. Washington, DC: National Center for Analysis of Longitudinal Data in Education Research.

Lafer, G. (2014, April 24). *Do poor kids deserve lower-quality education than rich kids? Evaluating school privatization proposals in Milwaukee, Wisconsin*. Washington, DC: Economic Policy Institute.

Lamberti, C. (n.d.). *Selling choice: Marketing charter schools in Chicago*. Chicago, IL: Chicago Public Schools. Retrieved from www.ctunet.com/quest-center/research/Selling-Choice-Marketing-Charter-Schools-in-Chicago.pdf

Lawyers' Committee for Civil Rights and Economic Justice. (2016a). *Lawyers' committee moves to intervene in charter cap case on behalf of students of color, students with disabilities, and English language learners*. Retrieved from lawyerscom.org/lawyers-committee-moves-to-intervene-in-charter-cap-case-on-behalf-of-students-of-color-students-with-disabilities-and-english-language-learners

Lawyers' Committee for Civil Rights and Economic Justice. (2016b). *Court to hear argument in charter cap lawsuit* [Press release]. Retrieved from lawyerscom.org/court-to-hear-argument-in-charter-cap-lawsuit

Leung, V., & Alejandre, R. H. (2016). *Unequal access: How some California charter schools illegally restrict enrollment*. Los Angeles, CA: ACLU of Southern California and Public Advocates. Retrieved from www.publicadvocates.org/wp-content/uploads/Report-Unequal-Access-080116.pdf

Loeb, S., Valant, J., & Kasman, M. (2011, March). Increasing choice in the market for schools: Recent reforms and their effects on student achievement. *National Tax Journal, 64*(1), 141–164.

Losen, D. J., Keith, M. A., II, Hodson, C. L., & Martinez, T. E. (2016, March). *Charter schools, civil rights and school discipline: A comprehensive review*. Los Angeles, CA: The Civil Rights Project.

Loudenback, J. (2016, June 9). *Compton trauma lawsuit near resolution?* Retrieved from laschoolreport.com/compton-trauma-lawsuit-near-resolution

Loveless, T. (2013). *Charter school study: Much ado about tiny differences*. Washington, DC: Brookings Institution.

Lustig, M. (2016, March 2). *Rethinking equity in Philadelphia: The Philadelphia case* [Student paper]. Graduate School of Education and Human Development, The George Washington University, Washington, DC.

Malkus, N. (2016, November 30). *Unlike their neighbors: Charter school student composition across states*. Washington, DC: American Enterprise Institute.

Mathis, W. J., & Powers, J. M. (2015). *Charter researchers promoting "no-excuses" schools republish inflated claims* [Press release]. Boulder, CO: National Education Policy Center.

Mathis, W. J., & Welner, K. G. (2016, March). *Research-based options for education policymaking: Do choice policies segregate schools?* Boulder, CO: National Education Policy Center. Retrieved from nepc.colorado.edu/files/publications/Mathis%20RBOPM-3%20Choice%20Segregation.pdf

McCoy, D. P. (2016, August 29). How charters became the most segregated schools in Indianapolis. *Chalkbeat*. Retrieved from www.chalkbeat.org/posts/in/2016/09/29/ips-board-approves-changes-to-magnet-admission-opening-doors-to-more-diverse-schools

Minnesota Legislative Reference Library. (2016). *Resources on Minnesota issues: Charter schools*. Retrieved from www.leg.state.mn.us/lrl/issues/issues?issue=charter

Miron, G., & Gulosino, C. (2013, November). *Profiles of for-profit and nonprofit education management organizations: Fourteenth edition—2011–2012*. Boulder, CO: National Education Policy Center.

Miron, G., Urschel, J. L., Mathis, W. J., & Tornquist, E. (2010). *Schools without diversity: Education management organizations, charter schools, and the demographic stratification of the American school system*. Boulder, CO: Education and the Public Interest Center & Education Policy Research Unit.

Mississippi Legislature. (2016). *House Bill 989*. Retrieved from billstatus.ls.state.ms.us/documents/2016/html/HB/0900-0999/HB0989PS.htm

Movement for Black Lives. (2016). *A vision for black lives: Policy demands for black power, freedom, & justice*. Retrieved from policy.m4bl.org

National Alliance for Public Charter Schools. (2016). *A growing movement: America's largest charter school communities*. Washington, DC: Author. Retrieved from www.publiccharters.org/wp-content/uploads/2015/11/enrollmentshare_web.pdf

National Alliance for Public Charter Schools. (2017). *Estimated charter public school enrollment, 2016–2017*. Washington, DC: Author. Retrieved from www.publiccharters.org/wp-content/uploads/2017/01/EER_Report_V5.pdf

National Association for the Advancement of Colored People. (2016, October 15). *Statement regarding the NAACP's resolution on a moratorium on charter schools* [Press release]. Retrieved from www.naacp.org/latest/statement-regarding-naacps-resolution-moratorium-charter-schools

National Center for Education Statistics. (2015). Table 216.20, Number and enrollment of public elementary and secondary schools, by school level, type, and charter and magnet status: Selected years, 1990–91 through 2013–14. In *Common core of data, public elementary/secondary school universe survey, 1990–91 through 2013–14*. Retrieved from nces.ed.gov/programs/digest/d15/tables/dt15_216.20.asp

National Center for Education Statistics. (2016, April). Charter school enrollment. In *The condition of education*. Retrieved from nces.ed.gov/programs/coe/indicator_cgb.asp

Nevada Department of Education. (n.d.). *Nevada Achievement School District*. Retrieved from www.doe.nv.gov/ASD

Nevarez, G., & Wyloge, E. (2016, February 13). Charter student populations don't match state demographics. *The Arizona Republic*. Retrieved from bit.ly/2lfbWk3

Orfield, G., & Ee, J. (2017). *Our segregated capital: An increasingly diverse city with racially polarized schools*. Los Angeles, CA: The Civil Rights Project.

Orfield, G., & Frankenberg, E. (2013). *Education delusions: How choice can deepen inequality and how to make schools fair*. Oakland, CA: University of California Press.

Poverty & Race Research Action Council. (2015). *Annotated bibliography: The impact of school-based poverty concentration on academic achievement & student outcomes*. Washington, DC: Author. Retrieved from school-diversity.org/pdf/annotated_bibliography_on_school_poverty_concentration.pdf

Prothero, A. (2015, December 17). Wash. court ruling could be roadmap to charter opponents in other states. *Education Week*. Retrieved from www.edweek.org/ew/articles/2015/12/17/wash-court-ruling-could-be-roadmap-to.html

Prothero, A. (2016, July 13). Mississippi lawsuit says charter schools are unconstitutionally funded. *Education Week*. Retrieved from blogs.edweek.org/edweek/charterschoice/2016/07/mississippi_lawsuit_says_charter_schools_are_unconstitutionally_funded.html

Public Counsel. (2015, September 15). *Historic ruling in landmark complaint on unique learning needs of children affected by trauma*. Retrieved from www.publiccounsel.org/stories?id=0172

Raghavendran, B. (2016, July 13). Judge refuses to dismiss Minnesota desegregation suit. *Star Tribune*. Retrieved from www.startribune.com/judge-refuses-to-dismiss-minnesota-desegregation-suit/386712411

Raise Your Hand for Illinois Public Education. (n.d.). *On the elected representative school board campaign*. Retrieved from www.ilraiseyourhand.org/content/elected-representative-school-board-campaign

Reardon, S. F. (2011). The widening academic achievement gap between the rich and the poor: New evidence and possible explanations. In R. Murnane & G. Duncan (Eds.), *Whither opportunity? Rising inequality and the uncertain life chances of low-income children* (pp. 91–116). New York, NY: Russell Sage Foundation Press.

Rotberg, I. C. (2014). Charter schools and the risk of increased segregation. *Phi Delta Kappan, 95*(5), 26–30.

Sanchez, M., & Belsha, K. (2015, July 13). Neighborhood schools' budgets decline with enrollment loss. *Catalyst Chicago*. Retrieved from catalyst-chicago.org/2015/07/neighborhood-schools-budgets-decline-with-enrollment-loss

Sattin-Bajaj, C., & Suarez-Orozco, M. (2012). *English language learner students and charter students in New York state: Challenges and opportunities*. Report from the NY Governor's Leadership Team for High Quality Charter Public Schools. Albany, NY: New York State Department of Education.

Schrag, P. (2010). America's orgy of reform. In I. C. Rotberg (Ed.), *Balancing change and tradition in global education reform* (2nd ed.). Lanham, MD: Rowman & Littlefield Education.

Scott, J. (2013). Educational movements, not market moments. In M. B. Katz & M. Rose (Eds.), *Public education under siege* (pp. 84–90). Philadelphia, PA: University of Pennsylvania Press.

Southern Poverty Law Center. (2016, July 11). *SPLC lawsuit: Mississippi charter school funding violates state constitution*. Retrieved from www.splcenter.org/news/2016/07/11/splc-lawsuit-mississippi-charter-school-funding-violates-state-constitution

Stokes, K. (2016, May 10). *Teachers union: Enrollment loss to charter schools costs L.A.*

Unified at least $500 million. Retrieved from www.scpr.org/news/2016/05/10/60491/
teachers-union-enrollment-loss-to-charter-schools

U.S. Department of Education. (2016, September 28). *U.S. Department of Education awards
$245 million to support high quality public charter schools* [Press release]. Retrieved
from www.ed.gov/news/press-releases/us-department-education-awards-245-million-
support-high-quality-public-charter-schools

Welner, K. G. (2013, April). The dirty dozen: How charter schools influence student enrollment. *Teachers College Record* [online], ID Number 17104.

Whitehurst, G. J., Reeves, R. V., & Rodrigue, E. (2016). *Segregation, race, and charter schools:
What do we know?* Washington, DC: Center on Children and Families at Brookings.

Woodworth, J. L., Raymond, M. E., Chirbas, K., Gonzalez, M., Negassi, Y., Snow, W., &
Van Donge, C. (2015). *Online charter school study.* Stanford, CA: Center for Research
on Education Outcomes. Retrieved from credo.stanford.edu/pdfs/Online%20Charter
%20Study%20Final.pdf

Zernike, K. (2016, August 20). Condemnation of charter schools exposes a rift over black
students. *The New York Times.* Retrieved from www.nytimes.com/2016/08/21/us/
blacks-charter-schools.html?_r=0

Zgainer, A. C., & Kerwin, K. (Eds.). (2015). *Charter school laws across the states: 2015 rank-
ings & scorecard.* Washington, DC: Center for Education Reform. Retrieved from
www.edreform.com/wp-content/uploads/2015/07/CharterLaws2015.pdf

CHAPTER 5

Shaping Charter Enrollment and Access

Practices, Responses, and Ramifications

Wagma Mommandi and Kevin Welner

Things are not always as they seem.

—Plato, "Phaedrus"

In the fall of 2015, *The New York Times* broke a story about a "got to go" list generated by leaders of the Success Academy charter school in Fort Greene, Brooklyn (Taylor, 2015). The article described how the elementary school used a variety of discipline-related approaches to pressure families to withdraw the listed children. The targeted children were, it seems, not achieving or behaving as well as the school wished. Several parents interviewed by the *Times* said that Success Academy employees explicitly told them the school was not right for their children. Nine of the 16 students on the Fort Greene list eventually withdrew from the school.

Eva Moskowitz, founder and director of the Success Academies, explained that her charter schools are "not the right fit for every student, and that [she believes] in having honest conversations with parents about what is best for their children" (Chadha, 2015). Similarly, reacting to the "got-to-go list," James D. Merriman, the chief executive officer of the New York City Charter School Center, a group that advocates and supports charter schools, said it was "unrealistic to expect any given school to be a good fit for every child" (Taylor, 2015).

As Merriman's statement suggests, this got-to-go list illustrates a broader set of problems around "fit." Operators of charter schools presumably define "fit" nonrandomly; lower-scoring students, those who require additional supports, and those seen as behavioral problems are generally seen as poorer fits. This leads to serious access issues and, from a researcher's perspective, results in selection bias. Consider, for example, the following:

- Great Hearts Academies, a network of charter schools enrolling more than 13,000 students at 29 schools in Arizona and Texas, is highly acclaimed for its results and its popularity. In 2015, Great Hearts' pass rates on Arizona's statewide achievement tests were double those of peer district schools at the secondary level. The average SAT of Great Hearts students in recent years was 1830, nearly 300 points higher than the national average. Almost all graduates (98%) immediately attend colleges or universities. But who is served by these schools? It turns out that while "more than half of Arizona's public school students qualify for free or reduced-price lunches, . . . only two of 19 Great Hearts schools in the Phoenix area participated in the National School Lunch Program and received federal Title I funding for at-risk populations" (Malik, 2015). Additionally, the *Phoenix New Times* reported that these Arizona and Texas charter schools spent no money on English-language learner instruction in 2014 (Alonzo, 2014).
- Stargate School, a charter school in Colorado serves the gifted and talented; students must pass an IQ test to be accepted. In the 2015–2016 school year, approximately 84% of students were white or Asian, and 1.6% qualified for free- or reduced-price lunch. In comparison, Stargate's home district, the Adams 12 Five Star School district, had very different enrollment: 39.3% of students qualified for free- or reduced-price lunch, and only 56% were white or Asian (Colorado Department of Education, 2016).

These charter schools portray themselves to the public as exclusively for the academically elite in much the same way that, for example, Boston Latin or Bronx Science do. Other charter schools accomplish the same outcome in subtler ways— approaches that are uniquely available to charters.

- Green Woods Charter School in Northwest Philadelphia had a system where interested parents could get an application only if they attended an open house held at a private golf club in the suburbs (Herold, 2012).
- Longmont, Colorado's Flagstaff Academy gives enrollment priority for the few available kindergarten seats to students previously enrolled in Flagstaff Academy Preschool, an associated, private (tuition-charging) preschool (Flagstaff Academy, 2016a, 2016b). The Flagstaff Academy was just one of several charter schools we identified with such enrollment policies.
- In the Silicon Valley of California, Bullis Charter School, serving an elite K–8 clientele, asks families to donate $5,000 per child each year (Hechinger, 2011).

In this chapter, we explore and analyze these and other practices, attempting to understand how and why they arise. Charter schools exist within a school choice ecosystem shaped in part by incentives and disincentives that, in turn, shape those schools' approaches to access. Given that different students come with different financial costs, test scores, and behavior, they are differentially attractive as potential enrollees. To survive and to thrive, charter schools must compete; they are successful when they enroll a sufficient number of students and when those students' outcomes allow the school to attract a new group of students each year. Accordingly, success for a charter school depends on an ongoing public perception as a successful school within a test-based accountability system, and this reality creates strong incentives to attract and enroll students whose behavior aligns with school philosophy, who have no expensive special needs, and who have high test scores and fluency in English.

Predictably, charter schools have sometimes responded to these powerful incentives with policies and practices that limit access and diversity. This chapter, which arises out of our access research, describes these policies and practices as well as positive, mitigating steps taken by some in the charter school sector. We do not, in describing these practices, feign objectivity. That is, while we acknowledge the incentives that drive charter schools to limit access, we see these limitations as patently harmful. Because charter schools portray themselves as public schools, the barriers to access that we discovered undermine fairness and wound our democracy. Because these barriers distort enrollment, they also undermine attempts by researchers to compare relative effectiveness of schools in the charter and noncharter sectors. And because "creaming" practices depend on other schools to serve the students left behind, charter school reform cannot scale up if those schools are not broadly accessible.

ACCESS PRACTICES: A QUALITATIVE STUDY

In this chapter, we summarize some lessons from our 2-year qualitative study of charter schools' access practices. The overall aim of the study has been to build a more nuanced understanding of how charter school policies and practices can restrict access. We also asked our informants about steps that they and others have taken to recognize and address access issues, so that other schools and policymakers can learn from their experiences and ideas.

We conducted a total of 40 phone interviews with charter school experts (primarily charter officials, education and legal researchers, and attorneys). We began by identifying researchers who had a track record of publishing high-quality, peer-reviewed, and widely cited research on charter schools. Charter school educators and officials, as well as attorneys working in the charter-access realm, were also contacted early on. During this initial round, interviewees were asked for recommendations of other people to talk to regarding charter school policies and practices. This snowball sampling approach yielded further interviews, with this process continuing until the policies and practices being shared by new interviewees were consistently duplicating ones already documented.

Using a semistructured interview protocol, we probed for examples of restrictions, then for examples of practices that were remedial or broadening. We also sought documentation of policies and practices (e.g., charter legislation, contracts, applications, parent and student handbooks, and reports). We used these documents to clarify statements and corroborate claims made by interviewees. Finally, we gathered online news articles on issues of charter access for the period from 2002 to 2015. Whenever possible, we cite published reports and news articles supporting the information provided to us by our interviewees. We analyzed these data with a coding scheme primarily derived from charter practices outlined in *The Dirty Dozen: How Charter Schools Influence Student Enrollment* (Welner, 2013).

The snowball approach we used for data gathering was necessary because random sampling was not realistic; it would not be productive to ask charter school leaders to report candidly about ways they limit or shape access. Yet the resulting data have both strengths and limitations. They allow for us to provide a rich picture of how access issues are playing out in charter schools around the country, but they do not allow for quantification, and we make no attempt to determine how many charter schools use a given approach.

We divided approaches into three rough time periods: preenrollment, enrollment, and postenrollment. We also classified the data based on "different approaches that charter schools use to structure their student enrollment," as previously identified by Welner (2013). We used the 12 approaches identified in 2013 and added two additional approaches that we identified during the course of our research.

In this chapter, we focus on three of the 14 ways charter schools shape student access—one from each phase. From the preenrollment period we chose description and design; from the enrollment period, conditions placed on enrollment; and from the postenrollment period, disciplinary practices. The remaining 11 practices are just as significant, however, and they are briefly described in Table 5.1. Note that a few of these practices are available to—and used by—public schools as well; while the flexibility granted charter schools allows greater leeway, schools in both sectors face similar incentives and sometimes respond in similar ways.

DESCRIPTION AND DESIGN: WHICH NICHE?

Choices made by a new charter school about the niche it will fill can send explicit and implicit messages about who is welcome and who is not. These choices can skew a school toward elite enrollment or can deliberately reach out to underserved populations. In New York City, Reinventing Options for Adolescents Deserving Success (ROADS) is a network of charter high schools with a mission to ensure that overage, undercredited students graduate from high school. ROADS has an admission priority for students who are involved in the juvenile or criminal justice system, who are homeless or in transitional housing, or who are involved in foster care or Child Protective Services (ROADS Charter High Schools, n.d.).

Table 5.1. Fourteen Approaches That Charter Schools Use to Structure Student Enrollment

PRACTICE	DESCRIPTION	EXAMPLE
Preenrollment		
Location	Strategic decisions made about school location that serve to either restrict access to undesired students or expand reach to desired populations (see Lubienski, Gulosino, & Weitzel, 2009)	Bullis Charter School in Los Altos, California, selected its population by locating in an affluent suburb and then using a hierarchy of enrollment preferences, including reserving half of all open seats for students residing in the wealthiest part of the Los Altos school district (Hechinger, 2011).
Marketing	Policies and practices related to marketing that serve to attract desired students and families and/or to dissuade undesired students and families	LISA Academy in Little Rock, Arkansas, recruited students by sending out mailers to area neighborhoods—except for the three zip codes representing the heavily Black and Latino parts of town, with the highest concentration of low-income housing (Petrimoulx, 2016). Jabbar (2015) documented invite-only school information nights in New Orleans where current school parents were asked to bring like-minded friends.
Description and design*	Decisions about a charter's thematic approach and curriculum that selectively appeal to different segments of the population	California's American Heritage Charter Schools have been accused of Christian messaging and curricular content, including a teacher giving a prayer in the name of Jesus at the school's commencement ceremony (Eakins, 2006). Military themes, language foci, and academic rigor are additional examples.
During enrollment		
Steering	The practice of selectively dissuading families during the enrollment stage (see Fiore, Harwell, Blackorby, & Finnigan, 2000)	Concerning Cambridge Lakes Learning Center in Illinois, the school board has heard complaints about special education services, including concerns that parents were being coached to modify their child's IEP in order to attend and that families were steered away because the school stated it could not serve their child's IEP needs (Community Unit District 300, 2016).

Table 5.1. Continued.

Denial of services	Not making available services to meet the needs of a given group of higher-needs children, including students with special needs and students whose first language is not English	At Dugsi Academy, only 4% of students were in special education, vs. 18% in Minneapolis and St. Paul district schools. The assistant director of Dugsi explained the school did not have the space to serve Level 3 special education students (Brown, 2012).
Illegal and dicey practices	Troubling and potentially illegal policies and practices that have the effect of discouraging or omitting less desired populations altogether	Interviewees told us it was common for charter schools to ask for Social Security numbers and birth certificates before enrollment, which goes against guidance from the U.S. Departments of Justice and Education (2014).
Conditions placed on enrollment	Conditions placed on enrollment that serve to turn away families or discourage families perceived to be less desirable	Benjamin Franklin Charter School (2016) in New Orleans requires students to take an admissions test in reading, language, and math and then screens out students whose test scores (combined with prior grade point averages) are insufficient.
Required volunteerism	Policies that state or imply that parents are required to commit hours of work as a condition of enrollment and thereby dissuade certain families at the enrollment stage (see Hammel, 2014)	At Keys Gate Charter School in Florida, parents must volunteer 20 hours of service for one child and 10 more for additional children, with half of the hours completed before winter break.
Conditions in applications˙	Requirements and conditions included within formal charter school application documents	This may include admissions essays, entrance exams, required in-person visits to the school at specified times, and short application windows. The application for Roseland charter in California is approximately 35 pages long and requires students to write an autobiography, five short essays, and six short response questions; parents are also required to write several essays of their own (*Los Angeles Times* editorial board, 2016).

Table 5.1. Continued.

	Postenrollment	
Counseling out	The practice of encouraging already enrolled students deemed to be a poor fit to consider different school options	At California's Accelerated Achievement Academy, students are individually told that the school is not meeting their needs if they are on academic probation for two consecutive semesters (Leung, Alejandre, & Jongco, 2016).
Grade retention	The practice of retaining students who do not meet proscribed academic benchmarks	One way to counsel out students is to tell them that they will not progress to the next grade if they remain. Students faced with this choice often opt to return to their neighborhood public school. At Freire Charter School in Philadelphia, a college preparatory school, if 5th- or 6th-graders fail two or more classes, they are retained with no summer school option.
Not backfilling student attrition	The practice of restricting new enrollment to only certain grade levels or refusing to accept new students during the school year, which reduces disruption but correspondingly shifts burdens to district schools and denies access to more mobile student populations	Latin American Montessori Bilingual Public Charter School in Washington, DC, takes no new students after prekindergarten (Chandler, 2015).
Charges	Burdensome costs, dues, and fees that amount to an informal tuition	Cambridge Lakes Charter School in Illinois mandated that each student's family invest in the company that built the school (Simon, 2013).
Discipline and punishment*	Expulsion, suspension, and other forms of harsh discipline that have the effect of pushing out students whose behavior does not align with school philosophy	A large percentage of Philadelphia charter schools have provisions in their disciplinary code that enable them to suspend or expel students for trivial acts such as untucked shirts, swearing, not having a belt, being disrespectful, folding arms, rolling eyes, or sucking teeth.

*These three approaches—description and design (preenrollment phase), conditions placed on enrollment (enrollment phase), and disciplinary practices (postenrollment phase)—are reviewed in depth in the chapter.

As another example, several interviewees pointed to the messages sent by certain language-immersion charter schools. An education researcher described a dual-immersion French school in East Oakland and rhetorically asked, "Who is that school designed for?" Another researcher pointed us to Washington Yu Ying Public Charter school, in Washington, DC, which uses a Mandarin-immersion approach. Although the population of Ward 5, home to Yu Ying, was 76% African American in 2010 (DC Office of Planning, n.d.), during the 2014–2015 school year only 37% of Yu Ying's enrolled students were African American (DC Public Charter School Board, 2016). A third researcher described a German-immersion charter school in the Minneapolis/St. Paul area:

> They were concerned from board level . . . about the school's lack of diversity, but clear steps that could have [been] taken . . . were not. [There were] lots of things that worked against them; [it's] not easy being a German immersion school [if seeking diversity].

There are clear academic benefits of immersion schools in languages such as French, German, and Mandarin. Yet, as the Minnesota researcher pointed out, being an immersion school influences who likely applicants will be, which counsels in favor of deliberate and active steps if the school's operators want to reach a broader swath of the community's student population.

Similarly, potential applicants are likely influenced when charter schools target a particular cultural or ethnic community via ethnocentric emphases. Eckes and Carr (2014) highlighted how these types of schools strive to preserve language and culture while also using their niche to improve learning for students underserved in other schools. Yet several of our interviewees stressed the importance of considering whether such schools limit access by discouraging students who do not identify with the culture or ethnicity the school is designed to serve. From this perspective, ethnocentric charter schools are mirror images of—or alternatives to—the eurocentricity of many traditional public schools. As with the language-immersion schools, an ethnocentric emphasis can provide clear benefits, but it can also shape enrollment.

These design influences are perhaps even clearer with a separate group of schools, where religion and language are tightly correlated. Interviewees called attention, for example, to the growth in the Hebrew-immersion charter movement and to an Arabic immersion charter school in Michigan (see Brownstein, 2014).

Christian messaging and curricular content came up the most in our research. Heritage Academy in Arizona (which runs three charter schools) was recently sued for Establishment Clause violations related to textbooks and other teachings that were allegedly overtly religious (Fisher, 2016a). California's American Heritage Charter Schools have engaged in comparable practices, including a teacher giving a prayer in the name of Jesus at the school's commencement ceremony (Eakins, 2006). Other charters, framed as "classical academies," have faced similar allegations. Two interviewees mentioned the Barney Charter School Initiative, a project of Michigan's conservative Hillsdale College that aims to advance the founding of classical charter schools (Hillsdale College, 2016). These schools project an underlying message to families that emphasizes a classical education but also has strong religious undertones. Seven Oaks Classical Academy in Bloomington, Indiana, is a member of the Barney Initiative and was designed to emphasize "America's founding principles" and to focus on traditional teaching methods and Latin. After it was denied a charter twice through the Indiana Charter School Board, the charter was granted by Grace College and Seminary, a private evangelical institution (Colombo, 2016).

"Hundreds of . . . charter schools are currently housed in former Catholic school facilities" (Brinson, 2011, p. 2). These schools did not convert into charter schools; rather, they shut down and charter schools opened up in the same space, often enrolling the same students, employing the same staff, and operating on church grounds (Decker & Carr, 2015). Similarly, Ohio's Patriot Preparatory Academy arose from the private Liberty Christian Academy in 2010. The charter school sets forth its "creed" as "Today I will act in wisdom, cooperation and faith" (Patriot Preparatory Academy, 2017), and when it converted from the private Christian school it kept the same building, many of the same teachers, the same founder, and half of the same students (Richards, 2010). Again, the contention here is not that these schools are out of compliance with the law; it is that they shape their enrollment in part via their outward projection as a religiously identified school.

Schools like these do not expressly identify as religious schools, and their teachings differ from those of private religious schools. Instead, the schools often focus on values and character and use curricula grounded in a given religion. This was the case with Colorado's Twin Peaks Charter Academy, which prohibited its 2016 valedictorian from including a mention of his (gay) sexual orientation during his speech (see Cheek, 2015).

Another group of schools label themselves as "academically rigorous," or as one interviewee put it, they "seek students who are gifted and talented." Perhaps the most prominent are the 21 charter schools that are part of the BASIS charter network. The BASIS approach is expressly demanding, even grueling. Expectations are that all students are at AP level in all subjects and that students test competitively on the Organization for Economic Co-operation and Development Test for Schools (McNeel, 2014). The BASIS parent–student handbook (n.d.) boasts, "The BASIS.ed program for grades 8–12 is widely recognized as one of the most academically-advanced high school programs in the world." The schools are marked by demographics strongly skewed toward families that are white, Asian, and wealthy, and by surprisingly high attrition rates given those demographics (Alonzo, 2014; Nevarez & Wyloge, 2016).

Like BASIS, the Great Hearts network of classical and highly rigorous charter schools (located in Phoenix and San Antonio) appeals strongly to parents who might otherwise seek out private schools for their classical or intensely advanced curricula (McNeel, 2014). The Charter School of Wilmington, another of the nation's most acclaimed high schools (Newsweek, 2015), focuses on math and science and prioritizes applicants who have a specific interest in the school; this interest is identified in part by student test scores (Wolfman-Arent, 2014).

Being academically demanding is, by itself, a positive characteristic for a school. But when those demands are coupled with a sink-or-swim approach (and message), as well as high attrition, it is easy to see how these schools actively shape their enrollment. When these schools then appear at the top of lists of America's top high schools, what we are seeing is the completion of a cycle, with elite enrollments leading to incredibly high measured outcomes, which leads back to more elite enrollments.

Charter schools have also become a small but growing area of K–12 military education. There are about 40 military-themed charter schools around the country, according to Ray Rottman, the president of the Association of Military Colleges and Schools of the United States. Then mayor of Oakland Jerry Brown started the first military-themed charter in 2001, the Oakland Military Institute. Brown explained that he chose to affiliate the school with the California National Guard because of its emphasis on ceremony, discipline, inspiration, and leadership training (Brown, 2001). Similarly, at Maritime Charter School in Buffalo, students wear $500 uniforms courtesy of the U.S. Navy. Maritime had the highest attrition rate of all of Buffalo's charter schools in 2015, and in the previous year one of every four students was either expelled, suspended, or withdrew. The charter school's leaders openly acknowledge the school's strict approach to discipline, which emphasizes that students must follow the rules, succeed academically, and commit to physical fitness (Tan, 2015). Again, a niche emphasis such as this will predictably yield a niche enrollment.

HOOPING IT UP: CONDITIONS PLACED ON APPLICATIONS

Through the application process, charter schools can control the pipeline that leads to enrolled students. If less desirable students do not apply, they will not be enrolled. Charter schools are usually in charge of their own application processes, and many impose a daunting array of conditions. These include lengthy application forms such as a required essay simply to get into the lottery, mandatory character references, a requirement for parents to visit the school before applying, short time windows to file the applications, special preenrollment periods for insiders, and admissions tests to determine grade placement or learning group. These policies and practices can directly turn away families (*I'm sorry, but you can't enroll here because you didn't visit*). Further, they can serve their purpose by discouraging parents who lack the time, resources, or overall commitment to jump through the hoops (Welner, 2013).

Four notable application-process approaches for limiting access came up repeatedly during our study: long and burdensome applications, required in-person visits, entrance assessments, and application deadlines. Each one of these, by itself, could deter a family from applying, but when used in concert, they are particularly onerous and effective.

Applications for charters are sometimes straightforward and even uniform within a school district. But some charter schools have applications that are long and potentially burdensome to complete, making them inaccessible for many families. One example is Roseland Accelerated Middle School in Santa Rosa, California, whose intimidating online application form was highlighted in a 2016 *Los Angeles Times* editorial. The application was described as several-dozen pages long and mandatorily completed prior to a student being accepted. A "Getting to Know You" section required students to write five short essays in addition to six short response questions; parents were also required to write several essays of their own. To top it off, the application required a three-page minimum autobiography from the potential student that was "well-constructed with varied structure" (*Times* editorial board, 2016).

In several large cities (such as Denver, New Orleans, Philadelphia, and Washington, DC), a common application is made available to charter schools, as a resource for the schools and as a way to avoid such problems. But charter schools can usually opt out of that common application. For example, in Philadelphia, all of the Renaissance charters (which have catchment areas) participate in the common application; but as of 2016 only 23 of the 66 non-Renaissance charters in Philadelphia participated. This means that the other 43 charter schools had their own unique application requirements, some of which were remarkably burdensome. The 2013–2014 prelottery application for the Charter High School of Architecture and Design required a student's most recent report card, birth certificate, two short-answer questions, original student artwork, and a letter of recommendation from a school counselor rating a range of issues from "effort and drive" to "self-confidence" (Public Citizens for Children and Youth, 2014). In New Orleans, seven charter schools still do not take part in OneApp, the city's common application. Three of these schools, Audubon, Lake Forest, and Lusher, are among the highest-rated schools in the city. As explained in a *Times-Picayune* article, "These three schools impose mind-numbingly complex application processes that test a parent's savvy, access to transportation and ability to get to work" (Dreilinger, 2016).

Another practice that limits access during the application phase is requiring visits from interested families, as noted above regarding Green Woods in Philadelphia. In their study of Colorado charter schools, Weiler and Vogel (2015) identified 22 schools that required a visit from parents prior to registration. They explained that the "practice of requiring a visit not only creates a hardship for some families, but it also could provide school officials with extraneous information that might influence the student's ability to register or succeed at the school" (p. 45). A parent we interviewed described calling Edward Brooke Mattapan, a Boston-based charter school, after not finding an application on its website—only to be told that the only way she could get an application was to first show up for a meeting at the school.

Another practice that turns away families during the application process involves the use of an admissions test to determine grade placement or academic level (or actual eligibility for admission). In Delaware, an Enrollment Preferences

Task Force (2015) found that in 2013–2014, nine of the state's 33 charter schools administered entrance exams or admissions essays. These schools also happened to be high performing and had lower percentages of low-income students than other charter schools in the state. One of these nine, the Charter School of Wilmington—named the nation's 10th best high school in 2014 by *Newsweek*—enrolled only 2.4% of students from low-income families and 0.6% of students with special needs, and the students were disproportionately white (Wolfman-Arent, 2014). The Charter School of Wilmington has an enrollment preference for students who have a specific interest in their methods, philosophy, or educational focus, and this specific interest is gauged, in part, by a test. Another Delaware charter, called MOT Charter School, has similar preferences and was even more disproportionately white, and only 4.9% of students were from low-income families, while 5.9% had special needs (Enrollment Preferences Task Force, 2015).

Finally, we note that charter schools are generally able to set their own application deadlines. Several interviewees named early application deadlines and short application windows as factors that limit access to certain charter schools. In Philadelphia, 36 of the 66 non-Renaissance charters have application deadlines in February or earlier for the following school year. The earliest deadlines belong to Boys Latin of Philadelphia and Franklin Towne Charter, where applications are due in October and November of the previous year, respectively (Great Philly Schools, 2016; School District of Philadelphia, 2016). This means that social capital and word-of-mouth information is at a premium—and that preexisting demographics are likely to be reproduced each year. Similar problems were identified in Minnesota as well as in Detroit, where a 2014 report revealed the following:

> Even popular [charter] schools that wind up fully enrolled, almost never use lotteries to fill seats. The decentralized structure of the enrollment and choice process in Detroit leads to opaque admissions in general—applying for a seat is a transaction conducted between family and school, without oversight. Beyond the basic structural issues, there are mechanisms that allow, and in fact encourage schools to do their enrollment without any transparency. This, in the end, allows individuals at schools to have essentially complete discretion regarding admissions. Families are in a compromised position—there are no guarantees that admissions decisions are made justly and there is no accountability mechanism for families to access.
>
> [As explained by Jeremy Vidito, executive director of strategic planning and new schools, Starr Commonwealth Educational Services:] "All that our authorizer requires is a two-week window for accepting applications, along with one public notice in a publication with 'wide distribution.' So charters can schedule the two-week window in March or April, way before many families are making decisions, and advertise this in the *Michigan Chronicle*, *Detroit News* or *Free Press*, papers with a large segment of readers but readers who are not our families. In the end this reduces the window where transparency and true randomness is used to enroll in schools. After the two weeks, the rest of enrollment is first come, first served." (Institute for Innovation in Public School Choice, 2014, pp. 20–21)

Small changes can make a big difference in leveling the access playing field during the enrollment process. Our interviewees pointed, for example, to the adoption of common enrollment procedures and applications in places such as Newark, Washington, DC, Denver, and New Orleans. A common process helps to eliminate the imposition of particularly burdensome provisions imposed by individual schools, and it adds transparency. Further, it eases the burden on parents who no longer need to seek out individual schools and figure out confusing and varied requirements.

Some districts that have adopted a common enrollment system use it just for charter schools; others (e.g., Denver) include the broad array of choice options within the "portfolio" systems. We have serious concerns about the overall impact of choice (or portfolio) districts, one of which is simply that the access problems long associated with charter schools are scaled up to other types of choice schools (see Disare, 2016a, 2016b, 2016c). However, the unified enrollment systems deserve praise for increasing clarity, efficiency, and fairness. Parents fill out a single application, and a single application deadline applies for all schools in the district. Citywide school fairs, resource centers, and published guides in multiple languages to help families access information go hand in hand with a common enrollment system (Poiner, 2015). In Denver, all charter schools are required to participate; in New Orleans, as noted above, a handful of charters do not participate in One-App—and this has led to documented abuses.

DISCIPLINE AND PUNISH

Expulsion, suspension, and harsh discipline regimes allow charter schools "to maintain a more controlled school environment through the selective removal of students who these schools deem as more disruptive" (Welner, 2013, p. 4). Disproportionately, this disciplinary clampdown is felt by black students and students with special needs.

Analyzing discipline data from nearly 5,000 charter schools gathered from the Department of Education's Office for Civil Rights, the Civil Rights Project at UCLA found that black students are four times as likely to be suspended from charter schools as their white peers. They also found that students with disabilities are suspended two to three times the rate of their nondisabled peers in charter schools (Losen, Keith, Hodson, & Martinez, 2016). A report by Equip for Equality also found that in Chicago, harsh charter school discipline policies disproportionately affect students with disabilities. While only about 12% of charter school students had an IEP in 2015, 26.2% of students expelled from charter schools had an IEP the previous year (Shapiro & Wysong, 2015).

In 2015, at KIPP DC AIM Academy, a middle school in Washington, DC, special education students were suspended at a rate of 48.2%, significantly higher than the 28.2% average for DC Public Schools (Abdul-Alim, 2015). The *New York Times* reported that Crossroads Charter School in Charlotte, North Carolina, suspended nearly three-quarters of its black students in 2011–2012 (Rich, 2016).

The same types of troubling inequities are found in traditional public schools, but charter schools suspend at higher rates than traditional public schools. A 2016 CityLab geographic analysis of school discipline in Boston, New York, and Washington, DC, showed that in all three cities charter schools out-suspended and out-expelled their district counterparts and that the hyperdisciplinary schools in all three cities were all charter schools located in concentrated majority-black neighborhoods (Joseph, 2016). Below, we outline four types of troubling disciplinary practices that research suggests are used by charter schools.

Death by Demerits

One way charter schools use discipline to shape their student population is what one interviewee called "death by demerits." In this point-based system, tallies are kept for each student for seemingly minor behavior infractions. Students who do not adapt to these regimes continuously accumulate demerits and then frequently face out-of-school suspension as a consequence. The cyclical process of accumulating demerits, attending required parental meetings, and missing instructional time not only wears families down and leaves students behind, but also informally pushes them out of these schools.

In an op-ed she penned in *The Washington Post*, a former charter school English teacher explained, "I once gave out 37 demerits in a 50-minute period. This was the sort of achievement that earned a new teacher praise in faculty-wide emails at Achievement First Amistad High School, in New Haven, Connecticut" (Fisher, 2016b).

In a 2016 study, researchers found 16 Philadelphia charter schools that used a point-based system in which students had to always carry identification cards that showed the penalties they received for minor incidents of misbehavior. The researchers found that these and other types of demerit systems, which they described as similar to disciplinary systems used in military academies, were surprisingly common in Philadelphia charter schools (DeJarnatt, Wolf, & Kalinich, 2016).

The Noble network of charter schools in Chicago issued demerits for such acts as not sitting up straight or not wearing a school uniform, or for "rowdy" or loud behavior, and charged fines to offending students. The superintendent of Noble defended this approach to discipline: "We absolutely live by that. If you allow a lot of windows to be broken, soon that house is going to turn into one where lots of damage is going on" (Ahmed-Ullah, 2014).

Sweating the Small Stuff

As suggested by the Noble superintendent, there is a theory behind these point-based behavior systems, which are commonly found in no-excuses charter school networks. They are philosophically committed to "sweating the small stuff." This approach to discipline is rooted in the theory of "broken windows" first introduced in 1982, applied to building maintenance and policing (Wilson & Kelling,

2015). When charter schools sweat the small stuff, they often punish actions that are not inherently wrong in order to dissuade worse actions.

It is no surprise, then, that charter networks that adhere to this philosophy have some of the highest rates of suspensions. In New York, for example, five of the 10 schools with the most total suspensions in 2013 were part of two prominent charter school chains, Achievement First and Democracy Prep (Joseph, 2016). A review of New York City charter school discipline policies found that exactly half of the 164 city charter schools permit suspension or expulsion as a penalty for lateness, absence, or cutting class (Advocates for Children New York, 2015).

An attorney we spoke with explained how one of her clients was penalized for not complying:

> I had a client, [a] 6-year-old kid the school wanted to sit in scholar-ready position. Acronym: it's called SLANT [Sit up, Listen, Ask questions, Nod, and Track speaker with eyes]. This kid, he has ADHD, cannot do it. He just can't, and he is constantly redirected to look at teacher. He has a whole series of diagnoses, and he—there is no way he can constantly stare at the teacher. [The] school wants [his] parent to medicate the kid. The psychiatrist didn't think it was necessary because he was 6, and [the] parent didn't want to medicate him because he was 6. I think you shouldn't have to throw a pharmacological intervention to make a 6-year-old follow a teacher. He was listening. [He] just wouldn't look at teacher ever, and he would get redirected so many times, and then he would be suspended, multiple times in a week, over and over and over.

Similarly, a researcher interviewee explained that a huge percentage of Philadelphia charter schools have provisions in their disciplinary code that enable them to suspend and even expel kids for incredibly trivial acts, including untucked shirts, swearing, not having a belt, being disrespectful, folding their arms, rolling their eyes, or sucking their teeth. At least 28 charter schools in Philadelphia schools allow a student to be expelled for chronically failing to wear a uniform properly. In addition to directing students how to sit and walk, the discipline code for Young Scholars-Douglass charter school dictates the proper width of a girl's headband, and specifies that students' shoes must be entirely black, including "laces, eyelets, buckles, soles, designs and emblems" (DeJarnatt et al., 2016, pp. 39–40).

These approaches to discipline have a racially disparate impact because, as several interviewees noted, "no-excuses" charter schools are almost exclusively located in low-income, segregated neighborhoods of color.

Zero Tolerance

Interviewees also pointed to the persistence of zero tolerance policies in the charter sector as a mechanism by which charter schools shape their student population. The 2015 annual report published by the Office of the DC Ombudsman for Education (n.d.) cautioned that some DC charter schools overused school exclusion through the use of zero-tolerance policies and concluded zero-tolerance policies run counter to national research and federal school discipline guidance. More than 64% of DC charter school discipline codes use zero-tolerance provisions for acts (including nonviolent acts) that result in automatic expulsion; meanwhile, rules for schools operated by the school district do not have zero-tolerance provisions in any circumstance (Council for Court Excellence, 2015).

In Philadelphia, researchers found that "zero tolerance" was explicitly mentioned in 38% of discipline codes, but twice that number (74%) of charter school discipline codes included categories of offenses that result in some form of automatic suspension or expulsion. The researchers called these "de facto zero tolerance policies" (DeJarnatt et al., 2016, p. 30).

Due Process Violations

A troubling way many charter school discipline policies differ from those of nearby district schools is in the protection of students' due process rights. These differences allow charter schools to suspend and expel students in a much more indiscriminate manner than do traditional public schools. A California-based attorney explained to us that although many charter schools have official policies that provide a right to a hearing, almost none have a right to appeal. Further, the hearing policies are not necessarily followed. The result is that students are given a perfunctory hearing, expelled, and "dumped back into [the] traditional school system."

A 2015 analysis of New York City charter schools' discipline policies by Advocates for Children reviewed 164 such policies, of which 59 failed to include the right to appeal charter school suspensions or expulsions, 36 failed to include any additional protections before suspending or expelling students with disabilities, and 52 failed to include the right to alternative instruction during the full suspension period—all in violation of state law (Advocates for Children New York, 2015). Similarly, a 2015 report by the Council for Court Excellence found that charter school discipline codes in Washington, DC, varied in their adherence to due process procedures, including the right to receive notice of a disciplinary infraction, the right to a hearing or to respond to behavioral allegations, and the right to appeal. Just 52% of charter school discipline codes allowed for additional due process protections for students with special needs (Council for Court Excellence, 2015). In contrast, the discipline code that governs DC Public Schools adheres to these due process procedures.

However, some charter schools are part of a national movement to change exclusionary discipline practices. In Washington, DC, for instance, Next Step Public Charter School significantly reduced its suspension rate when it implemented restorative justice as a schoolwide model. Several other DC public and charter schools have also embraced restorative justice, due to the availability of support and training from the Office of the State Superintendent of Education (DC Board of Education, 2016).

CONCLUSION

The National Alliance for Public Charter Schools (NAPCS), the sector's primary advocacy organization, contends that charters are beneficial because, among other things, they are "open to all children [and do] not have special entrance requirements" (NAPCS, n.d.). Charter schools, the NAPCS continued, are helping all children "have the opportunity to achieve at a high level," as demonstrated by the fact that "charter schools are some of the top-performing schools in the country," "charter schools are closing the achievement gap," and "a higher percentage of charter students are accepted into a college or university."

But claims like these are undermined—sometimes directly and sometimes indirectly—when charter schools use access-shaping approaches such as those outlined in this chapter. The truth is that some charters do have special entrance requirements and are not open to all children. Also, because charter schools often shape their enrollment, outcomes such as college matriculation and test scores are not comparable for researchers. That is, when enrollment patterns are biased by the approaches set forth in this chapter, researchers are only able to statistically account for all the important differences among the students.

NAPCS also insists that charter schools be referred to as, and understood to be, *public* schools (NAPCS, 2014). Such a characterization is supported by key features of charter school laws, primarily the requirement that charters cannot charge tuition. But charter schools also have features that look nonpublic, since they are privately operated, often by privately owned education management organizations, with teachers generally considered employees of those private companies and with public transparency laws not applicable to the private companies.

But it is the issue of access that lies most at the core of the public/private distinction. Public schools should, as fundamental institutions within our democracy, minimize barriers to access. Accordingly, a school's "publicness" includes at least two elements: legal status as public and behavior as public, in service of public goals. As research and policy both move forward, the future of charters—what role they play within our democracy and our educational system—will crucially depend on levels of actual access.

NOTE

The research reported here was supported by a grant from the Atlantic Philanthropies.

REFERENCES

Abdul-Alim, J. (2015, December 2). KIPP DC's high suspension rates raise alarms. *Afro.* Retrieved from afro.com/kipp-d-c-s-high-suspension-rates-raise-alarms

Advocates for Children New York. (2015). *Civil rights suspended: An analysis of New York City charter school discipline policies.* Retrieved from bit.ly/2kHznyV

Ahmed-Ullah, N. (2014, April 7). Chicago's Noble charter school network has tough discipline policy. *Chicago Tribune.* Retrieved from trib.in/2cxIOfS

Alonzo, M. (2014). Arizona charter schools often ignore Latino students and English-language learners. *Phoenix New Times.* Retrieved from bit.ly/2lNlRd9

BASIS Charter Schools. (n.d.) *Parent student handbook 2015–2016.* Retrieved from bit.ly/2kQhNeK

Benjamin Franklin Charter School. (2016). *Parent handbook.* Retrieved from bit.ly/2kQs0YF

Brinson, D. (2011). *Turning loss into renewal: Catholic schools, charter schools, and the Miami experience.* Retrieved from bit.ly/2lf3tgO

Brown, A. (2012, September 30). Counseled out: How some Twin Cities charter schools push kids with disabilities towards district schools. *TC Daily Planet.* Retrieved from bit.ly/2lNoUlR

Brown, J. (2001). A few good schools. *Education Next.* Retrieved from educationnext.org/a-few-good-schools

Brownstein, A. (2014, February 9). Hebrew charter school movement shows signs of growth and growing pains. *Forward.* Retrieved from goo.gl/raKuDq

Chadha, J. (2015, October 30). Success Academy founder responds to criticisms it weeds out students. *WNYC News.* Retrieved from bit.ly/1RUSos1

Chandler, M. A. (2015, October 31). Charters grapple with admissions policies, question how public they should be. *The Washington Post.* Retrieved from wapo.st/1l3t1tA

Cheek, T. (2015). Lessons learned: Censorship of a gay valedictorian. *The Colorado Independent.* Retrieved from goo.gl/GXkvxQ

Colombo, H. (2016, February 6). Charter school approval fuels new questions. *Indianapolis Business Journal.* Retrieved from bit.ly/2kodrgc

Colorado Department of Education. (2016). *Pupil membership district data.* Retrieved from www.cde.state.co.us/cdereval/pupilcurrentdistrict

Community Unit District 300. (2016). *May 19 special meeting presentation.* Retrieved from www.d300.org/document/18140

Council for Court Excellence. (2015). *Equity in school discipline.* Retrieved from bit.ly/2kHCJBY

DC Board of Education. (2016). *Annual report.* Retrieved from bit.ly/2l5QrQo

DC Office of Planning. (n.d.). *Population by race and Hispanic or Latino origin, for all ages and for 18 years and over, and housing units, for the District of Columbia—Ward 5: 2000 and 2010* [Data file]. Retrieved from bit.ly/2lhaXj4

DC Office of the Ombudsman for Public Education (n.d.). *2015 annual report.* Retrieved from bit.ly/2knGBfB

DC Public Charter School Board. (2016). *Washington Yu Ying PCS school performance.* Retrieved from www.dcpcsb.org/school/washington-yu-ying-pcs

Decker, J. R., & Carr, K. A. (2015). Church-state entanglement at religiously affiliated charter schools. *Brigham Young University Education & Law Journal, 2015*(1), 77–105.

DeJarnatt, S. L., Wolf, K., & Kalinich, M. K. (2016). Charting school discipline. *The Urban Lawyer, 48*(1), 1.

Disare, M. (2016a, September 8). Open houses and closed doors: How the first step toward high school can become a stumbling block. *Chalkbeat*. Retrieved from bit.ly/2lf7rpN

Disare, M. (2016b, September 29). New York City's high school fair could help simplify the admissions process. Instead, it adds to the confusion. *Chalkbeat*. Retrieved from bit.ly/2kQPgWq

Disare, M. (2016c, December 19). Great divide: How extreme academic segregation isolates students in New York City's high schools. *Chalkbeat*. Retrieved from bit.ly/2hZJCky

Dreilinger, D. (2016, May 26). How 3 top New Orleans public schools keep students out. *The Times-Picayune*. Retrieved from bit.ly/1OPOSNq

Eakins, P. (2006, June 11). Intolerance, or a strict education?—Students, parents concerned about prayer at Escondido Charter High. *San Diego Union Tribune*. Retrieved from bit.ly/2lf7lP0

Eckes, S., & Carr, K. (2014). Niche charter schools: Legal and policy considerations. In R. A. Fox & N. K. Buchanan (Eds.), *Proud to be different* (pp. 167–185). Lanham, MD: Rowman Littlefield.

Enrollment Preferences Task Force. (2015, December). *Final report*. Retrieved from udspace.udel.edu/handle/19716/17397

Fiore, T. A., Harwell, L. M., Blackorby, J., & Finnigan, K. S. (2000). *Charter schools and students with disabilities: A national study*. Retrieved from files.eric.ed.gov/fulltext/ED452657.pdf

Fisher, H. (2016a, September 16). Mesa charter school sued, accused of teaching religious doctrine. *East Valley Tribune*. Retrieved from bit.ly/2lhGH7G

Fisher, J. (2016b, August 11). Schools that accept "no excuses" from students are not helping them. *Washington Post*. Retrieved from bit.ly/2lNCk1P

Flagstaff Academy. (2016a). *About our enrollment process*. Retrieved from bit.ly/2kvl8fY

Flagstaff Academy. (2016b). *Flagstaff Academy open enrollment FAQs*. Retrieved from bit.ly/2lhBcGc

Freire Charter School. (n.d.). *Student and family handbook 2016–2017*. Retrieved from bit.ly/2lOh2Ai

Great Philly Schools. (2016). *2017–18 charter school common application*. Retrieved from bit.ly/2kQXcXP

Hammel, H. (2014). *Charging for access: How California charter schools exclude vulnerable students by imposing illegal family work quotas*. Retrieved from bit.ly/2leZOzM

Hechinger, J. (2011, November 14). Taxpayers get billed for kids of millionaires at charter school. *Bloomberg News*. Retrieved from bloom.bg/2lNOYhl

Herold, B. (2012, September 14). Questionable application processes at Green Woods, other charter schools. *The Notebook*. Retrieved from bit.ly/2kI7R4i

Hillsdale College. (2016). *The Barney charter school initiative*. Retrieved from bit.ly/1SUDlTX

Institute for Innovation in Public School Choice. (2014). *A current state assessment of public school enrollment and choice in Detroit*. Retrieved from bit.ly/2lhr93I

Jabbar, H. (2015). Competitive networks and school leaders' perceptions: The formation of an education marketplace in post-Katrina New Orleans. *American Educational Research Journal, 52*, 1093–1131.

Jabbar, H. (2016). Selling schools: Marketing and recruitment strategies in New Orleans. *Peabody Journal of Education, 91*(1), 4–23.

Jennings, J. L. (2010). School choice or schools' choice? Managing in an era of accountability. *Sociology of Education, 83*, 227–247.

Joseph, G. (2016, September 16). Where charter-school suspensions are concentrated. *The Atlantic*. Retrieved from theatln.tc/2d3GoHx

Keys Gate Charter School. (n.d). *About Keys Gate Charter School*. Retrieved from www.keyscharter.org/about-keys-gate-charter-school/

Leung, V., Alejandre, R., & Jongco, A. (2016). *Unequal access: How some California charter schools illegally restrict enrollment*. Retrieved from bit.ly/2apyOnu

Losen, D., Keith, M., Hodson, C., & Martinez, T. (2016). *Charter schools, civil rights and school discipline: A comprehensive review*. Retrieved from bit.ly/2lO1w7U

Lubienski, C., Gulosino, C., & Weitzel, P. (2009). School choice and competitive incentives: Mapping the distribution of educational opportunities across local education markets. *American Journal of Education, 115*, 601–647.

Malik, A. (2015, July 25). Top charter schools in town teach very different groups of students. *San Antonio Express-News*. Retrieved from bit.ly/1MwGrZY

McNeel, B. (2014, March 27). At BASIS San Antonio, intellectual engagement is the norm. *The Rivard Report*. Retrieved from therivardreport.com/basis-san-antonio

National Alliance for Public Charter Schools. (2014). *Separating fact from fiction: What you need to know about charter schools*. Retrieved from bit.ly/VcZUa1

National Alliance for Public Charter Schools. (n.d.). *About charter schools*. Retrieved from www.publiccharters.org/get-the-facts/public-charter-schools

Nevarez, G., & Wyloge, E. (2016, February 13). Charter student populations don't match state demographics. *The Arizona Republic*. Retrieved from bit.ly/2lfbWk3

Newsweek. (2015). America's top high schools 2015. *Newsweek*. Retrieved from www.newsweek.com/high-schools/americas-top-high-schools-2015

Patriot Preparatory Academy. (2017). *Annual report: Fiscal year 2016–2017*. Retrieved from goo.gl/bUJDfy

Petrimoulx, D. (2016, May 11). Charter school apologizes for recruiting mailer. *Arkansas Matters*. Retrieved from bit.ly/2kvikiE

Poiner, J. (2015, May 22). Common enrollment, parents, and school choice: Early evidence from Denver and New Orleans [Blog post]. Retrieved from bit.ly/2kvaCFp

Public Citizens for Children and Youth. (2014). *Performance audit of the ten charters seeking renewal*. Retrieved from bit.ly/2l6nbJ9

Rich, M. (2016, March 16). Charter schools suspend black and disabled students more, study says. *New York Times*. Retrieved from nyti.ms/1SUTzLj

Richards, J. S. (2010, September 8). Charter's ties to Christian school draw state scrutiny. *Columbus Dispatch*. Retrieved from bit.ly/2lNBG4G

ROADS Charter High Schools. (n.d.). *About us*. Retrieved from roadsschools.org/about-us

School District of Philadelphia. (2016). *2017–2018 charter school applications*. Retrieved from www.philasd.org/about/#schools

Shapiro, B., & Wysong, C. (2015). *Charter school enrollment in Illinois: Ensuring that admissions practices welcome all students*. Retrieved from bit.ly/2lNrKrL

Simon, S. (2013). *Special report: Class struggle—how charter schools get students they want*. Retrieved from goo.gl/5U782S

Tan, S. (2015, May 10). High number of expulsions at Western New York Maritime Charter School draw questions. *Buffalo News*. Retrieved from bit.ly/2lOhZZo

Taylor, K. (2015, October 15). At a Success Academy charter school, singling out pupils who have "got to go." *New York Times*. Retrieved from nyti.ms/1NDuyjo

Times editorial board. (2016, August 10). The bias inherent in some charter schools' admissions process [Editorial]. *Los Angeles Times*. Retrieved from lat.ms/2bfJ4S6

U.S. Department of Justice & U.S. Department of Education. (2014, May 8). *Dear colleague letter: School enrollment procedures.* Retrieved from bit.ly/1sqr0Gh

Weiler, S. C., & Vogel, L. R. (2015). Charter school barriers: Do enrollment requirements limit student access to charter schools? *Equity & Excellence in Education, 48*(1), 36–48.

Welner, K. G. (2013, April). The dirty dozen: How charter schools influence student enrollment. *Teachers College Record* [online], ID Number 17104.

Wilson, J. Q., & Kelling, G. L. (2015). Broken windows. In R. G. Dunham & G. P. Alpert (Eds.), *Critical issues in policing: Contemporary readings* (pp. 395–407). Long Grove, IL: Waveland.

Wolfman-Arent, A. (2014, December 15). Delaware school entrance assessments face tough test. *Newsworks.* Retrieved from bit.ly/2lhvMLb

CHAPTER 6

"Blended Learning"

The Education Technology Industry and the New Segregation

Gordon Lafer

What was educationally significant and hard to measure has been replaced by what is educationally insignificant and easy to measure. So now we measure how well we taught what isn't worth learning.

—Arthur Costa and Bena Kallick,
Dispositions: Reframing Teaching and Learning

Over the past decade, school systems across the country have been swept up in a technology craze. The education press, along with scores of reports and conferences, have focused increasingly on technological solutions to educational problems. And charter schools—particularly those in poor cities—have been leading this charge. At its boldest, education technology promises to make poverty irrelevant by simultaneously raising student achievement and lowering the budgetary cost of schooling for poor urban districts.

In this chapter, I explore why technology has become such a central focus of education reform, what digital pedagogy looks like in practice, how digital instruction serves to redefine the act of learning and the role of teachers, and how its adoption in urban charter schools contributes to new forms of educational segregation. I focus particularly on the Rocketship chain of charter schools, a darling of the technology and venture capital industries, which has often been upheld as a model of "blended learning," and which, in 2014, was at the center of a legislative proposal in Wisconsin that would have forced the conversion of "persistently failing" city schools to privately run charters.

From the viewpoint of educators, it is not obvious that technology is the right direction to turn toward in seeking improved education. Of the scores of educational applications developed in recent years, very few were created by teachers or scholars of education or tested for efficacy before being deployed in classrooms. And to the extent that these products have been subject to rigorous evaluations, the results are not promising. After a decade of experimentation, a Silicon Valley promoter of blended learning concluded in 2015 that "we don't have definitive evidence that blended learning works" (Sparks, 2015, p. 12). Similarly, Bill Gates—whose foundation is one of the largest supporters of both charter schools and digitized instruction—conceded in 2016 that the field had failed to live up to its promise, noting that to date, "we really haven't changed [students' academic] outcomes" (Molnar, 2016).

By contrast, research suggests that any number of school models might be more beneficial than digital instruction. To cite just a few recently successful innovations: one study found that intensive small-group tutoring allowed low-income black high school students in Chicago to learn the equivalent of 3 years of mathematics in one academic year—and at least one school successfully recruited a corps of retirees to serve as tutors at modest cost, thus making the program budgetarily viable (Rich, 2014); in Jennings, Missouri—next door to Ferguson—a low-income district witnessed a dramatic turnaround in academic performance after the school opened an on-site homeless shelter, food pantry, and medical services for students whose families couldn't provide these needs (Brown, 2015); and in Baltimore, where only 15% of 8th graders read at grade level, a new summer school program for failing middle school students made dramatic gains when participants were placed in classes limited to 20 students, with two teachers per class (Kolodner, 2016). Each of these innovations builds on established research documenting the importance of small classes and wraparound social services for students from poor families—and each one's results far surpass those of digital applications.

Why, then, are charter schools rushing headlong into a digital future, rather than seeking to replicate these more effective innovations? Unfortunately, the answer to this question is not to be found in any classroom experience, parent survey, or scholarly research, but instead in the halls of the nation's largest corporate lobbies.

EDUCATION POLICY MADE BY CORPORATE LOBBYISTS

In recent years, education policy and funding streams have been dramatically reshaped through a wave of new laws in state legislatures. While debates over education policy have engaged thousands of parents, students, teachers, and district officials and scores of advocacy groups, the most powerful voices weighing in on these topics come from the country's business lobbies, which together constitute the best-funded and most powerful force in state politics. At first glance, it might seem odd that organizations such as the Chamber of Commerce, the American Legislative Exchange Council (ALEC), and the Koch-funded Americans for Prosperity would care to get involved in an issue as far removed from commercial activity as school reform. In fact, they have each made this a top legislative priority. And following the Supreme Court's 2010 *Citizens United* decision allowing for unlimited corporate money in politics, these efforts have reaped widespread results. From 2011 to 2015, at least nine states increased the use of student test scores for teacher evaluation, 17 expanded online instruction, and 29 passed laws encouraging the privatization of education through vouchers or charter schools (Lafer, 2017). Most importantly for digital instruction, corporate lobbyists have worked to ensure that schools receive the same per-pupil funding for digital courses as for in-person classes taught by certified teachers. Indeed, ALEC model legislation—now adopted in five states—requires that even entirely virtual schools be paid the same dollars per student as traditional schools (Lafer, 2017). As a result, profit margins for digital products are enormous. As Netflix CEO and education technology entrepreneur Reed Hastings explained, the great financial advantage of digital education is that "you can produce once and consume many times" (Crotty, 2012, p. 3). It's no wonder, then, that investment banks, hedge funds, and venture capitalists have all flocked to this market.

In 2010, investment banker Michael Moe launched the first conference bringing education policymakers together with technology firms and investors. By 2014, nearly 300 companies were offering new education technology products to potential customers and investors (Fang, 2014). Applications are now being sold for almost everything—an app for student behavior management, an app for English-language learners, an app for 9th-grade reading, an app to replace guidance counselors. Very few of these have been tested by any education authority or are the products of teachers or education scholars. Their promotion and adoption is driven not by a need identified in the classroom, but by a combination of venture capital and technology firms eager to tap an emerging market with unrivaled potential. "Education is a $3.8 trillion industry globally," the organizers of Moe's Education Innovation Summit explained, but "the industry is significantly undercapitalized" (Sarley, 2010, para. 11). Rupert Murdoch likewise pronounced U.S. education "a $500 billion sector . . . waiting desperately to be transformed" (Fang, 2011, para. 46).

The finance industry looks at education the same way it regards Social Security—a huge flow of publicly guaranteed funding just waiting to be privatized, if only the politics can be worked out. At a meeting of New York investors in 2010, one advisor gushed that "you start to see entire ecosystems of investment opportunity lining up" in K–12 education (Simon, 2012). Indeed, over the past 10 years, venture capital investments in education have grown nearly tenfold, from $13 million to $1.25 billion (Fang, 2014; Simon, 2012). At the heart of these opportunities, *Princeton Review* founder and education entrepreneur John Katzman explained, is the question: "How do we use technology so that we require fewer highly qualified teachers?" (Simon, 2012).

This is the essential education policy goal of the financial sector: to replace costly and idiosyncratic human teachers with mass-produced and highly profitable digital products and to eliminate the legal and political structures that inhibit a free flow of public tax dollars to these private products. Any number of educational innovations might hold more promise than technology—but such programs have no place in the portfolio of reforms called for by corporate advocates because there is no way to make profit from them. To the extent that investors influence education policy, then, we are witnessing the redesign of elementary and high school pedagogy around a financial bottom line: Teach whatever you want, however you want, as long as it generates a financial return.

In this way, the charter industry and its corporate backers have been advocates for lowering the professional standards for teachers. In recent years, five states have adopted legislation loosening teacher certification requirements, all with the support of pro-charter business groups. Many more have exempted charter schools from certification requirements and have allowed Teach for America staff to take sole responsibility for a class after no more than 6 weeks of training (Lafer, 2017). The emphasis on technology helps explain this advocacy. Whether in virtual or real classes, the charter school model most often being advocated entails a curriculum narrowly focused on test preparation, delivered by a largely inexperienced staff designed to be replaceable after 2 or 3 years. From the point of view of charter corporations, it is irrational to develop long-term and highly skilled teachers who will each develop his or her own means of teaching the laws of physics or the history of the American Revolution. Instead, education is being reconfigured as a combination of corporate content providers and low-cost content deliverers.

For low-income students, the high turnover of teachers in the big charter management organization (CMO) chains of schools poses a particular concern. As the National Commission on Teaching and America's Future reported:

> Staff churn . . . is concentrated . . . in chronically underperforming schools serving low-income children. These schools rarely close the student achievement gap because they never close the teaching quality gap. . . . [T]heir students struggle year after year with a passing parade of inexperienced beginners, while students in high performing schools enjoy the support of teams of accomplished veterans. (Carroll & Foster, 2010, p. 4)

Particularly for the neediest students, who are often facing personal and family challenges in addition to academic goals, the presence of a mature stable adult who knows the student's family and community is often critical, yet it is most lacking precisely in the charter networks being promoted across the nation's poor cities.

THE ROLE OF CHARTER SCHOOLS IN THE
EXPANDING EDUCATION TECHNOLOGY MARKET

Even with their rapid growth, charter schools still educate a small minority of American students, and the ed-tech industry looks to the broader public school system as its ultimate market. But the governance structure of charter schools makes them uniquely valuable vehicles for introducing the technologies that investors hope will ultimately sweep the school system as a whole. In public school districts, ed-tech ventures face several critical hurdles. School districts are under pressure to adopt curricula with proven track records—a barrier to most tech products. Public officials are also typically prohibited from having any financial relationship with vendors, while charter schools often develop corporate partnerships with specific content providers. Finally, each school district is charged with evaluating and selecting the curricular products best suited to its particular student body, requiring vendors to negotiate a fragmented market composed of thousands of small-volume buyers. By contrast, as CMO chains expand, they offer investors the possibility of a single point of sale covering hundreds of schools, locked in by a corporate partnership that ensures brand loyalty beyond the vagaries of unpredictable product evaluations. It is charter schools' governance structure that makes them such a desirable partner for investors, and investors hope to use the charter sector as a wedge to open up the broader "education space" to private entrepreneurs.

The education technology industry is explicit about the fact that its market expansion depends on political reform and that the charter industry functions as the leading edge of this effort. As one venture capitalist explained, market growth depends on overcoming opposition from "unions, public school bureaucracies and parents" (Fang, 2014). Netflix CEO and charter investor Reed Hastings explained that "selling to school districts . . . [is] a very inefficient market," because they

> are really reacting to voter forces more than to market forces. . . . The best friend of the [education] technology movement . . . are charter schools. . . . You'll [still] get most of your money from the school district. But it's what you pioneer with charter schools that will drive that adoption [of technology products]. (Crotty, 2012, p. 2)

For this same reason, Hastings and others have promoted a vision of doing away entirely with publicly run schools and democratically elected school boards. Hastings has urged that the role of school boards be limited to "bringing to town more and more charter school networks. Sort of like a Chamber of Commerce would to develop business" (Crotty, 2012, p. 2).

FROM VIRTUAL SCHOOLS TO "BLENDED LEARNING" AND THE RISE OF ROCKETSHIP

The charter school industry's growth has been concentrated in poor cities. It is here that public schools have been poorest and the allure of something new is greatest; it is also here where local communities are least likely to have the political power to resist a market invasion by large CMO chains. In some jurisdictions, the path to charter privatization is straightforward: use standardized tests to declare poor schools "persistently failing"; put these under the control of a special, unelected authority; and then have that authority replace the public schools with charters. In its most ambitious version, this takeover strategy is being forced on dozens of schools at a time. In 2011, both Tennessee and Michigan created special districts to take over low-scoring schools; in both cases, the superintendent was specifically authorized to replace public schools with charters (Smith, 2013). In 2014–2015, corporate lobbyists and Wisconsin legislators promoted bills to bypass the middle step and simply require that low-performing public schools be replaced by privately run charters.[1] Since test scores are primarily a function of poverty, it's no surprise that 80% of Tennessee's schools targeted for charter privatization are in Memphis, nor that the Michigan and Wisconsin bills focus respectively on Detroit and Milwaukee (Lafer, 2017; Rich, 2013). Thus, what "slum clearance" did for the real estate industry in the 1960s and 1970s, high-stakes testing promises to do for the charter industry: wipe away large swaths of public schools, enabling private operators to grow not school by school, but 20 or 30 schools at a time.

The fastest-growing sector of the charter industry—and the most profitable— is online education (Miron, Urschel, Aguilar, & Dailey, 2012). However, the market for entirely virtual schools is limited, particularly in poor cities where fewer parents can serve as the stay-at-home tutors required to supplement online modules. Investors thus face a contradiction: The greatest opportunity for charter industry growth is in poor cities, but these settings are where wholly online schools—the most profitable model for investors—are least likely to flourish.

The solution to this problem has appeared in the emergence of "blended learning" schools, where students attend physical schools but spend a portion of their day online. One of the leading exemplars of this model is the Rocketship corporation, based in Silicon Valley and operating schools in Milwaukee, Nashville, and Washington, DC, as well as in California. In 2014, Rocketship was at the heart of a legislative proposal to forcibly replace low-scoring Milwaukee schools with privately run charters. The president of the Metropolitan Milwaukee Association of Commerce sits on Rocketship's board, and the company's model was put forth both in Milwaukee and by national corporate lobbyists as a model for what should replace troubled schools.[2]

From its inception, Rocketship has been championed by both technology executives and venture capitalists. Its earliest funders included Netflix CEO Reed Hastings, Facebook CEO Sheryl Sandberg, SurveyMonkey CEO Dave Goldberg, and Skype CEO Jonathan Chadwick, along with a number of leading venture capital firms (Bowman, 2011). It is possible, of course, that these executives provided financial support for Rocketship out of purely altruistic motives, the same way they might give to an art museum or a children's hospital. In at least some cases, however, it is more likely that they saw in Rocketship's growth a potential customer base for their own products.

Rocketship's model is based on four principles. First, the company cuts costs by replacing teachers with technology. Starting in kindergarten, students spend one-quarter of their class time in teacherless computer labs, using video game–based math and reading applications. The company has voiced hopes of increasing digital instruction to as much as 50% of student learning time. Second, Rocketship relies on a corps of young, inexperienced, and, therefore, low-cost teachers (Bernatek, Cohen, Hanion, & Wilka, 2012). Teacher turnover is dramatic—nearly 30% in some years—but the company pays Teach for America to supply a steady stream of replacements. Third, the school has narrowed its curriculum to a near-exclusive focus on math and reading. Since both Rocketship's marketing strategy and teachers' salaries are based on reading and math scores, other topics are treated as nonessential. There are no dedicated social studies or science classes, and the schools have no music, no foreign languages, no guidance counselors, and no libraries. Finally, Rocketship maintains a relentless focus on teaching to the test. Students take standardized tests every 8 weeks; following each, the staff spends a full day revising lesson plans with an eye to improving scores. Rocketship boasts of its "backwards mapping" pedagogy—starting with test standards and then developing lesson plans to meet them. Rocketship is, as near as possible, all test prep, all the time.[3]

The Rocketship model points to a critical distinction in the role of technology. Students in privileged schools often make extensive use of technology. But while these students are encouraged to be *active* users of technology—writing code, editing films, recording music, and designing graphics—Rocketship's students are *passive* users of technology, essentially plugged into video game–based applications designed to drill them for upcoming tests.

Charter school advocates frequently tout the value of digital instruction as providing "individualized" learning. In fact, however, test-based digital curricula are individuated only along one dimension: how quickly or slowly children make their way through the prescribed steps. In the broader sense, digital curricula are rigidly narrow. Children differ not only in how much they learn, but in *how* they learn. When kindergartners and 1st-graders are first grappling with basic math concepts, some do well by practicing equations, others by making and crossing off marks on paper, others through stories about quantities of things gained or lost, others by physically manipulating sticks or blocks. This is part of what makes it impossible for teachers to assign even the best-conceived lesson plan to all students, all the time. Part of the task of a good teacher is to determine which mode of learning is best suited to which children. For several decades, educators have sought to identify the specific different ways that children learn, in order to help teachers provide appropriate pathways for each child. One recent study suggested that the range of preferred student learning strategies might include verbal/linguistic, bodily/kinesthetic, musical/rhythmic, naturalist, visual/spatial, interpersonal, logical/mathematical, and intrapersonal (Gregory & Chapman, 2013, p. 164).

Due to the difficulty of identifying the precise dividing line between various ways of learning, as well as the difficulty of running controlled experiments with young children, no conclusive statistical proof can identify a specific set of "learning styles" that teachers should build curricula around, although most parents and teachers agree that different children learn in different ways. In Rocketship, a single mode of learning is imposed on all children. Indeed, while charter boosters often decry public schools as anachronisms of an earlier era, the principal at the Waldorf School famously favored for the children of Silicon Valley executives turned this assumption on its head: "Teaching to the test is . . . left over from the industrial age, an age of mass production. . . . Technology is a tool. . . . Education is done human to human, not through a machine" (S. Rynas, Administrator, Waldorf School of the Peninsula, telephone interview with J. Smith, University of Oregon, March 14, 2014).

So too, "school choice" is often touted as providing a degree of pedagogical flexibility that is supposedly impossible in traditional public schools. Thus, when the ALEC-affiliated Wisconsin Policy Research Industry first promoted a voucher system for Milwaukee, it stressed:

> Autonomy is vital to school organization . . . [because] successful teaching is probably more art than science. . . . Teaching is a highly contingent process, its results depending on the interaction of the methods used and the students those methods are used on. No one method, employed inflexibly, will work for all students. Unfortunately, when officials outside of schools try to direct teaching, they inevitably push teachers toward the utilization of one best method. In the extreme, the well-intentioned regulation of curriculum and instruction so limits teacher flexibility that the quality of teaching deteriorates for many students, especially those whose needs are not met by the one best method. (Chubb & Moe, 1989, p. 12)

Yet where charter advocates may criticize public school districts for imposing top-down control, Rocketship has, at best, substituted a corporate bureaucracy for a political one. If teachers or even principals in Rocketship schools believe a given software product is not appropriate for a set of students, they are not permitted either to select a different program or to provide an alternative to online instruction; all students are required to use the products assigned by the company's corporate office. In this way, Rocketship represents an even more centralized, command-and-control system than the public school districts charter advocates are wont to criticize.

CORPORATE PARTNERSHIPS AND PEDAGOGICAL RIGIDITY

The refusal to allow teachers or principals to experiment with alternative instructional materials might be a simple reflection of business realities: the corporate office signs contracts with financial partners that obligate all of the company's schools to use a given product. If individual schools were allowed to use their own judgment in evaluating the products best suited to their students, vendors might be faced with the same frustrations they voice about elected school boards.

Rocketship itself is a nonprofit, but its operation blurs the line between profit and nonprofit. For instance, Rocketship has benefited from financial support from both Reed Hastings and a fund headed by venture capital executive John Doerr. In turn, Doerr and Hastings are among the primary investors in DreamBox—a for-profit math application that Rocketship uses in its computer labs.[4] The U.S. Department of Education reviewed DreamBox in December 2013, concluding that it has "no discernible effects on mathematics achievement." After Rocketship-commissioned consultants offered further data, the Department of Education upgraded its assessment of DreamBox to "potentially positive" impacts based on "small evidence." Normally, if superintendents were presented with a curriculum rated somewhere between "no discernible effect" and "potentially positive" based on "small evidence," they might choose to look elsewhere. But if Rocketship rejects DreamBox, it might endanger financial support. Thus, pedagogical choices are made not on the basis of what's best for students, but at least partially on the financial interests of private investors.

Education reform advocates sometimes promote charter schools as the research arm of the education system—a place where new ideas can be tested, freed from the normal constraints of district policies, with the findings fed back to the rest of the system so that other schools can replicate charters' successes and learn from their failures. Imagining Rocketship as that type of endeavor, its loyalty to DreamBox might appear puzzling. But its behavior becomes understandable when we look at Rocketship first and foremost as a *business*, where the interests of key financial backers may trump the judgments of impartial educational research.

Thus, Rocketship continues to employ DreamBox as a standard part of its math program. Furthermore, both Rocketship and the DreamBox company itself continue to promote the software on the basis of "studies" of computer programs that federal researchers concluded showed little evidence of effectiveness. Rocketship parents curious about the software their children are using are directed to the DreamBox website, which declares that the software produces a "50% increase in student proficiency in math" and features a testimonial by Rocketship founder John Danner—a member of the DreamBox board of directors—touting the program's effectiveness. Nowhere on either Rocketship's nor DreamBox's website is there any reference to the Department of Education's review of their product (DreamBox Learning, 2016).

If charter chains were truly devoted to improving poor children's education and nothing more, they might experiment with some of the strategies described earlier—small classes, intensive tutoring, and wraparound social services. But while these initiatives may mark proven successes, they will never be entertained by Rocketship executives because there is simply no way for either technology startups or venture capital firms to profit from this model of education. Rocketship students are, indeed, participants in an experimental and developing pedagogy. But the question that experiment aims to answer is not simply "How can we do better by poor kids?" but rather, "How can we educate poor kids while generating a profit for investors?"

POVERTY AND THE NEW SEGREGATION:
"GOOD SCHOOLS" IN POOR CITIES AND RICH SUBURBS

Decades of studies confirm that the single most important factor affecting educational achievement is the inequality of wealth and poverty. Since the inception of testing under No Child Left Behind, for example, students from economically disadvantaged families have *never* scored higher than their better-off peers—at any age, in any state (Tienken & Zhao, 2013).

Thus, the single most important steps policymakers could take to improve the education of low-income students would be to make it easier for these children's parents to earn a living wage. Instead, some of the most influential corporate organizations promoting charter schools also support economic policies that make it more difficult for families to pull themselves out of poverty. It is simply impossible to declare oneself against the minimum wage, against food stamps, against public housing, against mass transit, against unemployment insurance, and against wage theft enforcement—as ALEC, Americans for Prosperity, and the Chamber of Commerce have all done—and simultaneously proclaim one's commitment to closing the education gap.

The corporate lobbies' proposals to replace public schools with privately run charters are presented as a needed response to "failure." Yet, by supporting reduced school funding and opposing economic standards that make it easier for families to work their way out of poverty, these same organizations are helping to create the conditions most likely to ensure educational failure. Indeed, the business lobbies appear to be in the odd position of first advocating policies that deny schools and families the resources they need to succeed and then proposing to sweep in and solve the problem through privatization.

Decades of scholarly research aimed at defining what constitutes a "good school" point in part to the importance of small classes, experienced teachers, and broad curricula. But research aside, we can answer this question in a simple way: Look at where wealthy people send their own children. While these schools include technology, it is not used to substitute for teachers. On the contrary, *Forbes* magazine's review of the country's top schools stresses that it is "tiny classes" and "individualized attention" that "help students earn their way into the best colleges" (Laneri, 2010).

In Wisconsin, Rocketship's most important backer is Metropolitan Milwaukee Association of Commerce (MMAC). In 2013, MMAC testified in support of a bill that would make it easier for companies like Rocketship to expand, dubbing such schools "the best of the best" (Baas, 2013). Yet the suburban hometown schools of MMAC's president and chairman—both among the state's best—look very different. Both schools have approximately 15 students for every licensed teacher, or half the Rocketship ratio. Both provide music, art, and libraries with professional librarians. And both boast veteran teaching staffs, with 90% of teachers at one school holding graduate degrees.[5] Thus, what is promoted as the gold standard for poor neighborhoods is deemed intolerably substandard for the children of more affluent families.

In this way, the charter industry is building a new system of segregated education—divided by class and geography rather than explicitly by race. The "blended learning" model of charter schools exemplified by Rocketship is being promoted only in poor neighborhoods—because it's a model that wealthier parents reject for their own children. But while some school districts might not be able to afford what wealthy children have, we should not be confused by this into believing there are different definitions of good education for rich and poor children. There can be only one standard for what constitutes a good school, and the goal for poor cities should be obvious: to get as close as possible to the type of education provided wealthier suburban kids. This means rejecting the profit-driven obsession with technological fixes and investing in the same type of skilled and experienced teachers, broad curriculum, pedagogical sophistication, and personal attention for poor students that is demanded for the rich.

NOTES

1. The most sweeping version of this legislation is described in Lafer (2014). A slightly more modest version—the "Opportunity Schools and Partnership Program"—was adopted as part of the 2015–2017 budget signed into law in July 2015.

2. In 2014, ALEC advertised a presentation titled "On the Rocketship: Expanding the High-Quality Charter School Movement," sponsored by the Thomas B. Fordham Institute, a member of ALEC's Education Task Force (American Legislative Exchange Council, 2014).

3. Rocketship Education and the proposed 2014 Wisconsin legislation are described in detail in Lafer (2014).

4. The relationship between Doerr, Hastings, DreamBox, and Rocketship, as well as DreamBox's record of performance and review by the U.S. Department of Education, is documented in detail in Lafer (2014).

5. This information is based on interviews with both hometown schools conducted by Jennifer Smith of the University of Oregon. The chair and president of the Metropolitan Milwaukee Association of Commerce do not have kids in these schools—they are beyond the age of having elementary school–aged kids—but these are the schools that would be their neighborhood schools based on where they live.

REFERENCES

American Legislative Exchange Council. (2014, June 12). *ALEC digital exchange.* Retrieved from www.alec.org/alec-exchange-06-12-2014

Baas, S. (2013, October 3). Statement on behalf of Metropolitan Milwaukee Association of Commerce before the Senate Committee on Public Education, Hearing on Senate Bill 76.

Bernatek, B., Cohen, J., Hanion, J., & Wilka, M. (2012, September). *Blended learning in practice: Case studies from leading schools, featuring Rocketship Education.* Retrieved from 5a03f68e230384a218e0-938ec019df699e606c950a5614b999bd.r33.cf2.rackcdn.com/msdf-rocketship_04.pdf

Bowman, M. (2011). Silicon Valley leaders invest over $3M in Rocketship education. *Venture Beat*, May 12. Retrieved from venturebeat.com/2011/05/12/silicon-valley-leaders-invest-over-3m-in-rocketship-education

Brown, E. (2015, December 20). This superintendent has figured out how to make school work for poor kids. *The Washington Post*. Retrieved from www.washingtonpost.com/local/education/this-superintendent-has-figured-out-how-to-make-school-work-for-poor-kids/2015/12/20/cadac2ca-a4e6-11e5-ad3f-991ce3374e23_story.html?utm_term=.0839b9a9f55c

Carroll, T., & Foster, E. (2010). *Who will teach? Experience matters*. Arlington, VA: National Commission on Teaching and America's Future. Retrieved from nctaf.org/?s=Who+will+teach%3F+Experience+matters&x=0&y=0

Chubb, J., & Moe, T. (1989, March). Educational choice: Answers to the most frequently asked questions about mediocrity in American education and what can be done about it. *Wisconsin Policy Research Institute Report, 2*(3). Retrieved from https://files.eric.ed.gov/fulltext/ED314518.pdf

Costa, A. L., & Kallick, B. (2014). Introduction. In *Dispositions: Reframing teaching and learning* (p. 14). Thousand Oaks, CA: Corwin.

Crotty, J. M. (2012). Reed Hastings on how to build a $20 billion education juggernaut. *Forbes*, May 11. Retrieved from www.forbes.com/sites/jamesmarshallcrotty/2012/05/11/reed-hastings-on-what-it-takes-to-grow-a-20-billion-education-company/2

DreamBox Learning. (2016). *DreamBox is proven effective at math instruction*. Retrieved from www.dreambox.com/research

Fang, L. (2011, November 16). How online learning companies bought America's schools. *The Nation*. Retrieved from www.thenation.com/print/article/164651/how-online-learning-companies-bought-americas-schools

Fang, L. (2014, September 25). Venture capitalists are poised to "disrupt" everything about the education market. *The Nation*. Retrieved from www.thenation.com/article/venture-capitalists-are-poised-disrupt-everything-about-education-market

Gregory, G., & Chapman, C. (2013). *Differential instructional strategies: One size doesn't fit all*. Thousand Oaks, CA: Corwin.

Kolodner, M. (2016, August 8). Baltimore summer school does the seemingly impossible—the kids actually want to be there. *Hechinger Report*. Retrieved from hechingerreport.org/baltimore-summer-school-does-the-seemingly-impossible-the-kids-actually-want-to-be-there

Lafer, G. (2014, April 24). *Do poor kids deserve lower-quality education than rich kids? Evaluating school privatization proposals in Milwaukee, Wisconsin*. Washington, DC: Economic Policy Institute.

Lafer, G. (2017). The destruction of public schooling. In *The one percent solution: How corporations are remaking America one state at a time* (chap. 4). Ithaca, NY: Cornell University Press.

Laneri, R. (2010, April 29). Special report: America's best prep schools. *Forbes*. Retrieved from https://www.forbes.com/2010/04/29/best-prep-schools-2010-opinions-private-education.html#49f9b3615027

Miron, G., Urschel, J., Aguilar, M., & Dailey, B. (2012). *Profiles of for-profit and nonprofit education management organizations, thirteenth annual report, 2010–11*. Boulder, CO: National Education Policy Center. Retrieved from nepc.colorado.edu/publication/EMO-profiles-10-11

Molnar, M. (2016, April 21). Bill Gates: Ed tech has underachieved, but better days are ahead. *EdWeek Market Brief.* Retrieved from marketbrief.edweek.org/marketplace-k-12/bill-gates

Rich, M. (2013, April 2). Crucible of change in Memphis as state takes on failing schools. *New York Times.* Retrieved from www.nytimes.com/2013/04/03/education/crucible-of-change-in-memphis-as-state-takes-on-failing-schools.html?_r=1&

Rich, M. (2014, January 26). Intensive small-group tutoring and counseling helps struggling students. *New York Times.* Retrieved from www.nytimes.com/2014/01/27/education/intensive-tutoring-and-counseling-found-to-help-struggling-teenagers.html

Sarley, D. (2010, December 2). *Innovators convene to discuss ways to improve education* [News Release, Arizona State University]. Retrieved from asunews.asu.edu/20101129_educationinnovators

Simon, S. (2012, August 2). Privatizing public schools: Big firms eyeing profits from U.S. K-12 market. *Reuters.* Retrieved from www.huffingtonpost.com/2012/08/02/private-firms-eyeing-prof_n_1732856.html?view=print&comm_ref=false

Smith, N. (2013). *Redefining the school district in Tennessee.* Washington, DC: Thomas B. Fordham Institute. Retrieved from edexcellencemedia.net/publications/2013/20130423-Redefining-the-school-district-in-tennessee/20130423-Redefining-the-School-District-in-Tennessee-FINAL.pdf

Sparks, S. (2015, April 13). Blended learning research yields limited results. *Education Week.* Retrieved from www.edweek.org/ew/articles/2015/04/15/blended-learning-research-yields-limited-results.html

Tienken, C., & Zhao, Y. (2013). How common standards and standardized testing widen the opportunity gap. In P. Carter & K. Welner (Eds.), *Closing the opportunity gap: What America must do to give every child an even chance* (pp. 111–122). Oxford, UK: Oxford University Press.

CHAPTER 7

Charter Schooling in a State-Run Turnaround District

Lessons from the Tennessee Achievement School District

Joshua L. Glazer, Diane Massell, and Matthew Malone

> We have great charter networks like Aspire, KIPP, Achievement First and Uncommon Schools. You are steadily getting to scale. Today, I am challenging you to adapt your educational model to turning around our lowest-performing schools. I need you to go outside your comfort zones and go to underserved rural communities and small cities.
>
> —U.S. Secretary of Education Arne Duncan (2009)

With mounting evidence of promising results in some charter schools that serve poor and disadvantaged students (Center for Research on Education Outcomes [CREDO], 2015; Gamoran & Fernandez, 2018; Hoxby, Murarka, & Kang, 2009; Sims & Rossmeier, 2015; Tuttle, Teh, Nichols-Barrer, Gill, & Gleason, 2010), federal policymakers, state leaders, and philanthropists have urged charter networks to take on the formidable task of turning around chronically low-achieving schools. They have extended financial inducements and made major modifications to law and regulation to spur charters to embrace this opportunity.

Despite these incentives, many charter organizations have shied away from the stricter conditions often imposed on turnaround schools (CREDO, 2015; Therriault, 2015). Their reluctance is not hard to understand. Whereas charters typically enjoy a wide zone of autonomy and independence, government authorities tend to limit the discretion of schools in turnaround situations. For example, policies of school choice and student enrollment are often more constrained and may limit the ability of charter leaders to control their student body. Likewise, while typical charter schools are "fresh starts"—that is, newly established schools—turnaround involves taking over existing schools along with their reputation, community expectations, and institutional history. In these situations, charter growth may be conditioned on a rapid rise in outcomes that is extremely difficult to accomplish (Glazer, Massell, & Malone, 2015). The complexity of these demands may make it more difficult for charters to expand and attain economic viability.

But these different conditions are those that charter advocates believe these organizations must learn to address. Skepticism about charters persists in part because of the flexibility that charters receive in their more typical operating environments. Critics frequently point to studies showing that charter schools have fewer students with disabilities, fewer English-language learners, and a less disadvantaged population of students than their surrounding public schools (Frankenberg, Siegel-Hawley, & Wang, 2010; Jabbar, La Londe, Debray, Scott, & Lubienski, 2014; Miron, Urschel, Mathis, & Tornquist, 2010; U.S. Government Accountability Office, 2012).

While some charter advocates believe that charter operators can and should overcome the obstacles that school turnaround presents, is it logical to expect charter organizations to improve schools in an environment fundamentally different from the one they were designed to operate in? Does taking away key elements of choice and tying charters to a larger set of community priorities undermine the theory of action meant to make them effective in the first place? And to the extent that charter organizations can rise to this challenge, what adaptations to their school models and organizational capacities are required?

We discuss the results of a study that sought to answer these questions by exploring charter organizations operating in the Tennessee Achievement School District (ASD), a state-run turnaround district that relies heavily on charters to improve schools classified as among the weakest in the state. Drawing on 3 years of research, we describe the ways in which the ASD environment replicates or departs from charters' more typical circumstances and consider the implications of those differences for charter organizations and for philanthropists and policymakers seeking to enhance these initiatives. We examine the complex constellation of resources and incentives generated by the institutional environment of the ASD, the pressures this has placed on charter operators, and the impact of these pressures on instructional and organizational designs, parental and community engagement, resource allocation, and collaboration with traditional local education agencies. On a practical level, we show how charter operators were pressed to substantially revise their core assumptions and strategies in response to an environment substantively different from and more complex than that to which they were accustomed.

STUDY CONTEXT

In January 2010, Tennessee passed the First to the Top Act, a sweeping reform of the state's education policy that was the cornerstone of its successful Race to the Top application. Among its numerous provisions, the legislation empowered the state commissioner of education to identify and intervene in the state's lowest-achieving 5% of Title I schools, referred to as "priority schools." Priority schools were then eligible for one of several interventions, including participation in a local education authority innovation zone (known as the iZone), a federal School Improvement Grant, a local education authority–led improvement process, and, most salient for this discussion, placement in the ASD.

The act granted the state commissioner the authority to remove priority schools from the local district, authorize charter management organizations (CMOs) to run schools and monitor their performance, and establish a limited system of parental choice. The state's initial blueprint for the ASD emphasized school autonomy, stringent accountability, and an aversion to school boards and traditional district bureaucracies (State of Tennessee, 2010; U.S. Department of Education, 2012). Practically, this meant that ASD schools were free to determine most curricular and instructional matters, hire and dismiss teachers and principals, extend the school day, and allocate internal budgets. An operator taking over an ASD school was not obligated to retain any of the school's teachers, though the law guaranteed teachers continued employment within the local district. Additionally, the ASD operated free from the oversight of school boards or any other local representative body (though individual charter operators did establish parent boards). The ASD superintendent would be accountable only to the state superintendent.

The ASD hired its first superintendent in August 2011 and entered into full operations with five schools in the fall of 2012. By 2015, the number of ASD schools had grown to 29, with four additional schools selected for conversion in 2016. As of the 2016–2017 school year, the 33 ASD schools were run by 14 different operators. Six of these operators were national organizations, whereas eight were local to Tennessee. Although the ASD is a statewide initiative, the primary focus of its efforts has been in the Shelby County Schools (SCS) district of Memphis, where most priority schools are located. As a result, our study looks exclusively at the ASD work in Memphis.

Since the ASD began operations, its leaders have adopted a "portfolio management model" of governance (Bulkley, Henig, & Levin, 2010; Hill, Pierce, & Guthrie, 1997) in which the role of the central office shifts from the direct supervision of schools toward a more hands-off approach to guidance and oversight with a portfolio of semiautonomous schools. Consistent with these ideas, ASD leaders attempted to replicate the environment that charters elsewhere have found conducive to their growth and development. The ASD pursued efforts to maximize operational autonomy, push down per-pupil funding to the school level, and pursue policies that would enable families to choose among schools more effectively (Glazer et al., 2015). Results have thus far been sobering. An independent evaluation determined that ASD schools, over a three-year period, performed no better on average than other priority schools and worse than schools in Shelby County's own turnaround initiative known as the iZone (Zimmer et al., 2015).

ASD leaders pointed to specific areas of improvement, but it is far from certain that ASD students, in general, are on route to the top quartile that leaders had confidently predicted.

The case of the ASD vividly illustrates how a state-run turnaround district confronts charter operators with an array of incentives, resources, and pressures markedly different from their more typical environment. We found that despite the ASD's substantial efforts to encourage operators to focus on academic achievement, the operators' ability to plan or dedicate resources to their original vision was strained by an eclectic institutional environment composed of competing logics. In addition, the turnaround mission greatly expanded operators' scope of work and placed new and often extraordinary demands on their organizations. Even the most seasoned CMOs were pressed to make significant adaptations to an environment characterized by an absence of a voluntary client base or robust conditions of choice, an extreme depth of student needs, a contentious relationship with the traditional local school district and broader community, and a high degree of uncertainty in a new and largely unmapped territory.

Under these conditions, some charter operators walked away, slowed expansion plans, or withdrew their bids for authorization. But others persisted and adapted to the challenges, and we broadly analyze their actions here. Our findings shed light on what policymakers, CMOs, and independent operators may expect to encounter in similar terrain and enable them to draw from the experiences and lessons learned in the ASD.

METHODS AND SAMPLE

Our research on the Tennessee ASD began in the spring of 2013, toward the end of the ASD's first fully functional school year. The overall study explores the policies, designs, and practices of both the ASD and the school operators within its jurisdiction. This article is informed by 140 interviews completed between 2013 and winter 2016 with members of the ASD executive team, leaders from nine school operators,[1] state officials, leaders from SCS, and several community organizations.

The study team conducted extensive semistructured interviews with charter operators two to three times per year to elicit the ideas and understandings that informed the charters' design, how they perceived practice and results in their schools, and the strategic adaptations leaders were making. Our interviews also explored how operators engaged with the ASD, SCS, the community, and parents and the implications of those relationships for their work and organizations. In addition, we observed meetings between the ASD and school operators, school performance reviews, professional development sessions, and community meetings open to the public, and we collected extensive operator and ASD documents and media reports.[2]

ASD MANAGEMENT:
CREATING A CHARTER-FRIENDLY TURNAROUND ENVIRONMENT

ASD leaders, many of whom were closely tied to the charter movement, embraced the core principles of portfolio management. Echoing the assertions set out in Chubb and Moe's (1990) seminal argument for a market-based system of schooling, Malika Anderson, former superintendent of the ASD, articulated the rationale for minimal central bureaucracy and operator autonomy:

> One of the primary benefits of our autonomous schools and operators is our promise that we will . . . rapidly develop innovative, student-centered responses. This is going to enable the schools to perform much better and much faster than they would within a bureaucracy where all of the decisions are centrally made and are playing to the middle.

To accomplish this vision, ASD leaders offered operators broad discretion over hiring, curriculum, instruction, and budgeting. They assiduously avoided mandating interventions or requiring actions outside the legal minimums. They maximized the flow of state per-pupil funding to operators by maintaining a lean central office and initially paying for these staff positions with federal and philanthropic dollars. Rather than providing direct guidance to school leaders, they restricted their own central office role to brokering resources that support operators or to leveraging collaboration among operators. In this system, organizational experience, learning, and adaptation were the province of providers, not the ASD central office.

ASD leaders also sought to establish a political space that protected operators from competing political agendas. The ASD does not have a democratically elected or permanent representative body, a move meant to decouple operators from the interest group politics and competing pressures that vie for schools' attention and a place on their agenda (Cohen & Spillane, 1991). In exchange for this wide scope of autonomy, the ASD set ambitious accountability targets—to move priority schools from the bottom 5% of performance in the state to the top 25% within 5 years. Operators that failed to meet growth targets risked not being permitted to open new schools and even closure of existing schools. The high bar for performance and the stringent sanctions were meant to create a sense of urgency, exceeding the targets typically set by other states or charter authorizers.[3]

Institutional Dynamics in the ASD Turnaround Environment

Urban and high-poverty communities have long posed extraordinary and often debilitating challenges to district officials, school leaders, and teachers. High rates of student mobility, extreme poverty, and a wide array of academic and psychological needs are challenges not uncommon in these schools. These circumstances frequently overwhelm the professional and organizational capacity of urban school systems and trigger turnaround interventions. Many charter schools have located in these same communities, and some have proven successful in delivering high-quality educational services to disadvantaged students (CREDO, 2013, 2015; Tuttle et al., 2010).

Yet charters typically have access to mechanisms that can shelter them from some of the more pernicious elements of public school environments that undermine teaching and learning. While charters have a legal obligation to admit all classifications of students, they are usually authorized to recruit students without the constraints of attendance areas. This gives them access to a broad pool of families from various neighborhoods who are actively seeking out educational opportunities for their children. This flexibility to recruit students from different locales—along with the ability to impose early registration requirements, limit specific types of services, and demand parent involvement—allows charters to engage with a more stable and academically motivated population and potentially reduces the numbers of students whose language or disabilities make them harder to educate (Goldring & Hausman, 1999; Lacireno-Paquet, Holyoke, Moser, & Henig, 2002; Rotberg, 2014).

But as we discuss in this section, the ASD environment neutralized many of the social and political resources that charters were designed to leverage. Despite the ardent commitment of ASD leaders to create the conditions for success, the inherited rules of the game, the dynamics of the institutional environment, and the stresses of an impoverished community presented even the most experienced providers with steep challenges. The ASD experience demonstrates the difficulty that charter operators confront when they are unable to create buy-in through meaningful choice, stabilize the treatment population, and focus on a more circumscribed set of activities.

Neighborhood Enrollment Zones and Constraints on Choice

Exposure to instruction. The neighborhood enrollment system in the ASD greatly altered operators' ability to provide the kind of intensive treatment interventions that give charters a distinct advantage over traditional public schools in similar high-poverty settings. Under the original Tennessee statute, ASD schools were set up to serve students from their respective neighborhoods and required to admit students who arrived at any time.[4] By contrast, charter schools in other Tennessee districts may open their doors to students from any geographic area. Similarly, in most settings, charter administrators can fix their enrollment at the beginning of the school year and require late applicants to wait until the following year. Many charter organizations also refrain from enrolling students in upper grades ("backfilling") even when they experience attrition and have open seats (Democracy Builders, 2015; Hill & Maas, 2015). The ASD's zoned enrollment system prohibited these practices. One CMO leader explained:

I think the biggest difference [in the ASD] is that we can't turn students away. So when I was a [charter school] principal, . . . I could say in January, we're not going to take new students. If they came in to register they would go on the wait list for next year. . . . We can't do that in neighborhood turnaround schools, even if we are full.

These restrictions weakened ASD operators' ability to stabilize a core treatment population. Operators reported that many Memphis students did not enroll until several weeks after school had begun, and more than one-third of students (36%–37%) in ASD schools moved in or out of their schools during the school year. This figure represents an improvement over student mobility prior to ASD intervention and is comparable to that of schools with similar demographics in the region (Henry, Zimmer, Attridge, Kho, & Viano, 2014).[5] However, it dwarfs the rate of student mobility for the state's overall charter sector, which in 2013–2014 averaged only 11% for K–8 schools and 9% for high schools (Tennessee Department of Education, 2015).

This extreme mobility presented tough challenges for CMO leaders, who had built their designs to address learning gaps early in a student's career and concentrate on nurturing those gains steadily over time. A leader from one ASD operator captured the comments made by many:

One of our big takeaways from last year was the effect that mobility of students has on our work. . . . Last year was our third year, which we would have said going in was going to be the dream year because students would have adjusted to our culture and be getting close to grade level academically. Instead, it was very similar to our first year because of all the new students who arrived on our campus.

Another operator elaborated on this point and the difficulty it presented to school managers:

In a traditional charter, if you're not enrolled by September 1, you can't come. If kids leave, we don't replace them. Here we have kids that come in in February. No telling what they've had all year long. They don't know your culture, they don't know your school. They bring in their past practice, and now they're your student and you're responsible for making sure they grow a grade level.

Student and family buy-in. The neighborhood enrollment system, compounded by poverty and other systemic barriers to choice, also altered the dynamics of family and student buy-in. In a more typical open-choice environment, charters educate students whose families have voluntarily elected to place them in the school and have committed to the school's educational approach and values. Parents and students who actively choose are more likely to understand a school's philosophy, participate in school-related activities, be involved in their child's education, and adhere to school expectations (Bifulco & Ladd, 2006; Martinez, Thomas, & Kemerer, 1994; Smrekar & Goldring, 1999).

In the ASD, however, traditional zoning rules made most ASD schools the *de facto* option for students in their catchment zone. Absent a student population whose families sought out schools that met their values and priorities, providers struggled to engender parent buy-in and engagement. Said one provider:

> The parent's engagement level is lower, their initiative is lower, we're teaching in a way that's very different from what was taught in this building prior, so it's a big change for parents. So that makes it really, really hard. So you have to win the parents; you have to convince them.

Pressure to minimize suspensions and expulsions. Under their usual conditions, charters have the option of removing students who do not adhere to the rules or are otherwise disruptive to the learning culture they are trying to establish. From the outset, the ASD warned operators to refrain from removing students, in part because these were neighborhood schools and students and families did not necessarily actively choose them. As Malika Anderson articulated it:

> The model has to recognize that if students have not affirmatively selected in, they have to have different ways of reaching them, of motivating them, of encouraging them to go above and beyond—without the stick of being able to kick them out. . . . So if the student doesn't fit into your program, it doesn't mean the student changes; it means the program changes.

Nevertheless, during the 2013–2014 school year, 21% of ASD students were suspended, and 2% were expelled and remanded to alternative school settings. Fourteen of the expelled students were in grades pre-K to 3, a problem that led the ASD to form an advisory group and double down on the message that operators should refrain from such actions. This pressure, along with the absence of a more voluntary client base, created a different balance of power between parents and school officials. Explained one CMO leader:

> In your traditional charter, parents . . . are taking an initiative to buy into what you're doing, and if it doesn't go well, then a traditional charter can say, "You're not doing what you promised to do, so you're no longer a student." As an ASD school, you don't have that option.

In sum, while a focus on school climate and family buy-in is common within the larger charter movement, the conditions in the ASD presented challenges to these usual strategies. The combination of zoned neighborhood enrollment, high mobility, weak control over student entry, and a press to lower suspensions and expulsions meant that ASD operators lacked the leverage to establish the kind of school culture and behavioral routines they felt were essential and that charters typically enjoy. The ASD set remarkably high expectations for its operators, yet shrunk the array of tools at their disposal for accomplishing these ends.

Special Education

For traditional and charter public schools alike, marshaling the economic and organizational resources to meet the needs of students with disabilities is often a vexing problem. But delivering special education services has been particularly daunting for ASD operators because of the extreme levels of special-needs students in Memphis schools, the funding model, the difficulty of leveraging economies of scale in the ASD, and the perceived lack of strong external service providers.

Large special education population. In 2013–2014, 15.2% of students across the ASD schools were identified for special education services. While these proportions were on par with other priority schools in Memphis,[6] they were much higher than the norm in charter or traditional public schools.[7] Overall, ASD operators in Memphis served about 5% more students with disabilities than other charters in the state of Tennessee in 2014 (Tennessee Department of Education, 2015). Further, ASD data show that these percentages have risen steadily over time, are more concentrated in some schools, and mask the depth of students' needs. For example, 15% of ASD students requiring services in 2014–2015 were classified as having "severe" disabilities, thereby requiring 32.5 hours of special education and related services per week.

Even those operators with a long history in Memphis did not appreciate how their status as a neighborhood school, versus an open-choice school, would affect the numbers and types of students with special needs. A leader from a CMO with schools in SCS and the ASD commented:

> Probably the biggest difference between our open enrollment school and an ASD school . . . is that we just have a higher number of students with high needs [in the ASD], whether they are identified as special education students or not special education students. . . . And a zoned school costs us more for special education because we have to be able to meet the needs of all the students.

Financial model. Even in typical charter settings, establishing a financially viable model of service for special education has proven difficult (Gross & Lake, 2014). But under the zoned enrollment system, ASD operators were financially responsible for meeting the special education needs of all students in their attendance areas, even if students received services in another setting. Further, the range and high level of needs among students with disabilities presented operators with significant resource challenges.

The problem might be particularly acute in Tennessee, where the state provides a flat per-pupil amount of $8,100 to ASD schools (2014–2015), regardless of the number or type of students served. Operators did receive federal funding from the Individuals with Disabilities Education Act (IDEA), but this fell far short of operators' costs, did not account well for growth, and was difficult to fully recoup. Operators' ability to create a solid financial plan to serve these students was further exacerbated by the high level of student mobility, since students with disabilities can arrive at any time of the year. Moreover, budget estimates vacillate from one school year to the next, since the enrollment of just a few students with severe needs can cause sharp increases in expenditures.

Weak economies of scale. Although special education poses challenges to traditional public schools, these schools benefit from the ability of their parent districts to exploit economies of scale by pooling resources into a single school or across a few schools (Miron & Urschel, 2010). In contrast, the ASD is a lean organization that values autonomy, pushes down per-pupil funding to operators, and has minimal involvement in school-level processes. It has neither the capacity nor the inclination to actively broker collaborative relationships, compromises, or cost-sharing arrangements among operators. Consequently, to enable an economy of scale or cost-sharing measures, each operator would have to determine whether and how to collaborate. Moreover, such agreements are further complicated by charters' varying capabilities and needs, as well as their different views of effective practice.

A District Among Districts

The dynamics of charter schooling were also dramatically altered by the fact that the ASD is a school district inserted into the territories of traditional public school districts that retain considerable formal and informal authority. As such, the ASD and its operators have been highly vulnerable to those districts' priorities and the dynamics of local politics. Moreover, local resistance to the ASD in Memphis has contributed to an environment where the legitimacy of ASD operators has been highly contested and community support must be actively constructed (Glazer & Egan, 2016). This combination of interdependence with the local district and community pushback against the ASD has further weakened operators' control over their environment, increased uncertainty, and placed additional demands on their organizations.

One example regards the SCS's legal authority to draw the neighborhood attendance boundaries that determine school enrollment and feeder patterns. Operators reported that these changes influenced their budgeting and ability to plan based on student enrollment. In one case, the SCS board passed a resolution expanding grade levels served by its own schools to enable parents to bypass a priority school assigned to an ASD provider (Pignolet, 2016). In another case,

SCS refused to provide the ASD with contact information for families that were recently zoned into ASD schools (Kebede, 2016).

SCS's informal powers were also considerable and were amply demonstrated in highly charged negotiations over which schools would be absorbed into the ASD. Although the ASD leaders legally could have selected any priority school they wanted, SCS's local legitimacy and informal authority meant that it wielded considerable leverage in these negotiations. Some CMO leaders believed that SCS was claiming the most economically viable schools, narrowing providers' path to economic viability. Said one:

> There's a fight for kids with a district that's just trying to stay afloat, and then you've got this ASD coming in that's only making that harder. So I know that there's been a lot of effort and there's been a lot of rhetoric around improving the relationship. But when I look at the actual benefits of those relationships, I feel like Shelby County has played the better strategy throughout this whole past 3 years. . . . So, not only would we get access to smaller schools, but also they would be ones that are super underenrolled.

Another district-level decision about colocating ASD charters in the same buildings as SCS schools further strained operators' resources and compromised their turnaround strategies. The "phase-in" strategy allows ASD operators to take over a school one grade at a time, thereby enabling operators to incrementally build up a corps of students with common learning and behavioral norms. It also allows operators to gradually expand their capacity and refine their strategy. But the fact that phase-in required several years of colocation with an SCS school created a contentious and volatile situation in the school and in the community. The SCS superintendent depicted colocation as "awkward, demoralizing, and expensive" for the district (as quoted in Burnette, 2014). In 2014, vocal community opposition to colocation ultimately led one provider to withdraw from Memphis altogether, despite significant planning, investments, and a plan to open in a different site (Dries, 2015).

But community resistance was motivated by more than concerns about colocation. The conversion of schools into the ASD engendered fierce outcries and mistrust about ASD intentions. Many in Memphis saw the ASD as a hostile state takeover of their schools—not, as ASD managers argued, a return of schools back to the parents and students. To many, the ASD was the latest chapter in a long history of white racism, reckless social engineering, and paternalism (Glazer & Egan, 2016). One operator contrasted the backlash in Memphis with the support and tranquility they were accustomed to in their home state:

> This has been humbling for me. We've been quite shielded from a lot of the politics and press. . . . I've learned so much about just how complex education can be in particular landscapes. We're very fortunate that our home state kind of lets us have the number of kids we want. We buy our own buildings. We kind of own the whole process.

The tense atmosphere and delicate coexistence with SCS constitutes a key part of the charter environment in the ASD. The charged political environment adds substantial operational uncertainties and further erosion of operators' control over an environment in which they clearly do not "own the whole process." Operators have little choice other than to make painful accommodations to political resistance and to a local district whose ties to the community afford it considerable legitimacy.

ADAPTATIONS

As the previous section has shown, the turnaround environment of the ASD imposed unusual conditions for charter operators that substantially departed from a more conventional charter environment. Nevertheless, some operators have responded to these challenges with more sophisticated school-level designs, instructional adaptations, and expansions to their organizational capabilities. In this section, we take a broad look at several of the modifications operators made to cope with the lack of parent buy-in, student mobility, the depth and diversity of student needs, and the ASD's lack of social legitimacy at the local level.

Stretching the Instructional Design

The transience of the student population meant constant uncertainty and a body of students with a disparate array of learning challenges. This upheaval and instability posed two core dilemmas for the operators. One was an urgent need to expand and refine their instructional infrastructure—for example, curriculum, materials, instructional strategies—in ways that would effectively address students with more varied academic issues. The other was to determine whether these expanded efforts were effective—that is, whether poor results were due to a lack of exposure to treatment or bad treatment designs.

To handle the problem that student churn posed to understanding treatment effects, the leaders of one charter began analyzing student results in cohorts according to how long they had been in the school. They used this strategy to help distinguish between the potency of their model and the extent of students' exposure to it.

> We changed our understanding of how to measure our success, which means there is not really a steady trend of overall school growth but rather growth of cohorts. It also means there is no such thing as getting to the place where the culture is set and the gaps are closed. Every year is a first year.

Operators experimented with a complement of initiatives to identify and target knowledge and skill gaps with more individualized learning opportunities and tailored, small-group instruction. The process of creating and implementing these new strategies required sustained effort, expertise, and adaptations to practice. For example, to more precisely pinpoint students' learning needs, one CMO developed a refined learning scale with eight ability levels. It found, however, that teachers were overwhelmed by identifying and providing instruction at each level. This implementation problem led to the design of new, more specific instructional routines to reduce the complexity of practice. As one operator explained:

> What happens when you don't teach at grade level is that the deficit becomes even deeper. And it is a struggle for teachers to figure out how to teach eight different lesson plans. That is the reason why we went to a small group blended learning type of instruction. . . . You have the personalized computer part plus a really in-depth intervention block where the group is even smaller. . . . Every teacher in the building is an interventionist, . . . so the groups that are typically in the class are 8 to 10 kids.

Other operators also sought new curricula and programs tailored to low-performing students. For example, whereas this operator combined computer-assisted instruction with a new intervention block involving every employee in the building, another developed a coteaching model to reduce the cognitive demand on teachers required by extreme differentiation. As stated by Chris Barbic, a former ASD superintendent:

> You're not going to find enough teachers who can differentiate at the level that our teachers need to differentiate at. It's an impossible feat. Folks are figuring out ways to do that through both technology and how you structure and organize your staff—and no one has figured it out yet, but I think people are starting to.

On the one hand, our data support Barbic's observation that some operators were starting to devise school-level designs that addressed the greater depth and concentration of student needs. On the other, it would be difficult to overstate the demands this placed on organizational capability, and the far-reaching extent of expertise, time, and money required to devise complex instructional systems. Some of the CMOs had large hub offices and the capacity to address them, whereas others were independent charters without substantial resources.

Stretching School Wraparound Supports

ASD operators understood that they would have to provide more than intensive academic supports to address some of the fundamental challenges impeding their students' opportunities to learn. While some operators began with an understanding of the wraparound services that would be needed, others were pressed to develop new services or adapt existing ones. This occurred in part because the supports that might have been provided by traditional districts were noticeably absent or compromised in the ASD. Operators arranged or contracted for wrap-around services to address health and social service needs, student safety, parent employment, and housing stability. One operator conducted home visits to connect families to these services, while others created after-school options, partnered with food banks, created financial literacy programs for parents, and more. A staff member from a national charter philanthropy explained that these community outreach efforts were highly atypical of the foundation's experience with charters in other settings. But operators believed that without them their work at the school would regress. As one operator put it, "It's like a revolving cycle—like you're pressing play and rewind again and again." Here too, however, providing more support placed more demands on the organization. Partnerships with external service organizations arose to alleviate some of the burden on operators, yet these relationships had to be brokered, coordinated, and managed, further taxing operators' organizational resources.

Stretching the Designs for Serving Students with Special Needs

Operators expanded their internal capacity to provide instructional services and supports to address the challenges of students with disabilities and extreme needs. For example, at least four operators in our sample developed functional skills classrooms, and several operators created self-contained classrooms or pre-K programs for students with disabilities. They also coordinated supports across schools within their own network, or across networks with similar approaches and needs, to generate mini-economies of scale. For example, one operator assigned students with specific disabilities to one of its five schools. Three other operators agreed to share the costs of an enrichment teacher for gifted students rather than each paying one teacher for a small segment of their students.

Adapting Behavioral Routines

Operators responded in various ways to the challenge of a nonelective student population. To encourage alternatives to expelling disruptive students, the Operator Advisory Council, a group comprising representatives from each provider, recommended a set of behavioral assessments and disciplinary practices for grades pre-K to 3. The ASD offered professional development on the positive behavior intervention supports program, and two operators in our sample adopted restorative justice practices to empower students to resolve conflicts. Moreover, the ASD and the Operator Advisory Council also sought to restrict exclusionary practices by collectively developing clear, voluntary guidelines.

These adaptations appeared to be motivated by providers' commitment to equality and fairness, but at the same time, they diminished operators' ability to manage and actively shape their student culture and climate. Providers were seeking alternative ways to develop their envisioned learning environment, but in the meantime, the task of inculcating shared norms was more complex for ASD operators than for typical charter school operators.

Stretching Parent Engagement and Community Outreach

Resentment toward the ASD and anger about the removal of specific schools from local control meant that operators began their work with a deficit of community support and social legitimacy. To build that trust, operators launched more extensive outreach campaigns and developed new methods of soliciting parental buy-in and community support. This involved establishing and nourishing an array of institutional and personal relationships with parents and other key stakeholder groups. For example, one CMO developed new formal structures within and across schools to generate regular parent input and guidance and created more occasions for social interaction and celebration with families.

> There are a couple of things that we did in addition to the kind of traditional things that we do at our [non-ASD] schools to engage families. Each school has an advisory school council and parents are officers. . . . We're creating a regional parent council . . . to have parents who know what's going on, can give us input, and also parents who are willing to speak up and say something about the school. We also have a lot more community events at each school.

Providers looked for new ways to communicate with and engage families. After disappointing participation in traditional open houses, leaders of one network found that parents were much more likely to attend sporting events. They strategically used these opportunities to communicate with parents about their programs and their students. Another charter official reported encouraging "teachers to step up and own different events at the school," adding that although "it's hard in the beginning . . . it is not really optional. It's something that we have to prioritize." Thus, while some charter organizations have been known to cut back on the "frill" of sports and similar activities to focus their resources more intensively on academics, ASD operators sought to maintain or build nonacademic programs and assign teachers to these events.

This work extended beyond parents to include a broader swath of the community. For example, one operator dedicated a staff member to develop community partnerships with a local university, churches, businesses, and civic groups; engage in community walks; and visit students' homes to hear parents' concerns. Several operators expanded their mission from school turnaround to neighborhood turnaround. One CMO purchased and cleaned up abandoned homes and lots near the school and even invested in building new housing. A different operator hired a local organization that employed neighborhood people for its lawn work and other maintenance.

The face-to-face contact and programs that facilitated communication and engagement were critical to operators' efforts to build local legitimacy and support. At the same time, they strained operators' organizational capabilities and stretched the attention of their leaders across a wider, more diffuse array of purposes that diverted resources from schools and classrooms. What for many operators was initially a laser-like focus on academic achievement expanded into a more varied set of activities. Not surprisingly, operators reported that they struggled to balance outreach efforts with the imperative to build a strong academic program. These examples show not only how operators have embraced these challenges, but also how allocating staff, effort, and money to outreach and engagement taxes their capacity to confront formidable educational challenges.

CONCLUSIONS

Operators in the ASD have been compelled to devise more varied instructional strategies and interventions to address a broader spectrum of student learning needs, bolster their organizational capabilities, and take extraordinary measures to increase public support and their own legitimacy. As Chris Barbic, the former ASD superintendent, observed, few could really anticipate the implications of a turnaround environment:

> We could tell people it was hard, we could talk about how this was different than charter schools prior to this and how charter schooling was done. But until you open up the school and get the students and start understanding what the work is like, you just can't appreciate it.

While some might argue that the conditions for charters in the ASD put them on an even playing field with their public counterparts in high-poverty neighborhoods, the reality for ASD charters was in many ways more complex. ASD operators had to contend with many of the constraints that impede traditional schools yet without the benefits that a conventional district could provide. For one thing, traditional public schools have the advantage of being just that—traditional. Regardless of their performance, these schools and their employees have the imprimatur of long local standing and the social and political capital that accrue with this resident identity. As outsiders tainted by the perception of state takeover, ASD charters were looked on with suspicion and did not enjoy this taken-for-granted legitimacy.

Similarly, ASD operators were dependent on a school district where factions could be indifferent, if not hostile, to their success (Glazer & Egan, 2016). Although the ASD had considerable statutory authority, SCS retained substantial control and informal power, which left operators vulnerable to its decisions about neighborhood zoning, school phase-ins, and the pool of priority schools to which they could be matched. Charters' work was also influenced by SCS's inactions, such as the district's decision not to develop a common application system or common school accountability framework.

In special education and other domains, the ASD operators initiated numerous changes and made extensive efforts to respond to these instructional and organizational demands. They added or reallocated resources to expand their own special education classrooms and collaborated with other operators to leverage some efficiencies of scale. They reorganized assessment and instruction, introduced computer-assisted learning, added wraparound services for students and families, and developed new strategies for communicating with parents and building trust in their neighborhood communities. These adaptations are reminiscent of a handful of successful comprehensive school reform initiatives that also had minimal control over their environment but that compensated with highly sophisticated, complex designs for teaching, learning, and leadership (Cohen, Peurach, Glazer, Gates, & Goldin, 2014).

The expansion of operators' products and services is encouraging, but they come at a cost. Whereas charters usually have the leverage to tighten their focus and strategically allocate resources, the ASD operators had to broaden their goals and scope of activity. This diffusion of purpose and activity is reminiscent of traditional schools whose efforts to meet the diverse needs of multiple constituencies have earned them the label of "shopping malls" in which the breadth of academic and nonacademic offerings come at the expense of focus and clarity of purpose (e.g., Powell, Farrar, & Cohen, 1985).

That said, enthusiasm for ASD-style turnaround districts has continued, as other states have established independent turnaround districts explicitly modeled (and named) after the ASD. But the turnaround space for charters is indisputably different from their usual circumstances, and as such calls for a very different type of schooling operation. As Chris Barbic cautioned, playing in the "big leagues" of school turnaround is not suitable for every charter organization:

> Three years ago we would have been in sell mode as to why you need to come here. When I'm talking to people now, I'm like, this is the big leagues. Do you want to play the equivalent to basketball for the Kentucky Wildcats where every single game is huge, it's a circus, you're under intense scrutiny, and the pressure to perform is incredible? . . . I think the pitch now is if you think you're ready for the big leagues, come to Memphis.

Yet beyond the challenge that Barbic aptly described, another more fundamental issue has not been fully recognized by advocates of ASD-like initiatives. The press to expand purposes and offerings, the limits on creating a voluntary and stable client base, and the need to negotiate complex political dynamics in the ASD environment are precisely what charter schools were designed to avoid. The improvements to practice that charters were meant to deliver were to emerge from an institutional arrangement that would enable charter schools to do precisely what traditional schools cannot—maximize resources and focus on a clear and limited set of goals.

In this sense, there is a great irony to ASD-like reforms. Their emergence reflects impatience if not disdain for traditional districts, which are viewed as incompetent, bureaucratic organizations with little ability for self-improvement. But in asking charter organizations to operate neighborhood schools, in which choice is more illusion than reality and the demands of variable stakeholder groups are acutely felt, reformers have inadvertently created an environment strikingly similar to the one they are seeking to replace. The fact that ASD charters, many of which demonstrate remarkable drive and commitment to innovate, have assumed organizational characteristics reminiscent of traditional public schools is not surprising, given such similarities.

We do not conclude from this that every school operator working in an ASD-like environment is destined to fail. In fact, we have encountered operators with sophisticated and thoughtful designs. We do contend, however, that re-creating charter-like flexibility inside state turnaround districts is more difficult than proponents might suppose, and that even charter organizations with a track record of success can be expected to encounter unfamiliar challenges that will require substantial adaptations. Those operators that do succeed will do so not because their status as charters provides advantages over traditional schools. They will do so because they have devised highly sophisticated school-level designs buttressed by extraordinary organizations capable of adapting to their complex institutional environments.

NOTES

The research on which this chapter is based was funded by the Walton Family Foundation and the Spencer Foundation.

1. The ASD has authorized schools that are part of CMO networks as well as single independent nonprofits. Some operate under different types of contracts. For linguistic ease, we use the term "charter" or "operators" to generically refer to all types.

2. For a full discussion of our research methods, see Massell, Glazer, and Malone (2016).

3. For a detailed analysis of student achievement in the ASD, see Zimmer, Kho, Henry, and Viano (2015).

4. The legislature later allowed charters to enroll up to 25% of their students from other designated low-performing schools.

5. In 2011–2012, the year before schools came into the ASD, this cohort of schools experienced 46% mobility. That rate dropped to 37% by the 2013–2014 school year and has hovered between 36% and 37% for subsequent cohorts (Henry et al., 2014).

6. In district-run innovation zone schools, 15.7% of enrolled students were identified as having special needs, while 17.5% of students in other Memphis priority schools were so designated (Henry et al., 2014).

7. One national study found that special-needs students comprised only 8% of public charter school enrollments in 2009–2010, compared to 11% in traditional schools (U.S. Government Accountability Office, 2012). In most school settings, 2% to 7% of enrolled students qualify for the highest level of intensive special education supports (Ervin, 2008).

REFERENCES

Bifulco, R., & Ladd, H. F. (2006). Institutional change and coproduction of public services: The effect of charter schools on parental involvement. *Journal of Public Administration Research and Theory, 16*(4), 553–576.

Bulkley, K. E., Henig, J. R., & Levin, H. M. (Eds.). (2010). *Between public and private: Politics, governance, and the new portfolio models for urban school reform.* Cambridge, MA: Harvard Education Press.

Burnette, D. (2014, December 31). Best of 2014: Colocation presents hurdles, opportunities. *Chalkbeat Tennessee.* Retrieved from co.chalkbeat.org/posts/tn/2014/12/31/colocation-presents-hurdles-opportunities/

Center for Research on Education Outcomes. (2013). *National charter school study 2013.* Stanford, CA: Author. Retrieved from credo.stanford.edu/documents/NCSS%20 2013%20Final%20Draft.pdf

Center for Research on Educational Outcomes. (2015). *Urban charter school study report on 41 regions.* Stanford, CA: Author. Retrieved from urbancharters.stanford.edu/download/Urban%20Charter%20School%20Study%20Report%20on%2041%20Regions.pdf

Chubb, J. E., & Moe, T. M. (1990). *Politics, markets and America's schools.* Washington, DC: Brookings Institution Press.

Cohen, D. K., Peurach, D. J., Glazer, J. L., Gates, K. E., & Goldin, S. (2014). *Improvement by design: The promise of better schools.* Chicago, IL: University of Chicago Press.

Cohen, D. K., & Spillane, J. P. (1991). Policy and practice: The relations between governance and instruction. In S. H. Fuhrman (Ed.), *Designing coherent education policy: Improving the system* (pp. 35–95). San Francisco, CA: Jossey-Bass.

Democracy Builders. (2015). *No seat left behind: The unfilled potential of empty seats in charter schools.* New York, NY: Author. Retrieved from democracybuilders.org/no-seat-left-behind-report-view-now/

Dries, B. (2015, March 25). YES Prep says no to Memphis school. *Memphis Daily News, 130*(58).

Ervin, R. A. (2008). *Considering tier 3 within a response-to-intervention model.* New York, NY: RTI Action Network. Retrieved from www.rtinetwork.org/essential/tieredinstruction/tier3/consideringtier3

Frankenberg, E., Siegel-Hawley, G., & Wang, J. (2010). *Choice without equity: Charter school segregation and the need for civil rights standards.* Los Angeles, CA: Civil Rights Project.

Gamoran, A., & Fernandez, C. M. (2018). Do charter schools strengthen education in high-poverty urban districts? In I. C. Rotberg & J. L. Glazer (Eds.), *Choosing charters: Better schools or more segregation?* (pp. 133–152). New York, NY: Teachers College Press.

Glazer, J. L., & Egan, C. (2016). *The Tennessee Achievement School District: Race, history, and the dilemma of public engagement.* Nashville, TN: Tennessee Consortium on Research, Evaluation, and Development.

Glazer, J. L., Massell, D., & Malone, M. (2015). *Research into Tennessee's Achievement School District: First year results.* Nashville, TN: Tennessee Consortium on Research, Evaluation, and Development.

Goldring, E., & Hausman, C. (1999). Reasons for parental choice in urban schools. *Journal of Education Policy, 4*(5), 469–490.

Gross, B., & Lake, R. (2014). *Special education in charter schools: What we've learned and what we still need to know.* Seattle, WA: Center on Reinventing Public Education.

Henry, G., Zimmer, J., Attridge, J., Kho, A., & Viano, S. (2014). *Teacher and student migration in and out of Tennessee's Achievement School District.* Nashville, TN: Tennessee Consortium on Research, Evaluation, and Development.

Hill, P., & Maas, T. (2015). *Backfill in charter high schools: Practices to learn from and questions to be answered.* Seattle, WA: Center on Reinventing Public Education.

Hill, P. T., Pierce, L., & Guthrie, J. (1997). *Reinventing public education: How contracting can transform America's schools.* Chicago, IL: University of Chicago Press.

Hoxby, C. M., Murarka, S., & Kang, J. (2009). *How New York City's charter schools affect student achievement: August 2009 report.* Cambridge, MA: New York City Charter Schools Evaluation Project.

Jabbar, H., La Londe, P. G., Debray, E., Scott, J., & Lubienski, C. (2014). How policymakers define "evidence": The politics of research use in New Orleans. *Policy Futures in Education, 12*(8), 1013–1027.

Kebede, L. F. (2016, July 21). "We just want our kids back": Charter leaders respond to student retention tactics used by Shelby County Schools. *Chalkbeat Tennessee.* Retrieved from www.chalkbeat.org/posts/tn/2016/07/21/we-just-want-our-kids-back-charter-leaders-respond-to-student-retention-tactics-used-by-shelby-county-schools

Lacireno-Paquet, N., Holyoke, T. T., Moser, M., & Henig, J. R. (2002). Creaming versus cropping: Charter school enrollment practices in response to market incentives. *Educational Evaluation and Policy Analysis, 24*(2), 145–158.

Martinez, V., Thomas, K., & Kemerer, F. (1994). Who chooses and why: A look at five choice plans. *Phi Delta Kappan, 9,* 678–681.

Massell, D., Glazer, J. L., & Malone, M. (2016). *"This is the big leagues": Charter-led turnaround in a non-charter world.* Nashville, TN: Tennessee Consortium on Research, Evaluation, and Development.

Miron, G., & Urschel, J. L. (2010, June). *Equal or fair? A study of revenues and expenditures in American charter schools.* Boulder, CO, and Tempe, AZ: Education and the Public Interest Center & Education Policy Research Unit. Retrieved from nepc.colorado.edu/files/EMO-RevExp.pdf

Miron, G., Urschel, J. L., Mathis, W. J., & Tornquist, E. (2010). *Schools without diversity: Education management organizations, charter schools, and the demographic stratification of the American school system.* Boulder, CO, and Tempe, AZ: Education and the Public Interest Center & Education Policy Research Unit.

Pignolet, J. (2016, April 18). SCS plan would bypass ASD school in Raleigh. *Commercial Appeal.* Retrieved from archive.commercialappeal.com/news/schools/scs-plan-would-bypass-asd-in-one-neighborhood-30c546c9-e918-6397-e053-0100007fc091-376092841.html

Powell, A. G., Farrar, E., & Cohen, D. K. (1985). *The shopping mall high school: Winners and losers in the educational marketplace.* Boston, MA: Houghton Mifflin.

Rotberg, I. C. (2014). Charter schools and the risk of increased segregation. *Phi Delta Kappan, 95*(5), 26–31.

Sims, P., & Rossmeier, V. (2015). *The state of public education in New Orleans.* New Orleans, LA: Cowen Institute for Public Education Initiatives, Tulane University.

Smrekar, C., & Goldring, E. (1999). *School choice in urban America: Magnet schools and the pursuit of equity.* New York, NY: Teachers College Press.

State of Tennessee. (2010, January). *Race to the Top: Application for initial funding*. Retrieved from www2. ed.gov/programs/racetothetop/phase1-applications/tennessee.pdf

Tennessee Department of Education. (2015). *Charter schools annual report 2015*. Nashville, TN: Office of Research and Policy, Tennessee Department of Education.

Therriault, S. B. (2015). *A new approach to school turnaround: Charter operators managing district schools*. Washington, DC: American Institutes for Research.

Tuttle, C. C., Teh, B., Nichols-Barrer, I., Gill, B. P., & Gleason, P. (2010). *Student characteristics and achievement in 22 KIPP middle schools*. Washington, DC: Mathematica Policy Research.

U.S. Department of Education. (2012). *ESEA flexibility request (Tennessee)*. Washington, DC: Author.

U.S. Government Accountability Office. (2012). *Charter schools: Additional federal attention needs to help protect access for students with disabilities*. Washington, DC: Author.

Zimmer, R., Kho, A., Henry, G., & Viano, S. (2015). *Evaluation of the effect of Tennessee's Achievement School District on student test scores*. Nashville, TN: Tennessee Consortium on Research, Evaluation, & Development.

CHAPTER 8

Do Charter Schools Undermine Efforts to Create Racially and Socioeconomically Diverse Public Schools?

*Roslyn Arlin Mickelson, Jason Giersch,
Amy Hawn Nelson, and Martha Cecilia Bottia*

Unless we change directions, we are likely to end up where we are headed.

—Chinese proverb

Since the last decades of the 20th century, many of the nation's public education systems have been resegregating. At the same time, the U.S. student population is becoming increasingly ethnically and racially diverse and socioeconomically polarized (Fiel, 2015; Frankenberg & Siegel-Hawley, 2013; Logan & Burdick-Will, 2015; Orfield, Ee, Frankenberg, & Siegel-Hawley, 2016). In this chapter, we investigate the relation between racial segregation in public education and the growth of charter schools. Charters are among a suite of choice reforms introduced as solutions to perceived shortcomings in many public school systems' capacities to deliver equitable and excellent education to every student. However, the preponderance of empirical research demonstrates that equity and excellence are incompatible with almost every form of segregation (Bohrnstedt, Kitmitto, Ogut, Sherman, & Chan, 2015; Johnson, 2011; Mickelson & Nkomo, 2012; Reardon, 2016).

The tensions among equity, excellence, and segregation are germane to educational choice reforms such as charters for two reasons. First, school choice has a historical record as a conscious strategy used by white southerners to avoid *Brown's* (1954) mandate to desegregate (Bonastia, 2012). Second, most charter schools are more racially segregated than their local school system, or even their nearest traditional public school neighbors (Malkus, 2016). Yet these facts do not answer the title's question. Charters may reflect trends rather than influence them. We answer the title's question—do charter schools undermine efforts to create diverse public schools?—with a review of the literature regarding the relation of school choice to segregation by race and socioeconomic status (SES). Next, we examine research about charter schools and segregation in the state of North Carolina. We then turn to an examination of the relationship of charters to segregation in the Charlotte-Mecklenburg Schools (CMS) public school system itself.

Once renowned for successful desegregation, CMS resegregated by race and SES soon after it was declared unitary in 2002. In 2016, CMS began a multiphase redesign of its pupil assignment plan to address growth and segregation. Our case study permits us to look at the direct role of charters in fostering racial segregation through the mechanical relationship between charter transfers and the total enrollment of middle-class, white and Asian, and/or high-performing students who leave CMS. By examining the public discourse about the scope of equity initiatives and the policy process in CMS, we also examine the *indirect* effects of charter schools on segregation. Specifically, we present evidence of how the looming threat that middle-class white parents will exit CMS and enroll their children in charters influences Mecklenburg County policymakers' perceptions of politically viable options for effectively addressing segregation. We conclude with a consideration of how public school decisionmakers' capacity to pursue greater educational equity by combating segregation is deterred by competition from charter schools.

SCHOOL CHOICE AND SEGREGATION

Contemporary forms of school choice include inter- and intradistrict magnets, charters, home schooling, vouchers, and private schools. Not all choice options are publicly supported, but parents today can choose among publicly funded school choice options in 55% of the nation's largest districts (Whitehurst, 2016). Schools of choice—whether private schools, charters, homeschooling, vouchers, or intradistrict magnet programs—whose admissions processes do not require diversity are likely to be more segregated than the traditional public schools from which they draw their students (Frankenberg & Siegel-Hawley, 2013; Malkus, 2016; Mickelson, Bottia, & Southworth, 2012).

The choice-segregation nexus is structured by the interactions among federal, state, and local education policies and their implementation. Parental preferences, information networks, and differential capacities to exercise choice mediate the relationship between educational structures and enrollment patterns. Race and SES are key predictors of whether parents are likely to exercise their options, with affluent white families being disproportionately more likely to utilize school choice. Less prosperous whites and families of color typically have fewer financial resources, have less access to information about school choices, and are less likely to choose their children's school (Bifulco, Ladd, & Ross, 2009; DeJarnatt, 2008; Kimelberg, 2014; Roda & Wells, 2013; Sikkink & Emerson, 2008). Studies indicate that parents of English learners and children with disabilities often are dissuaded from certain choice options by providers who point out the absence of necessary services for their children (Miron & Urschel, 2012). Pattillo (2015) found that in the Chicago area, the choice process left black parents evaluating their experiences more as being chosen by a school rather than choosing a school for their child.

During the choice process, parents generally prioritize the school's proximity to home and academic quality (Cucchiara, 2013; DeJarnatt, 2008; Reback, 2008). A school's racial and ethnic composition matters, too. Parents typically choose schools with children who are demographically similar. While families of color at times consciously choose a racially segregated option, especially when the school of choice's theme addresses unique needs (Finley, 2016), white parents are more likely than any other racial or ethnic group to seek schools where their child is a member of a large racial majority (DeJarnatt, 2008; Ladd, Clotfelter, & Holbein, 2015; Liebowitz & Page, 2014; Weiher & Tedin, 2002).

Charter Schools and Segregation

The segregative patterns true of school choice in general are also true of charter schools. Reasons for charter segregation begin with the degree to which their enabling legislation requires attention to diversity. National data indicate that to differing degrees across school jurisdictions and states, charter schools are likely to be segregated by students' race, ethnicity, disability, English-learner status, disciplinary history, and SES (Bifulco et al., 2009; Lareau & Goyette, 2014; Malkus, 2016; Mathis & Welner, 2016; Ni, 2012; Roda & Wells, 2013; Scott, 2005; Sikkink & Emerson, 2008; Wells, Holme, Lopez, & Cooper, 2000; Whitehurst, 2016). Charter schools tend to be more segregated by race and SES than other public schools in the communities they serve (Malkus, 2016). Logan and Burdick-Will (2015) noted that for whites and Asians, attending a charter means lower exposure to peers in poverty. For blacks, Hispanics, and Native Americans, attending a charter means learning environments with higher concentrations of low-income classmates than in traditional public schools.

Charters and Segregation in North Carolina

North Carolina's mixed history with segregation and desegregation spans several decades (Ayscue et al., 2014). Following the *Brown* decision, several school districts in the state employed strategies that modestly integrated their public schools. After the Supreme Court upheld crosstown busing as a remedy for *de facto* segregation in the 1971 *Swann* decision, CMS became a national leader in desegregation for two decades. In 2000, the Wake County Public School System became the first metropolitan area to implement an assignment plan based on a mix of student SES and academic performance (Parcel & Taylor, 2015). Over the last two decades, North Carolina school systems have largely reverted back to neighborhood-based assignments, and education policies at both the state and local levels tend to deemphasize or ignore diversity (Ayscue et al., 2014). The typical white, black, Latino, and Asian student in North Carolina attends a public school with a disproportionate number of coethnics relative to their district's overall demographic mix. Black and Latino youth attend schools with larger shares of low-income peers than the state's average, while white and Asian students have smaller shares of low-income peers (Ayscue et al., 2014).

Market-inspired school reforms—including charter schools—have a growing role in the resegregation of North Carolina public education. After Republicans gained a majority in the North Carolina legislature in the mid-1990s, they considered a host of market-based education reforms. In 1996, the legislature passed its first charter school–enabling law but capped the total at 100 for the entire state, limited the number of charters to two per district, required strict oversight, required efforts to create a diverse student body, and allowed the local school district to weigh in on the local charter's possible impact. By the 1997–1998 school year, 33 charter schools were in operation. Within 10 years, the number of charters approached the law's 100-charter limit.

The Obama administration's Race to the Top reform initiative encouraged states to adopt charter school–friendly reforms. A key element of North Carolina's Race to the Top proposal was the removal of its 100-charter school cap. The legislature removed the cap in 2011, and the number of charters rapidly grew. By 2016, 167 charter schools were operating in the state. Fueling their proliferation was North Carolina's 2013 Senate Bill 8, which lowered the minimum percentage of certified faculty at a charter school from 75% to 50%, established a faster approval process, blocked local districts from adding impact statements to charter applications, and established a Charter Schools Advisory Board populated solely by charter advocates.

As North Carolina's charter schools proliferated, distinct racial and SES attendance patterns emerged (Ladd et al., 2015; Malkus, 2016). Charter schools tend to be less diverse in terms of student race and SES than their local schools despite wording in the original enabling legislation requiring charters to make reasonable efforts to create a student body resembling the demographics of the district in which it is located.

It appears that investors responding to opportunities for profit have been attracted by the state's less restrictive climate for charter school growth. The less restrictive climate has encouraged the placement of many new charters in affluent suburbs (Helms, 2016h). The extant charter policy appears to create a diversity policy vacuum into which middle-class white suburbanites and entrepreneurial charter providers have stepped. Within this larger state context, we now examine the relation of charter schools to CMS's efforts to reverse resegregation.

CHARTER SCHOOLS AND SEGREGATION
IN THE CHARLOTTE-MECKLENBURG SCHOOLS

A brief review of CMS's history is relevant to our discussion of racial segregation in the district. Once considered perhaps the nation's most successfully desegregated district, CMS operated under *Swann's* (1971) mandatory desegregation order for over 30 years. Mandatory busing as the key tool for desegregation was largely replaced with controlled choice among magnet schools in 1991. By 1999, the year CMS returned to court to fight against lifting *Swann*'s desegregation mandate, over two-thirds of CMS students attended desegregated schools. After being declared unitary in 2002, CMS implemented a neighborhood-based assignment plan that led to rapid school resegregation by race and SES, given that most neighborhoods were segregated (Mickelson, Smith, & Hawn Nelson, 2015).

But residential segregation is far from the only reason that in 2016 CMS was the state's most racially segregated large school system (North Carolina Department of Public Instruction, 2016a). In the past 25 years, the Charlotte metropolitan region has experienced dramatic demographic shifts and explosive growth. The Hispanic community grew from less than 2% of the county's population in 1990 to roughly 13% in 2016. The Asian population tripled during this time frame, while black and white communities grew but at a much slower rate. In 2016, the adult population of Mecklenburg County was 6% Asian, 32% black, 13% Hispanic, and 48% white (U.S. Census Bureau, 2016). Over three-quarters of Mecklenburg County's school-aged population—roughly 147,000 youths—attend one of CMS's 161 schools. The remaining 23% attend private, home, or charter schools (Helms, 2016i). Notably, the percentage of Mecklenburg County youth attending private schools has declined slightly during the last decade (Helms, 2016i). This decline is consistent with national private school enrollment trends among whites. A 2013 study conducted by the U.S. Census linked the decline in private school enrollment among whites to growth of charters (Ewert, 2013).

Resegregation of CMS

Under CMS's residential assignment plan, individual schools tend to be less diverse than the district's enrollment as a whole. For example, black students comprised 40% of the district's enrollment, yet eight schools were more than 75% black, and 17 suburban schools were less than 10% black. While whites comprised 29% of CMS's student population, 66 schools were less than 10% white, and four schools were at least 75% white. Hispanic students comprised 23% of CMS enrollments but made up more than 50% of the population in 18 schools, and Asian enrollment topped 20% in four schools even though the district was only 6% Asian overall. Roughly half of CMS's students qualified for free or reduced-price lunch. Because of the close correlation between race and SES in Mecklenburg County, in the 76 schools where all students qualified for free lunch, almost 87% of students were black or Latino (Helms, 2016j).

Despite its resegregation, CMS continues to be considered one of the nation's best large urban districts. It received the 2011 Broad Prize for Urban Education (Mickelson et al., 2015). In February 2017, the College Board awarded CMS national honors for boosting the number of students taking and passing Advanced Placement exams (Helms, 2017c). Students still do well in schools without concentrated poverty. White student proficiency rates on North Carolina's standardized End-of-Grade and End-of-Course exams are double the Hispanic and black rates.

White students' graduation rates exceed those of black and Hispanic youth (North Carolina Department of Public Instruction, 2016b).

At the same time, the academic consequences of segregation for students in high-poverty schools are striking. In 2005, Judge Howard Manning, who oversaw the state's *Leandro* (1997) fiscal adequacy case, observed that several high-poverty CMS high schools were committing "academic genocide" (Manning, 2005, p. 23). Even after controlling for student background and prior achievement, researchers find that achievement and attainment are worse for those who attended racially segregated CMS schools (Billings, Deming, & Rockoff, 2014).

Charters Available to Mecklenburg County Families

As described above, CMS parents face a complex demographic and academic context when they decide to send their child to a traditional public school or to a charter. By North Carolina law, students are entitled to an education provided by the school district in which they reside, but they also may attend any charter in the state as long as they obtain transportation. In 2015, families chose from 25 charters located in Mecklenburg County and from 11 in adjacent counties located within commuting distance. Table 8.1 presents charters' demographic, performance, and organizational characteristics. Calculating diversity or segregation based on whether the demographics of the charter are ±15% of the county's percent white, we see that 10 Mecklenburg County charters are segregated white, 11 are segregated black, and four are racially diverse, including the charter for highly gifted children, which is 51% Asian and 41% white. The counties adjacent to Mecklenburg are between 56% and 83% white. Nine of the 11 charters located in them are clustered close to CMS's wealthy white southern and northern suburbs. The nearby charters had student bodies that ranged from 65% to 88% white, reflecting the adjacent county's demographics. Two of the 11 have student bodies that serve disproportionately low-performing students of color and are not near the Mecklenburg County line.

Designing a New Pupil Assignment Plan

Under board policy, CMS reevaluates student assignment every 6 years and, in 2016, determined that it would be necessary to recalibrate CMS's pupil assignment plan because of enrollment growth, shifts in intra-urban ethnic residential patterns, the growing diversity of the student population, and concentrations of poverty in many schools. The persistent academic failures in the district's hypersegregated high-poverty schools prompted the CMS school board to include some efforts in its redesign plan to break up concentrations of poverty (CMS, 2016a). Referring to the academic failures of high-poverty schools described in previous paragraphs, a school board member representing demographically diverse neighborhoods explained the board's decision to address schools with concentrated poverty by saying "our community is crying out for solutions" (Henderson, 2016).

Table 8.1. Characteristics of All Charter Schools in Mecklenburg County and Adjacent Counties, 2015[1]

Charter school	School size	% Prof. EOG R	% Prof. EOG M	Lunch	Trans	County White (%)	Charter School			
							Hispanic	Black	White	Other
Mecklenburg County										
Aristotle Preparatory	180	45.7%	31.4%	Yes	Yes	29%	1%	90%	4%	4%
Bradford Preparatory School	741	71.0%	66.0%	No	No	29%	6%	15%	69%	9%
Charlotte Choice	334	33.1%	20.2%	Yes	Yes	29%	15%	83%	1%	1%
Charlotte Lab School	281	N/A	N/A	Yes	Yes	29%	9%	23%	64%	8%
Charlotte Learning Academy	214	28.4%	23.9%	Yes	Yes	29%	8%	83%	4%	5%
Charlotte Secondary	480	56.3%	41.4%	No	No	29%	11%	41%	41%	8%
Commonwealth High School	261	N/A	N/A	No	No	29%	22%	70%	3%	5%
Community Charter	105	34.1%	29.3%	No	No	29%	6%	77%	17%	0%
Community School of Davidson	1,342	82.6%	81.7%	No	No	29%	4%	4%	87%	5%
Corvian Community School	611	76.4%	78.8%	No	No	29%	5%	9%	78%	8%
Crossroads Charter[2]	180	N/A	N/A	No	No	29%	2%	97%	0%	1%
Invest Collegiate	794	81.7%	72.5%	No	Yes	29%	7%	66%	16%	10%
KIPP Charlotte	400	50.8%	45.1%	Yes	Yes	29%	5%	93%	1%	2%
Kennedy Charter[2]	346	25.3%	14.6%	Yes	Yes	29%	4%	94%	1%	1%
Lake Norman Charter	1,606	80.1%	77.7%	No	No	29%	4%	13%	74%	8%
Metrolina Regional Scholars Academy	368	95.0%	95.0%	No	Yes	29%	5%	3%	41%	51%
Pioneer Springs Community School	222	64.4%	31.1%	No	No	29%	6%	4%	80%	10%
Queen City STEM School	301	N/A	N/A	No	No	29%	7%	42%	19%	33%
Queen's Grant Community School	1,267	74.5%	71.1%	Yes	No	29%	8%	22%	66%	4%

School	Enrollment									
Socrates Academy	669	80.5%	81.3%	No	No	29%	7%	6%	76%	11%
Stewart Creek High School	117	N/A	N/A	No	No	29%	3%	91%	2%	3%
Sugar Creek Charter School	1,401	58.3%	58.5%	Yes	Yes	29%	6%	93%	0%	1%
Thunderbird Preparatory School	499	71.3%	61.5%	Yes	No	29%	8%	4%	82%	6%
United Community School	167	N/A	N/A	No	No	29%	6%	51%	34%	10%
VERITAS Community School	109	N/A	N/A	Yes	Yes	29%	7%	29%	51%	12%
Outside of Mecklenburg County										
A.C.E. Academy (Cabarrus County)	311	40.3%	32.3%	No	Yes	56%	8%	69%	14%	9%
Cabarrus Charter Academy (Cabarrus County)	1,122	79.9%	69.8%	Yes	No	56%	10%	23%	56%	12%
Carolina International School (Cabarrus County)	849	64.8%	47.1%	No	No	56%	10%	27%	47%	16%
Mountain Island Charter (Gaston County)	1,309	71.9%	67.2%	Yes	Yes	60%	5%	22%	65%	7%
Piedmont Community Charter (Gaston County)	1,245	70.9%	62.6%	No	No	60%	8%	17%	69%	5%
American Renaissance School (Iredell County)	542	71.2%	62.4%	No	No	83%	5%	8%	79%	7%
Langtree Charter Academy (Iredell County)	1,134	74.8%	71.1%	Yes	No	83%	8%	4%	74%	14%
Pine Lake Preparatory (Iredell County)	1,716	84.0%	81.0%	No	Yes	83%	3%	2%	88%	7%
Success Charter (Iredell County)	88	20.4%	24.1%	Yes	Yes	83%	3%	85%	7%	5%
Lincoln Charter School (Lincoln County)	1,926	83.0%	78.5%	No	Yes	78%	8%	4%	85%	4%
Union Academy (Union County)	1,399	82.1%	68.1%	No	Yes	65%	10%	8%	77%	5%

CMS engaged a consulting firm to assist with the redesign of the district's pupil assignment plan. The consultants' two-phase plan is premised on parental choice among expanded magnet offerings or a home school whose redrawn boundaries will be configured to address proximity to residence, shifts in the spatial demography of various ethnic groups, uneven growth patterns, and reductions in the most extreme concentrations of poverty. The proposal featured continuity of assignments for students and their siblings. In November 2016, the board unanimously approved the first phase of the plan that began with a January 2017 magnet school lottery that took students' socioeconomic status into consideration. The magnet phase was implemented for the 2017–2018 school year. The proposed plan also called for implementation of a second phase, a revised home school assignment plan for the 2018–2019 school year.

The details of the new boundaries are at the center of an intense public debate unfolding in CMS, in which charter schools directly and indirectly play a prominent role. The school board's announcement of its plan's equity and diversity goals (Helms, 2016b) spurred heightened interest in charter schools among families who perceived the board's intention to break up concentrated poverty in the district as a threat to their middle-class white suburban neighborhood school. The extent to which prosperous white suburbanites actually leave CMS and enroll their children in charters can have a *direct* effect on CMS's ability to create more diverse schools districtwide. CMS's goal of reducing concentrated poverty becomes more difficult if fewer nonpoor white youth are available to participate in either the magnets or the newly drawn pupil assignment plan. Mere expression of heightened interest in charters among middle-class white parents also *indirectly* contributes to segregation in CMS. If policymakers believe too ambitious a plan will trigger white, Asian, and middle-class flight to charters, they are likely to scale back their efforts to expand equity through creating more diverse schools.

Charters' Indirect Effects on Segregation in Mecklenburg County

Weakened Fiscal and Political Support for CMS. The school board is not the only policymaking board watching and weighing charter growth in Mecklenburg County. CMS's budget must be approved by the Mecklenburg Board of County Commissioners (BOCC). As growth in charter enrollment outstrips growth in traditional public schools, policy actors are less inclined to fund new district schools, improve old ones, or generally invest in public education. Such is the current situation in Mecklenburg County. Projected growth in CMS is one-fifth as large as projected growth in the charter sector (Helms, 2016d). This disparity made it difficult for the school board to ask Mecklenburg BOCC for a $100 million bond to build new schools and refurbish older ones required by the district's population growth, demographic transformation, and the board's equity goals. Commissioners are reluctant to invest in new school construction or renovations if student populations do not grow, and in some cases even decline (Helms, 2016d). However, despite these barriers, the bond passed in November 2017.

Fiscal Consequences Undermine Quality of Traditional Public Schools. When a student enters a charter school, money follows her from the district of her residence to the charter she attends. CMS educators note that the funding pass-through occurs while district operating costs remain unchanged (CMS, 2016b), complicating enrollment projections, budgeting, and instructional programming (Helms, 2016f). Any weakness in instructional programs understandably undermines confidence among families who may respond to perceived deterioration in CMS as a justification for sending their child to nearby charters.

For example, in a 2014 presentation to the Mecklenburg BOCC, CMS identified the significant adverse impact that Mecklenburg County charters, as well as charters "located just outside Mecklenburg County," have on the district. The presentation enumerated the many issues raised by charter growth, including its harmful financial impact (CMS, 2014, slide 21). Some BOCC members expressed little sympathy for CMS, noting that the increase in pass-through funding was caused by families choosing charters over their traditional public schools. Following the presentation, a commissioner who represented prosperous white suburbs urged her BOCC colleagues to remember that

> . . . the parents and guardians are the ones driving this data we're looking at. [The proliferation of charter schools in and around Mecklenburg County] tells us a story, and we need to understand what that story is. (Helms, 2014)

During a 2016 budget meeting between the BOCC and CMS, a BOCC member representing a prosperous suburb chastised CMS for appearing to cast charters as a burden because they draw public money from CMS's allotment: "They're as much a public school as any other school" (Helms, 2016g). He called CMS's efforts to create SES diversity a "shell game" and said it made sense that CMS was losing students to charters (Worf, 2016). He later described the proposed magnet plan as "more about marketing to counter the growing number of students fleeing CMS for charter, private and parochial schools than about education" (Henderson, 2016).

Deterring Flight to Charters by Circumscribing the Scope of Equity Plans. CMS board members know that aggressively pursuing SES desegregation policies that middle-class parents perceive as threatening access to and the quality of their neighborhood school may trigger exits from CMS. This possibility is central to the context in which CMS is redesigning its pupil assignment plan. During a discussion of these plans, a representative of a largely white and wealthy suburb warned her colleagues:

> If we do not have a guaranteed home school for every student, we don't need to go to the County Commission and ask for more money because they will not stay at CMS. As a matter of fact, [I] will probably be putting in an application to open a charter school. (Helms, 2016d)

Her remark linking future funding from the BOCC, a guaranteed seat in neighborhood schools, and the threat of middle-class white flight to charters captures the *zeitgeist* of many white suburbanites in CMS for whom restoring diversity is not a priority.

In fact, a number of suburbanites have organized into a group called CMS Families United for Public Education. The group identified three main objectives: (1) maintain existing neighborhood school assignments, (2) expand magnet school options, and (3) put resources and programs in place to assist the worst performing schools (Helms, 2016e). Another group, CMS Families for Close to Home Schools and Magnet Expansion, likewise supports assigning students to schools by neighborhood. Members of both groups showed up *en masse* at a public meeting to discuss school reassignment plans. The meeting, convened by a board member representing heavily white and prosperous suburbs, drew about a thousand people, the vast majority of whom expressed approval for the board member's promise to protect neighborhood schools in the new assignment plans (Helms, 2016a).

The board's goal of breaking up concentrated poverty through reconfigured pupil assignments rekindled discussions of splitting CMS into three new districts that would create a low-income heavily minority district sandwiched between wealthier and whiter districts in the northern and southern suburbs (Helms, 2016c). Two decades earlier, disgruntled suburbanites floated the possibility of deconsolidation, but their efforts were quashed by the reality that the state legislature, then in the hands of Democrats, would never permit the deconsolidation of CMS. In 2016, Republicans hold veto-proof majorities in both chambers of the state legislature. An ironic indirect effect of charters on segregation in CMS may be to temper the push for deconsolidation so long as expanding numbers of racially and economically segregated charters offer sufficient seat capacity to meet white suburban families' growing demands.

The Elephant in the Room

Charters' indirect influences on racial and SES segregation add a significant obstacle to the already divided district's efforts to diversify schools. Charters already influenced the design of CMS's expanded magnet program. At a December 2016 School Choice Fair sponsored by the *Charlotte Observer*, a CMS central office administrator conversant with the district's strategies for planning magnets acknowledged that the district took the location and themes of charter schools into account when planning magnet schools.

With the new magnet plan underway, CMS turned its attention to the redesign of pupil assignment boundaries to address the district's demographic changes. The new boundaries must also keep schools sufficiently appealing to middle-class families currently being lured to leave CMS for charter schools.

CMS leaders are keenly aware of the role charters will play in CMS's future vitality. Tensions became evident during the first school board meeting of 2017 when the board debated whether or not to continue to design the new assignment plan. A board member expressed a desire to "throw the brakes" on the process. She argued that CMS should first assess how well the new magnet plan addresses the district's goals and allow the incoming superintendent to acclimate to his new job. Opponents of delay argued that prolonging the decision on new boundaries would doom the forthcoming school bonds and undermine the consultants' previously approved two-pronged diversity strategy of magnets plus new boundaries (Helms, 2017a). Two weeks later, a split board voted to continue to design the new boundaries for 2018–2019. A suburban board member framed the task ahead by noting that if diversity becomes the driving force and boundaries are changed dramatically, "everybody with affluence will choose to go outside CMS" (Helms, 2017b).

The yearlong campaign by politically active suburban parents explicitly threatening a middle-class exodus from CMS to the charter sector if boundary changes altered their children's opportunities to attend their neighborhood schools with students similar to them paid off. The redrawn catchment areas adopted by the CMS school board in May 2017 altered the attendance boundaries of 21 of the 75 high-poverty schools (defined as those with between 70% and 100% of students who qualify for free or reduced-price lunch). The plan drew new attendance zones for only 7,000 of the district's approximately 55,000 students assigned to high-poverty schools. Thus, districtwide, the second phase will affect assignment boundaries for roughly 12% of CMS's 170 schools and 5% of CMS's 147,000 students (CMS, 2016c). According to a board member representing many of the outlying areas of the county, the adopted plan will be well received in the northern suburbs because it does not uproot the vast majority of students (Helms, 2017d).

CONCLUSION

We now return to our title's question: Do charter schools undermine efforts to create racially and socioeconomically diverse public schools? Overall findings that charter schools are, more often than not, themselves segregated by race and SES do not answer our question. Charters may merely reflect, not drive, the nation's trend toward resegregation. However, evidence from North Carolina suggests that charters complicate and may, in fact, directly and indirectly undermine policy actors' efforts to create more diverse traditional public schools.

Our case study of charter schools and segregation in CMS suggests that charters and the district are becoming two parallel, unequal, and segregated sectors of North Carolina public education. Increasingly, charters serve a bifurcated market, with a smaller portion serving largely low-income black families and a larger portion serving prosperous white families, some of whom are motivated, at least in part, by a desire to avoid their racially and socioeconomically diverse traditional public schools. Second, charters mechanically complicate CMS's capacity to create diverse schools because of the racial and SES characteristics of the students who exit to the charters. Third, the fiscal repercussions of fewer dollars for CMS due to funding pass-throughs to charters and policy actors' reluctance to invest in public education building and maintenance because of the growth of the charter sector contribute to a real and perceived decline in CMS's capacity to provide a top-notch education. And fourth, as our case study illustrates, the mere threat of charters luring students to enroll is an ever-present cloud hovering over the heads of Mecklenburg County's policy actors. This threat becomes part of the calculus of any reform strategy designed to reduce segregation in public schools and likely "puts the brakes" on considerations of bolder solutions.

Educational equity and excellence remain much sought after and elusive societal goals. Segregation is inimical to both goals, and charters exacerbate segregation trends. Policies that structure various choice options can stimulate or curtail the capacity of a particular form of choice to segregate. Without equity-oriented safeguards that ensure access to information, transportation, recruitment, inclusiveness, and equitable admissions criteria, the expansion of charter schools will likely correspond with increased segregation by race, class, English-language proficiency, and disability status in both the charter and traditional public school sectors. Moreover, as CMS illustrates, nearby charter schools deter public school decisionmakers' capacity to combat segregation. Individual charters undoubtedly may offer equity and excellence to their students. Yet, given the sector's relationship to segregation, charter schools generally do not appear to advance racial or SES diversity in either traditional or charter schools.

NOTES

The research in this chapter was supported by grants to the first author from the Poverty and Race Research Action Council and the National Science Foundation (RE-ESE-060562).

1. Table 8.1 is from the North Carolina Department of Public Instruction (2016c). EOG R indicates percent proficient on state standardized end-of-grade test in reading; N/A, not available since it was a new charter without testing results to report; EOG M, percent proficient on state standardized end-of-grade test in mathematics; lunch, whether the school offers a lunch program; trans, whether the school offers transportation.

2. Due to some combination of poor academic performance, financial scandal, or declining enrollment, Crossroads Charter and Kennedy Charter were closed as of the 2016–2017 school year. In 2014–2015, hypersegregated minority Concrete Roses Charter closed for similar reasons.

REFERENCES

Ayscue, J. B., Woodward, B., Kucsera, J., & Siegel-Hawley, G. (2014). *Segregation again: North Carolina's transition from leading desegregation then to accepting segregation now.* Los Angeles, CA: Civil Rights Project.

Bifulco, R., Ladd, H. F., & Ross, S. L. (2009). Public school choice and integration evidence from Durham, North Carolina. *Social Science Research, 38,* 71–85.

Billings, S. B., Deming, D. J., & Rockoff, J. (2014). School segregation, educational attainment, and crime: Evidence from the end of busing in Charlotte-Mecklenburg. *Quarterly Journal of Economics, 129*, 435–476.

Bohrnstedt, G., Kitmitto, S., Ogut, B., Sherman, D., & Chan, D. (2015). *School composition and the black-white achievement gap* (NCES 2015-018). Washington, DC: National Center for Education Statistics.

Bonastia, C. (2012). *Southern stalemate: Five years without public education in Prince Edward County, Virginia.* Chicago, IL: University of Chicago Press.

Brown v. Board of Education, 347 U.S. 483 (1954).

Charlotte-Mecklenburg Schools. (2014, March 25). *Impact of charter schools* [PowerPoint]. Presentation to the Board of County Commissioners.

Charlotte-Mecklenburg Schools. (2016a). *Goals for the student assignment plan developed by policy committee.* Retrieved from bit.ly/2l7X44D

Charlotte-Mecklenburg Schools. (2016b). *Board of Education 2016–2017 operating budget request.* Retrieved from bit.ly/2lPejYx

Charlotte-Mecklenburg Schools. (2016c). *Fast facts.* Retrieved from www.cms.k12.nc.us/mediaroom/aboutus/Documents/CMS%20Fast%20Facts%20Sheet%202015-2016.pdf

Cucchiara, M. B. (2013). *Marketing schools, marketing cities: Who wins and who loses when schools become urban amenities.* Chicago, IL: University of Chicago Press.

DeJarnatt, S. L. (2008). School choice and the (ir)rational parent. *Georgetown Journal on Poverty Law & Policy, 15*(1), 1–47.

Ewert, A. (2013). *The decline in private school enrollment* [SEHSD Working Paper FY12-117]. Washington, DC: Social, Economic, and Housing Division, U.S. Census Bureau.

Fiel, J. (2015). Closing ranks: Closure, status competition, and school segregation. *American Journal of Sociology, 121*(1), 126–170.

Finley, T. (2016, April 28). 100 percent of seniors at Chicago school admitted to college for 7th year in a row. *The Huffington Post.* Retrieved from www.huffingtonpost.com/entry/100-percent-of-seniors-at-chicago-school-admitted-to-college-for-7th-year-in-a-row_us_5722273ee4b0b49df6aa5aaa

Frankenberg, E., & Siegel-Hawley, G. (2013). A segregating choice? An overview of charter school policy, enrollment trends, and segregation. In G. Orfield & E. Frankenberg (Eds.), *Educational delusions? Why choice can deepen inequality and how to make schools fair* (pp. 119–144). Berkeley, CA: University of California Press.

Helms, A. D. (2014, March 25). Mecklenburg commissioners question charter school oversight. *The Charlotte Observer.* Retrieved from www.charlotteobserver.com/news/local/education/article9106883.html

Helms, A. D. (2016a, February 17). Push to protect neighborhood schools builds momentum. *The Charlotte Observer.* Retrieved from www.charlotteobserver.com/news/local/education/your-schools-blog/article60843187.html

Helms, A. D. (2016b, February 23). CMS Board votes 7–1 for assignment goals, with big questions ahead. *The Charlotte Observer.* Retrieved from www.charlotteobserver.com/news/local/education/article62091767.html

Helms, A. D. (2016c, February 24). Matthews mayor: It's time to explore a suburban split from CMS. *The Charlotte Observer.* Retrieved from www.charlotteobserver.com/news/local/education/article62279447.html

Helms, A. D. (2016d, February 24). Charter growth in Mecklenburg expected to outstrip CMS 5 to 1. *The Charlotte Observer.* Retrieved from www.charlotteobserver.com/news/local/education/your-schools-blog/article62255582.html

Helms, A.D. (2016e, March 11). Parent group offers a three-point plan for CMS assignment. *The Charlotte Observer*. Retrieved from www.charlotteobserver.com/news/local/education/your-schools-blog/article65434112.html

Helms, A. D. (2016f, May 4). As students choose CMS or charters, does money follow them? *The Charlotte Observer*. Retrieved from www.charlotteobserver.com/news/local/education/your-schools-blog/article75519577.html

Helms, A. D. (2016g, May 24). CMS gets little love from county at summit on budget and bonds. *The Charlotte Observer*. Retrieved from www.charlotteobserver.com/news/local/education/article79656117.html

Helms, A. D. (2016h, July 4). Chinese investors help fuel Charlotte's charter school boom. *The Charlotte Observer*. Retrieved from www.charlotteobserver.com/news/local/education/article87268177.html

Helms, A. D. (2016i, July 7). Home schooling grows, private schooling slumps in Mecklenburg County. *The Charlotte Observer*. Retrieved from www.charlotteobserver.com/news/local/education/your-schools-blog/article88173372.html

Helms, A. D. (2016j, December 2). CMS tally: More Hispanic and Asian students, fewer black and white. *The Charlotte Observer*. Retrieved from www.charlotteobserver.com/news/local/education/article118484453.html

Helms, A. D. (2017a, January 12). Boundary clash: CMS board members and staff split over whether to delay assignment work. *The Charlotte Observer*. Retrieved from www.charlotteobserver.com/news/local/education/your-schools-blog/article126138234.html

Helms, A. D. (2017b, January 24). CMS boundary study moves ahead, with timing and other big questions up in the air. *The Charlotte Observer*. Retrieved from www.charlotteobserver.com/news/local/education/article128565474.html

Helms, A. D. (2017c, February 2). Tackling tough work: CMS earns national honor for students taking and passing AP exams. *The Charlotte Observer*. Retrieved from www.charlotteobserver.com/news/local/education/article130409469.html

Helms, A. D. (2017d, April 20). Here's why neighborhood school advocates may like new CMS boundary plan. *The Charlotte Observer*. Retrieved from www.charlotteobserver.com/news/local/education/article145777814.html

Henderson, B. (2016, October 13). CMS magnet plan sparks debate with Mecklenburg County commissioners. *The Charlotte Observer*. Retrieved from www.charlotteobserver.com/news/local/article108107437.html

Johnson, R. C. (2011). *Long-run impacts of school desegregation & school quality on adult attainments* [NBER Working Paper No. 16664]. Cambridge, MA: National Bureau of Economic Research.

Kimelberg, S. M. (2014). Beyond test scores: Middle-class mothers, cultural capital, and the evaluation of urban public schools. *Sociological Perspectives, 57*(2), 208–228.

Ladd, H. F., Clotfelter, C. T., & Holbein, J. B. (2015). *The growing segmentation of the charter school sector in North Carolina* [Working Paper 133]. Washington, DC: National Center for Analysis of Longitudinal Data in Education Research.

Lareau, A., & Goyette, K. (2014). *Choosing homes, choosing schools: Residential segregation and the search for a good school*. New York, NY: Russell Sage Foundation.

Leandro v. State (Leandro I), 346 N.C. (1997).

Liebowitz, D. D., & Page, L. C. (2014). Does school policy affect housing choices? Evidence from the end of desegregation in Charlotte-Mecklenburg. *American Educational Research Journal, 51*(4), 671–703.

Logan, J. R., & Burdick-Will, J. (2015). School segregation, charter schools, and access to quality education. *Journal of Urban Affairs, 38*(1), 323–343.

Malkus, N. (2016). *Differences on balance: National comparisons of charter and traditional public schools.* Washington, DC: American Enterprise Institute. Retrieved from www.aei.org/publication/differences-on-balance-national-comparisons-of-charter-and-traditional-public-schools

Manning, J.H. (2005). *Report from the court: The high school problem. North Carolina General Court of Justice,* Superior Court Division, 95 CVS 1158, May 24.

Mathis, W. J., & Welner, K. G. (2016). *Do choice policies segregate schools?* Boulder, CO: National Education Policy Center. Retrieved from nepc.colorado.edu/publication/research-based-options

Mickelson, R. A., Bottia, M.C., & Southworth, S. (2012). School choice and segregation by race, ethnicity, socioeconomic status, and achievement. In G. Miron, K. Welner, P. Hinchey, & W. Mathis (Eds.), *Exploring the school choice universe: Evidence and recommendations* (pp. 167–192). Charlotte, NC: Information Age.

Mickelson, R. A., & Nkomo, M. (2012). Integrated schooling, life course outcomes, and social cohesion in multiethnic democratic societies. *Review of Research in Education, 36,* 197–238.

Mickelson, R. A., Smith, S. S., & Hawn Nelson, A. H. (2015). *Yesterday, today, and tomorrow. School desegregation and resegregation in Charlotte.* Cambridge, MA: Harvard Education Press.

Miron, G., & Urschel, J. (2012). The impact of school choice reforms on student achievement. In G. Miron, K. Welner, P. Hinchey, & W. Mathis (Eds.), *Exploring the school choice universe: Evidence and recommendations* (pp. 211–236). Charlotte, NC: Information Age.

Ni, Y. (2012). The sorting effect of charter schools on student composition in traditional public schools. *Educational Policy, 26*(2), 215–242.

North Carolina Department of Public Instruction. (2016a). *Grade, race, sex report, 2015–2016.* Retrieved from www.dpi.state.nc.us/fbs/accounting/data

North Carolina Department of Public Instruction. (2016b). *North Carolina 4-year cohort graduation rate report, 2014–2015.* Retrieved from www.dpi.state.nc.us/docs/graduate/statistics/2015cohort-report.pdf

North Carolina Department of Public Instruction. (2016c). *2015–2016 state, district, and school level summary data.* Retrieved from www.dpi.state.nc.us/accountability/reporting

Orfield, G., Ee, J., Frankenberg, E., & Siegel-Hawley, G. (2016). *Brown at 62: School segregation by race, poverty, and state.* Los Angeles, CA: Civil Rights Project/Proyecto Derechos Civiles.

Parcel, T. L., & Taylor, A. J. (2015). *The end of consensus: Diversity, neighborhoods, and the politics of public school assignments.* Chapel Hill, NC: University of North Carolina Press.

Pattillo, M. (2015). Everyday politics of school choice in the black community. *Du Bois Review: Social Science Research on Race, 12*(1), 41–72.

Reardon, S. (2016). School segregation and racial academic achievement gaps. *Russell Sage Foundation Journal of the Social Sciences, 50*(3), 497–531.

Reback, R. (2008). Demand (and supply) in an inter-district public school choice program. *Economics of Education Review, 27*(4), 402–416.

Roda, A., & Wells, A. S. (2013). School choice policies and racial segregation: Where white parents' good intentions, anxiety, and privilege collide. *American Journal of Education, 119*(2), 261–293.

Scott, J. (2005). *School choice and diversity: What the evidence says.* New York, NY: Teachers College Press.

Sikkink, D., & Emerson, M. O. (2008). School choice and racial segregation in US schools: The role of parents' education. *Ethnic and Racial Studies, 31*(2), 267–293.

Swann v. Charlotte-Mecklenburg Board of Education, 402 U.S. 1 (1971).

U.S. Census Bureau. (2016). *QuickFacts: Mecklenburg County, North Carolina.* Retrieved from www.census.gov/quickfacts/table/PST045215/37119

Weiher, G. R., & Tedin, K. L. (2002). Does choice lead to racially distinctive schools? Charter schools and household preferences. *Journal of Policy Analysis and Management, 21*(1), 79–92.

Wells, A. S., Holme, J. J., Lopez, A., & Cooper, C. W. (2000). Charter schools and racial and social class segregation: Yet another sorting machine? In R. Kahlenberg (Ed.), *A notion at risk: Preserving public education as an engine for social mobility.* New York, NY: Century Foundation Press.

Whitehurst, G. (2016). *Education choice and competition index 2015: Summary and commentary.* Washington, DC: Brookings Institution. Retrieved from www.brookings. edu/~/media/multimedia/interactives/2016/ecci/final/ecci_2015_final.pdf

Worf, L. (2016). *County commissioners give CMS a piece of their minds* [Transcript of news broadcast]. Charlotte, NC: WFAE.

CHAPTER 9

Do Charter Schools Strengthen Education in High-Poverty Urban Districts?

Adam Gamoran and Cristina M. Fernandez

> Schools teach those they think they must and when they think they needn't, they don't. That fact has nothing to do with social science, except that the children of social scientists are among those whom schools feel compelled to teach effectively. . . . Repudiation of the social science notion that family background is the principal cause of pupil acquisition of basic skills is probably prerequisite to successful reform of public schooling for children of the poor.
>
> —Ronald Edmonds, "Effective Schools for the Urban Poor"

In 1979, Harvard education scholar Ronald Edmonds published *Effective Schools for the Urban Poor* as a counter to the Coleman Report, a prominent national study that found that unequal achievement across the United States was more closely tied to differences in student background than it was to differences in school resources (Coleman et al., 1966). Edmonds argued that effective schools were a matter of political will, not research. He drew on correlational and case study findings to identify elements that characterized such schools, including strong administrative leadership, high expectations, an orderly environment, an emphasis on basic skills, and frequent monitoring of student progress (Edmonds, 1982).

Today, Edmonds's argument is echoed in the claims of charter school researchers and advocates who maintain that Coleman's conclusions, though unshaken by subsequent research (Alexander & Morgan, 2016; Downey & Condron, 2016), fail to allow for the possibility that the schools we *could have* need not be the same as the schools we *have now*. That is, just because most schools today carry along the inequalities that students bring with them, this does not belie the possibility that schools of a different kind could counter inequalities that originate outside schools (Gamoran, 2016). Moreover, many writers argue that such schools already exist in

133

the form of urban charter schools, and that essential aspects of successful urban charter schools are the very same elements identified by Edmonds nearly 40 years ago, particularly, high expectations, orderly environments, a relentless focus on instruction, and frequent assessment to gauge student progress (Dobbie & Fryer, 2013).

Does the evidence justify the view that urban charter schools elevate achievement for low-income minority students? If so, what are the sources of success? Do findings on test scores carry implications for longer-term outcomes, such as college completion? What lessons do these findings provide for the vast majority of urban schools that are not charters? And how should we understand the effects of charter schools on academic outcomes in light of increasing racial isolation in U.S. schools (An & Gamoran, 2009; Gamoran & An, 2016)? By addressing these questions, this chapter aims to shed light on whether charter schools are an effective strategy for reducing educational inequality in the United States.

CHARTER SCHOOLS AND STUDENT OUTCOMES

Early research on charter school effects on achievement yielded mixed results. Witte, Weimer, Shober, and Schlomer (2007), for example, found positive effects of charter schools in Wisconsin, whereas Bifulco and Ladd (2006) found no effects for charter schools in North Carolina, and Ballou, Teasley, and Zeidner (2007) reported positive effects for elementary but not middle school charters in Idaho. The first national study of students in charter schools found their achievement lagging behind that of comparable students in traditional public schools (Center for Research on Education Outcomes [CREDO], 2009). As others have noted (Clark, Gleason, Tuttle, & Silverberg, 2015; Epple, Romano, & Zimmer, 2015), such nonexperimental studies tended to show little or no effects of charter school attendance on student achievement, whereas early lottery-based studies that compared students who won enrollment to charter schools to those who did not often found that these oversubscribed charters outperformed traditional public schools (e.g., Hoxby, Murarka, & Kang, 2009; Hoxby & Rockoff, 2005).

A major landmark in charter school research occurred with the release of a national study of charter school lotteries. Originally published as a government report (Gleason, Clark, Tuttle, & Dwoyer, 2010) and 5 years later in revised form in an academic journal (Clark et al., 2015), the study gathered evidence from 36 lotteries in 15 states.[1] The results revealed no average effects of middle school charter lotteries on student achievement in reading or mathematics, and no average differences across student subgroups defined by race/ethnicity and gender. Rather, the main finding from this study was about variability: In some districts, lottery winners performed better than lottery losers, but in other districts the reverse held true. As a result, the overall effects averaged out to about zero. The lottery studies are important because the random assignment that occurs through the lottery process ensures that those who win and lose lotteries, all of whom attempted to exercise a choice to attend a charter school, are alike. Lottery-based findings are not distorted by selection bias—the fact that students who attend charter schools are different from those who do not—nor by selective attrition—the possibility that students in charter schools might leave those schools at different rates than students in traditional public schools.[2] However, the lottery studies cannot generalize to the full population of charter schools because they occur only in oversubscribed schools, where demand exceeds supply, and in specific locales that do not reflect the full range of areas in which charter schools are located. Nor do they necessarily generalize to the full population of students, since students who apply for charter school lotteries may differ from those who do not.

With the findings of Gleason and colleagues (2010), results from lottery-based and other studies seemed to converge on a conclusion that some charter schools are effective while others are not. Understanding this variation has become the central challenge for subsequent scholarship in this domain. Indeed, since the first national studies appeared in 2009 and 2010, research on the effects of charter schools on student achievement has become plentiful. The general pattern is consistent with the early national studies, that is, wide variability across contexts. However, schools in urban areas serving low-achieving, low-income, and African American and Hispanic students more consistently exhibit positive effects compared to traditional public schools.

Studies That Examine Charter Schools Across Multiple Contexts

Since variable findings are so common, perhaps the most relevant and useful studies are those that examine effects of charter schools compared to traditional public schools in multiple contexts. For example, Zimmer, Gill, Booker, Lavertu, and Witte (2012) examined charter schools in two statewide samples and five large districts. To broaden the generalizability of their findings, these authors did not restrict their samples to lotteries in oversubscribed schools; instead they included all charter middle and high schools in each jurisdiction. To address nonrandom selection into charter schools, they included student fixed effects, in which students serve as their own controls and charter school effects are identified on the basis of whether students' achievement trajectories shift as they move into and out of charter schools. These analyses yielded mixed results, with some positive and some negative effects and no consistency across settings. Likewise, Davis and Raymond (2012) examined charter schools in 14 states and two large districts. They adopted the fixed-effects design employed by Zimmer et al. (2012) and also used a matching approach in which charter students were compared to traditional public school students with similar observed characteristics.[3] The two methods yielded similar results: wide variability across settings, levels of schooling, and subject areas in effects of charter schools compared to traditional public schools. In the matching model, 19% of charter schools outperformed their local markets in reading, as did the same percentage in mathematics; by contrast, 21% of charter schools underperformed their local markets in reading and 33% underperformed in mathematics. Yet both methods returned positive charter effects for low-income students, English learners, and special education students. The authors concluded, "[t]he real insight from each of the models is that the effectiveness of charter schooling is widely varied" (Davis & Raymond, 2012, p. 233).

As a follow-up to the 2009 national study, CREDO released another national study in 2013, with data from 25 states and Washington, DC, areas that comprised over 95% of the nation's charter school students. Using their matching approach, CREDO once again reported wide variability in charter school effects. In the 2013 study, however, the charter school achievement deficits reported in 2009 were no longer evident, and reading achievement was higher in charter schools than in traditional public schools. Moreover, the 2013 report indicated that the relative performance of the charter sector had improved year by year, and black students, students in poverty, and English learners who attended charter schools exhibited higher test scores than comparable students in traditional public schools.

Two other studies of multiple contexts focused on urban schools. In 2015, CREDO released a study on student achievement in 41 urban areas in 22 states, focusing on achievement trends between the 2006–2007 and 2011–2012 school years. This study revealed significantly higher rates of math and reading growth in urban charter schools compared to traditional public schools in the same urban locales (the equivalent of 40 additional days of learning in math and 28 in reading). Moreover, the positive effects of charter schools increased over the school years examined in the study. Despite the strong positive effects on average, however, charter schools in some urban communities lagged behind the learning gains of traditional counterparts. Finally, Tuttle et al. (2013) examined achievement effects of 43 middle schools in the Knowledge Is Power Program (KIPP) Academy charter school network, which overwhelmingly serves low-income, black, and Hispanic students in urban districts. The researchers primarily relied on a matched comparison design; however, they replicated their results with a subset of 13 KIPP middle schools in which lotteries were used to enroll students. Both analyses yielded statistically significant and substantively meaningful positive effects for KIPP schools compared to the traditional public schools from which their students were drawn. A subsequent study of the continued expansion of KIPP schools yielded similarly positive results (Tuttle et al., 2015).

Studies That Examine Charter Schools in Single Districts or States

Lottery-based studies of urban charter schools have generally found positive effects on student achievement. In Boston, Abdulkadiroğlu, Angrist, Dynarski, Kane, and Pathak (2011) examined the effects of charter school attendance on student achievement. These writers adopted an instrumental variables approach in which success in a charter lottery serves as an indicator, or "instrument," for charter school attendance. Assuming the benefits of winning a lottery accrue solely through charter school attendance, this approach yields causal estimates of the effects of charter school attendance. Its advantage over the simpler comparison of lottery winners and losers is that because not all lottery winners end up attending charter schools (and some losers gain admission anyway), the comparison of lottery winners and losers, while not subject to selection bias, does not exactly measure the effects of *attending* a charter school, which is the question of policy interest. However, this type of instrumental variables approach is still subject to the limitation that it can be applied only in cases of oversubscribed charter schools.

The results showed clear achievement advantages for the Boston charter schools compared to traditional public schools. In reading, charter middle school attendance boosted achievement by a quarter of a standard deviation per year, and in math, the effect was over four-tenths of a standard deviation per year. (By comparison, the black–white test-score gap in Boston is about one standard deviation, so these are large effects.[4]) Effects in high school were smaller but still statistically significant and substantively meaningful. A later study of Boston's charter high schools found gains in state assessment and SAT scores, an increased likelihood of sitting for an AP exam, and higher pass rates on the state high school graduation examination (Angrist, Cohodes, Dynarski, Pathak, & Walters, 2013). Another Boston study that focused on a single middle school that converted from traditional public to charter also found large charter effects on achievement in reading and mathematics (Abdulkadiroğlu, Angrist, Hull, & Pathak, 2016).

In New York City, Dobbie and Fryer (2011) studied lottery data from the Promise Academy in the Harlem Children's Zone, concluding that Promise Academy schools were effective at increasing the achievement of the poorest minority children, with elementary and middle school students exhibiting gains in math and ELA, and middle school students showing gains in mathematics achievement. A later study of the Promise Academy schools, based on a survey of admissions lottery winners and losers, revealed that 6 years after the lottery, youth admitted to the middle school continued to exhibit higher test scores (Dobbie & Fryer, 2014). The results of these studies were consistent with earlier research on New York City charter schools (Hoxby et al., 2009).

New Orleans offers a particularly instructive case for analysis of charter school effects on achievement. Following Hurricane Katrina in 2005, nearly all public schools were converted to charter schools, so this city offers a unique instance of citywide conversion to charters. Harris and Larson (2016) used three strategies to compare achievement before and after the post-Katrina reform. First, they examined successive cohorts in New Orleans schools to see how achievement trajectories changed across grade levels before and after the reform. Second, they focused on the large subset of students who returned to New Orleans after the hurricane and compared their before and after achievement trajectories. Third, they compared change in achievement growth in New Orleans to that of other Gulf Coast districts that suffered the ravages of the hurricane but did not undertake the whole-scale charter reform. All three methods indicated higher achievement following the charter school reform in New Orleans. With cumulative effects estimated at between two-tenths and four-tenths of a standard deviation, the effects were smaller than those in the lottery studies, such as in Boston and New York, but they are substantively meaningful as well as statistically significant. In another analysis of post-Katrina charter schools in New Orleans, Abdulkadiroğlu and colleagues (2016) used a matching approach to compare students before and after the conversion to charter schools and found effects similar to those uncovered by Harris and Larson (2016).

Not all studies focused on urban school districts presented evidence of significant achievement gains. In a study of a large urban school district in the Southwest, Imberman (2011) compared charter schools that originated as traditional public schools with charter schools that began as charter schools and found that schools that began as charter schools generated large improvements in discipline and attendance but, for the most part, not on student test scores. Nisar's (2012) study of charter schools in Milwaukee found that, on average, charter schools had no significant effect on student achievement, but there was great variation in effectiveness across charter school type, with charter schools with higher autonomy from the local school district displaying the most effectiveness. In Memphis, low-performing schools operated by charter management organizations have not altered their achievement trajectories, although the researchers studying this reform suggested it may be too early to reach a conclusion (Zimmer, Kho, Henry, & Viano, 2015).

In addition, studies of charter school achievement at the state level are often less positive than studies of achievement in urban areas. Chingos and West (2015), for example, focused on the state of Arizona, which has the largest proportion of students attending charter schools compared to all other states. At every grade level, they found, charter schools were slightly less effective than traditional public schools in raising student achievement in some subjects, especially in nonurban areas. Overall, they found that achievement in the charter sector varied widely, more so than among traditional public schools. They noted, however, that the charter schools that closed over a 6-year span were significantly less effective than those remaining open, a pattern not visible in traditional schools.

Aspects of these findings were echoed in other states. Ni and Rorrer (2012) evaluated the effectiveness of charter schools in Utah from 2004 to 2009, finding that charter schools on average performed slightly worse than traditional public schools in math and language arts. They noted, however, that charter schools became more effective as they aged; students who enrolled in charter schools with more than 5 years of experience obtained greater gains in math than students in traditional public schools. Mills (2013) found that open-enrollment charter schools in Arkansas exhibited small but statistically significant negative impacts on student achievement in both math and literacy, but observed that the negative effects declined with the number of years of charter operation. Other statewide studies with zero or negative effects include North Carolina (Bifulco & Ladd, 2006; Ladd, Clotfelter, & Holbein, 2015), Florida (Sass, 2006), and Texas (Hanushek, Kain, Rivkin, & Branch, 2007).

Studies of Outcomes Other Than Achievement

An important limitation in research on charter school effectiveness is that, by and large, studies have focused on student achievement to the exclusion of other outcomes. While achievement can be an important predictor of long-term educational and occupational success, it does not offer a complete picture of students' experiences in school. Moreover, test scores can be manipulated, for example by emphasizing test preparation over deeper learning, so the validity of test scores as markers of charter school effectiveness is open to question. Unfortunately, few studies have examined social and behavioral outcomes of charter schools (Berends, 2015). However, as data on charter schools have come to span longer and longer time frames, evidence of effects on subsequent educational and occupational outcomes has begun to emerge. This evidence offers an important check on the test score findings.

Booker, Gill, Sass, and Zimmer have conducted several studies looking at the postsecondary outcomes of charter school students. In their first study on the effects of charter high schools on educational attainment, Booker and colleagues (2011) studied the effects of charter high school attendance on students in Florida and Chicago by restricting their samples to students who attended charter middle schools and comparing those who went on to charter high schools to those who attended traditional public high schools.[5] The researchers found that charter high school attendance was associated with a higher probability of high school completion (compared to charter middle school students who transitioned to traditional public high schools) and an increased likelihood of attending 2- or 4-year colleges. In the Florida analyses, effects on educational attainment were greatest for urban charter schools. In 2014, they extended their research to produce the first findings of the long-term effects of charter school attendance on earnings in adulthood. They found that charter high school enrollment was associated with increased probabilities of earning a high school diploma, attending college, and, in Florida, of college persistence (Booker et al., 2014). They also examined labor market outcomes from students in Florida, finding statistically significant estimated increases in annual earnings associated with charter school attendance, and a 12.7% increase in maximum earnings. Since college attendance alone could not explain the observed earning difference, they posited that charter schools might induce skills that enhance their students' value in the labor market.

In their most recent study of long-term attainment and earnings, Sass, Zimmer, Gill, and Booker (2016) built on the findings of Booker et al. (2011), following the longitudinal data available for former charter high school students in the state of Florida through the ages of 23 to 25. As in the earlier findings, the authors found that students who attended charter high schools had an increased probability of earning a high school diploma within 5 years, enrolling in college, and persisting in college for at least 2 years. Assuming a normal progression through schooling between ages 5 and 25, they found a statistically significant earnings advantage of about $2,300 for charter high school students, equivalent to about a 12% increase in maximum earnings over a 3-year span.

The results from Florida and Chicago are consistent with a small number of other studies that examined high school graduation and postsecondary outcomes (Berends, 2015). Furgeson and colleagues (2012) used a matching approach to compare students in charter schools to those in traditional public schools. These writers found mixed effects on high school graduation, but consistent positive effects on the likelihood of college enrollment. Comparing lottery winners and losers in one charter school in New York City, Dobbie and Fryer (2011) found positive effects on high school graduation and college attendance. Whereas Angrist, Cohodes, and colleagues (2013) did not find effects on high school graduation in their study of Boston charter lotteries, they found positive charter effects on students moving from 2-year to 4-year colleges. The consistency and breadth of these findings for educational attainment reinforce the achievement findings and suggest that achievement growth might be a valid indicator of charter school effectiveness, though more long-term studies are needed to have greater confidence in this conclusion.

MAKING SENSE OF VARIABILITY IN CHARTER SCHOOL EFFECTS

If the primary story of charter schools and achievement is about variability, a close second is the consistency of positive results for achievement in urban charters that serve predominantly low-income students (Betts & Tang, 2014). This pattern is especially evident in the large-scale multistate studies of charter schools, whether conducted with fixed-effects approaches, matching models, or randomized lotteries. For example, in their national study of charter school lotteries, which revealed wide variation in charter school effects overall, Clark and colleagues (2015) uncovered significant positive effects on mathematics test scores in charter middle schools with high concentrations of students on free and reduced-price lunch, and significant *negative* effects in reading and mathematics in schools with few such students. Likewise, effects on mathematics were positive in urban charter schools and negative in nonurban charters. Using both matching and fixed-effects approaches, the CREDO reports paint different pictures for the nation as a whole and for urban districts. Though their 2013 national study pointed to improvements over the 2009 national study, overall effects of charter schools were close to zero on average across the nation, and highly varied. By contrast, their 2015 study of urban charters uncovered positive effects that, though not universal, were considerably more consistent than those for the nation as a whole. Similarly, Tuttle and colleagues' (2013, 2015) studies of KIPP Academy schools serving urban, low-income, minority populations uncovered consistent positive effects for mathematics and reading scores. What clues does this pattern reveal about why some charter schools are effective and others are not?

What's the Alternative?

Before searching for specific characteristics of urban charter schools that might explain their relative effectiveness compared to other charters, an obvious though often overlooked possibility is that the difference might be found not in the charter schools themselves, but in the traditional public schools from which charter students are drawn. It is possible that the effectiveness of the alternative—that is, the school that charter students would attend if the charter were not present—varies across urban and nonurban contexts. That could explain the pattern of variability favoring charters in urban contexts. As Clark and colleagues (2015) explained:

> Because impacts are measured relative to the counterfactual in each site—the schools charter school students would have attended had they not attended a charter—variation in impacts could reflect variation in the effectiveness of the charter schools as well as variation in the effectiveness of the non-charter schools available to students in that area. . . . We are not able to rigorously disentangle these two possibilities in our data. (p. 431)

Although Clark and his colleagues (2015) could not pursue this question empirically, other researchers have begun to do so. Burdick-Will, Keels, and Schuble (2013) observed that charter schools were most likely to be found in urban areas with poor-performing traditional public schools and high proportions of nonwhite families. In a study of public school choice in Denver, Denice and Gross (2016) found that due to residential segregation, black and Hispanic children were "largely trapped in lower-performing schools" (p. 316). To attend higher-performing schools, they had to select a school that required them to travel farther from home than they otherwise would—and farther than the typical white student would need to travel to find a high-performing school.

Chabrier, Cohodes, and Oreopoulos (2016) explored the counterfactual hypothesis directly with secondary analyses of data from charter school lotteries drawn from the national lottery study (Gleason et al., 2010) and from Massachusetts (Angrist, Pathak, & Walters, 2013). They estimated regression analyses that predicted the size of charter school effects as a function of the average test performance in schools attended by students who were unsuccessful in the charter lotteries, which they termed the "fallback" schools. They found that the fallback indicator was strongly related to the charter school effect, that is, the higher performing the schools attended by those who did not win the charter lotteries, the smaller the apparent effect of the charter schools.

Despite this suggestive evidence, there are also reasons to suspect that the characteristics of some urban charter schools, rather than the poor quality of the alternatives, might contribute to charter school effects. First, longitudinal studies have found that the performance of charter schools tends to improve over time (CREDO, 2013; Ni & Rorrer, 2012). For this pattern to reflect the fallback schools rather than the charters, the fallback schools would have to be consistently declining in performance. Second, a number of studies have identified specific features of charter schools that are linked to success (Berends, 2015). These findings suggest that it is the strengths of some charter schools rather than the weaknesses of the alternatives that account for positive effects of urban charters. Most likely, both factors are at play.

Features of Effective Charter Schools

A number of writers have attempted to identify conditions associated with more and less effective charter schools. For example, Carlson, Lavery, and Witte (2012) considered whether achievement variation among charter schools corresponded to the ways charter schools were authorized. In Minnesota, where their study took place—and where the first charter school was established in 1991—charter schools may be authorized by local school boards, postsecondary institutions, nonprofit organizations, and the state department of education. These authors did not find a relationship between type of authorizer and average achievement, though they observed that schools authorized by nonprofit organizations exhibited more variability in achievement than schools authorized by local school boards. Another study focused on charter management organizations, which are nonprofit organizations that operate multiple charter schools (Furgeson et al., 2012). This study, too, found wide variation in performance, indicating that some charter management organizations systematically outperformed others (Furgeson et al., 2012). Considering these two studies together, it appears that variation within types of charter authorizers is more important than variation between types in explaining why some charters are effective and others are not.

Because the effects of charter schools are highly varied overall, yet effects of KIPP Academy schools appear persistently positive, researchers have speculated that the specific design elements of KIPP schools might account for their success (Angrist, Pathak, & Walters, 2013). Distinctive features of KIPP schools include their urban locale and low-income, predominantly minority populations, their relatively small size (middle schools averaged 314 students in the 2013 study), long school days (more than 9 hours per day), emphasis on schoolwide behavior systems, and relatively inexperienced teachers and principals who spend exceptionally long hours on the job (Tuttle et al., 2013). Reviewing the literature on urban charter schools, Angrist, Pathak, and Walters (2013) hypothesized that such elements as "discipline and comportment, traditional reading and math skills, instruction time, and selective teacher hiring" (p. 2) account for the success of KIPP schools and other urban charters. They labeled these features as the "No Excuses" model after Thernstrom and Thernstrom's (2003) book by the same title, which used vignettes of successful urban schools (including KIPP schools) to argue for the power of elements such as these to close the racial achievement gap. As Dobbie and Fryer (2013) recognized, these features are equally consistent with the "effective schools" model identified by Edmonds in 1979.

Pursuing this hypothesis, both Dobbie and Fryer (2013) and Angrist, Pathak, and Walters (2013) examined whether the "No Excuses" characteristics explain variation among urban schools. Unlike analyses of charter school effects, which rest on experimental or quasi-experimental designs, studies of the characteristics of effective charters are observational, relying on statistical controls to adjust for nonrandom selection of students into different charter schools. Hence, the findings may be regarded as suggestive though not conclusive.

In considering conditions that could account for positive effects of urban charters, Dobbie and Fryer (2013) contrasted an effective schools model that emphasized a well-ordered school and a relentless focus on instruction with a resource-based model as indicated by class size, per-pupil expenditures, and teacher qualifications. This is essentially the same argument offered by Edmonds (1979), though using correlational analysis instead of case studies. Edmonds argued that by focusing on resources, Coleman and colleagues (1966) reached the wrong conclusion, because whereas average school resources did not account for achievement variation, features such as good discipline, basic skills instruction, and monitoring student progress did. In testing conditions that account for charter school effects using data from 35 charter schools in New York City, Dobbie and Fryer (2013) found support for Edmonds's perspective: The benefits of urban charters were not linked to resources, but rather to frequent teacher feedback, high-dosage tutoring, use of data to guide instruction, increased instructional time, and high expectations. These conditions accounted for 50% of the variation in school effectiveness. Angrist, Pathak, and Walters (2013) reached similar conclusions, noting that "No Excuses" practices such as an emphasis on discipline, wearing uniforms, and a practice of teachers calling parents contributed positively to the effectiveness of charter middle schools in Massachusetts.

Summarizing this literature, Berends (2015) concluded that the key features of effective charter schools were extra instructional time (manifested in longer school days and tutoring), a schoolwide focus on achievement, schoolwide behavior policies, teacher feedback and coaching, and decisionmaking that takes student progress into account. As Table 9.1 shows, these elements map closely onto long-recognized characteristics of effective schools (Edmonds, 1979, 1982). The findings of Chabrier, Cohodes, and Oreopoulos (2016) inject a cautionary note into this conclusion, because when they added a "fallback school" indicator (i.e., an indicator of the achievement levels of schools attended by students who did not succeed in charter lotteries) into regression models predicting the size of charter school effects, the fallback school indicator was a more potent predictor than the specific school characteristics. The balance of the evidence thus suggests that urban charters studied via lottery designs show positive effects both because they embody characteristics of effective schools, and because the traditional public schools from which their students are drawn, though varied, tend to be low-performing on average.

Table 9.1. Similarities Between Edmonds's (1982) Elements of Effective Schools and Berends's (2015) Features of Effective Charter Schools

Edmonds (1982)	Berends (2015)
Instructional leadership	Teacher feedback and coaching
High expectations	Schoolwide focus on achievement
Good discipline and order	Schoolwide behavior policies
An emphasis on basic skills	Instructional time: long school days, tutoring
Frequent monitoring of pupil progress	Data-based instructional decisionmaking

THE CONTEXT OF EFFECTIVE SCHOOLS

Three conclusions stand out from recent research on achievement in charter schools. First, the effects of charter schools across the nation are highly varied, with rigorous studies showing as many negative effects as positive ones. Second, charter schools are most consistently effective where they are most needed: in urban districts that serve low-income, predominantly minority populations. Third, some combination of the weaknesses of traditional public schools in these areas and the ability of urban charters to adopt long-recognized elements of effective schools probably accounts for the success of many urban charter schools.

The research methods underlying the first two conclusions are strong, with experimental and quasi-experimental designs that allow for causal interpretations of the charter school effects under reasonable assumptions (Epple et al., 2015). Nonetheless, the findings are limited in important ways. They rest largely on test scores, although analyses of longer-term outcomes tend to corroborate the test score results. The strongest designs, based on lotteries, are the most limited in scope because only oversubscribed schools can be included, and the results pertain only to students who apply for charter schools. However, studies that relied on broader samples reached compatible conclusions about the benefits of urban charter schools serving low-income minority youth.

The third conclusion rests on correlational analyses of observed data, so more caution is warranted in the causal interpretation. Reading these results through the lens of Ronald Edmonds, however, it is less important to distinguish whether the relative benefits of urban charters reflect their strengths or the weaknesses of their counterparts than it is to establish that schools serving some of our most vulnerable populations are capable of achieving better results than what typically occurs. From this perspective, the second conclusion is most essential: The benefits revealed in urban charter lotteries do not reflect selective admissions or selective attrition, but the experiences students have in schools and their responses to those experiences.

In cases where urban charter schools are more effective than their traditional public counterparts, is the charter school impact large enough to matter?

Some studies have exhibited substantial effects, for example in Boston. But even where the effects are more modest, such as in New Orleans, the districtwide charter school reform was impactful enough to close the test score gap between New Orleans and the rest of Louisiana by just over one-third of a standard deviation between 2004 and 2011 (Harris & Larsen, 2016). This is a meaningful improvement: Whereas New Orleans ranked 67th out of 68 districts in the state in percent proficient prior to Katrina, it now ranks 39th. Yet it still leaves New Orleans below the midpoint in one of the lowest-performing states in the country, so much room for additional progress remains.

Despite the clarity of these conclusions, their implications are not self-evident. Two questions seem paramount. First, have the benefits of urban charter schools come with hidden costs, such as declining resources for traditional public schools and increased school segregation? Second, can the elements of successful charter schools be adopted by traditional public schools in order to reap the benefits while avoiding the social costs of charters?

Charter Schools, Resources, and Segregation

A key to contextualizing the effects of urban charter schools is understanding their place in the larger urban environments in which they are located. At least two conditions give cause for concern. First, urban charters tend to have higher concentrations of African American and Hispanic students and students on free and reduced-price lunch than the traditional public schools from which their students are drawn (Whitehurst, Reeves, & Rodrigue, 2016). This means that charter schools tend to increase levels of ethnic and economic segregation in districts that are substantially segregated already. Whether this is a positive or negative result depends in part on whether the expansion of charter schools has led low-income, minority students in urban districts to become overrepresented in schools that are more effective than the typical result. If so, this seems like a desirable outcome, though not as desirable as increasing the effectiveness of schools attended by such students *without* increasing segregation.

Second, as the number of charter schools in a district increases, public school funding shifts from the traditional public to the charter sector (Baker, 2016). In part, this is a simple reflection of funds following students from traditional public to charter schools. For a variety of reasons, however, these transfers result in reduced resources available to traditional public schools. Each school carries fixed costs, for infrastructure items such as heating and light and for administrative personnel. These costs do not diminish gradually with each student departure, so traditional public schools are left with fewer instructional resources per student (Epple et al., 2015). In some cases, moreover, special-needs and English-learner students are underrepresented in the charter sector, leaving public schools with proportionately greater costs associated with educating students in these population groups (Chingos & West, 2015; Dobbie & Fryer, 2013; Ni & Rorrer, 2012; Office of English Language Acquisition, 2015; Winters, 2013). Further, charter schools have access to private donations that increase their funding advantage over traditional public schools (Baker, 2016). These trends tend to undermine the traditional public sector. As Epple and colleagues (2015) explained:

> District administrators find themselves grappling with these financial impacts while, at the same time, attempting to maintain or increase quality so as to avoid loss of more students. If fixed costs imply [traditional public schools'] cost per student rises as students leave for charters, per student payment to charters will rise as well if, as is typically the case, charter funding per student is tied to district per student funding. This may stimulate a vicious (from the district perspective) cycle in which rising payments per student induce charter school entry, further district enrollment losses occur, district cost per student and associated charter payment per student rise, and so on. (p. 51)

These authors conclude that "there is no doubt that competitive pressures on [traditional public school] finances from charter schools are intense in urban districts experiencing rapid charter growth" (p. 51). Supporting this conclusion, Baker (2016) demonstrated that for a number of cities, a rising charter sector has indeed corresponded with declining funds for traditional public schools. Baker argued that this pattern is most problematic in districts with declining funding environments, such as Philadelphia and Detroit, where declining enrollments combined with declining state support for education have contributed to serious shortfalls for traditional public schools.

For advocates of school choice, this is how competitive pressures are supposed to work: Schools that are in less demand (presumably, though not assuredly, because they are less effective) will lose funding and ultimately be closed, whereas schools that are in more demand will be well funded and burgeoning with students. This model of market forces, however, fails to recognize that closing a school is not like letting a store go out of business—as enrollments fall, students who remain still need to be educated. These findings about segregation and funding pressures raise a new question about effective urban charter schools: Instead of expanding the charter sector, why have traditional public schools not adopted the characteristics of effective schools as presented, for example, in Table 9.1?

Effective Schools in the Noncharter Sector

Nearly 40 years ago, Ronald Edmonds identified characteristics of schools that he concluded were effective in raising achievement in urban districts. For the most part, these characteristics did not involve new resources, so they had been missed by the leading quantitative analyses of school conditions and student achievement. Instead, they were more about leadership and culture: a press for achievement, good discipline, and monitoring progress frequently. Edmonds did not have in mind a separate sector of public schools that would avoid the oversight of school districts. On the contrary, he sought to instill these changes in all public schools, or at least all urban public schools (Edmonds, 1982).

In principle, it would seem feasible to instill these characteristics in traditional public schools. This notion, however, is challenged by the fact that although the design has been known for almost four decades, schools along these lines have not been well established in the traditional public sector, and achievement in many urban schools has continued to lag. It may be that some of the distinctive features of charter schools, in particular the exceptionally high workload on average for teachers and principals compared to the average in traditional public schools (Zimmer et al., 2012), make it difficult to replicate the effective schools model in the traditional public sector. As Baker (2016, p. 6) put it, a reliance on extraordinary work hours, inexperienced staff, and high staff turnover is "not especially . . . informative for systemic reform."

Another reason that Edmonds's features of effective schools may be more evident in urban charters than in traditional public schools might be that charter schools have ways to shape their student populations that make it easier to institute the features that Edmonds stressed. Of course, neither charter schools nor traditional public schools may select students on the basis of test scores or other characteristics. However, charter schools have community-building tools at their disposal that public schools typically lack. This point is vividly illustrated in research on the Achievement School District (ASD) in Memphis, where the state of Tennessee has handed over schools in the lowest 5% of achievement performance to a range of charter operators (Glazer, Massell, & Malone, 2015; Massell, Glazer, & Malone, 2016). Although the charter operators have the autonomy to implement their models of curriculum, instruction, and assessment, they lack the control over student enrollment that charter schools typically enjoy. For example, charter schools often form slowly, adding one grade at a time, but in the ASD, they must open with all grades at once. Charters typically allow students to enter only at certain grades (for example, kindergarten, grade 5, or grade 9), but in the ASD they are required to take students whenever they present themselves, even in the midst of the school year. Many charters limit the services they offer to special-needs students or English learners, but that is not the case in the ASD. Moreover, students in charter schools (or their parents) have ordinarily made an active choice to enroll, whereas in the ASD, as in traditional public schools, students are assigned based on where they live. As one ASD charter operator explained (Massell et al., 2016):

> In a traditional charter, if you're not enrolled by September 1, you can't come; if kids leave we don't replace them. Here we have kids that come in in February. No telling what they've had all year long. They don't know your culture; they don't know your school. They bring in their past practice, and now they're your student and you're responsible for making sure they grow a grade level. (p. 12)

Lacking control over enrollment policies, struggling to fund services for special-needs students, and facing resistance from the traditional public school sector, ASD schools have not achieved the kind of success that urban charter schools have achieved elsewhere (Zimmer et al., 2015).

The case of New Orleans provides a useful counterexample to Memphis in that in New Orleans, as in Memphis, charter schools must ultimately accommodate all students. However, in New Orleans, students and families are able to select schools on a citywide basis. Moreover, New Orleans schools have benefitted from heightened levels of resources since Katrina: Not only have substantial private funds become available to support the charter school reform, but state and local funding became increasingly directed toward schools with the most disadvantaged populations (Baker, Farrie, & Sciarra, 2016).

Perhaps an infusion of additional resources into traditional public schools that allow them to stay open for longer days, provide tutoring for struggling students, and deliver tools and training that enable teachers to better monitor and respond to student progress could help traditional public schools realize the levels of success reported for urban charter schools. Combining research on effective charter schools with new studies showing that school funding is, after all, implicated in schooling outcomes (Jackson, Johnson, & Persico, 2015; Lafortune, Rothstein, & Schanzenbach, 2016) suggests that if additional resources were deployed in the most effective ways, it may be possible to bring more of the elements of effective charter schools to the traditional public sector. Lacking the ability to shape their student bodies as do typical charter schools, traditional public schools probably need even more resources than charter schools, but currently they must make do with less. By bridging the funding gap, it may be possible to bridge the achievement gap—but only if the new funds are spent in ways that support the structures and activities that matter for learning.

CONCLUSIONS

At a minimum, findings about the achievement effects of urban charter schools present a challenge to advocates for traditional public schools. Although charter school effects are highly varied across the nation, effects for some urban charters serving low-income minority students have been more consistently positive, thanks both to weak alternatives and to the presence of well-known features of effective schools in the urban charter sector. Charter schools remain a highly contentious policy, and many states and districts have elected to restrain their expansion to avoid the collateral consequences for segregation and public sector funding. These steps, however, must be paired with the development of effective schools in the traditional public sector if they are to meet the challenge laid forth by Edmonds to provide equal educational opportunities to urban disadvantaged students.

NOTES

1. The published version omitted three lotteries in two states for a total of 33 charter school lotteries in 13 states.

2. Studies that compare lottery winners and losers are not distorted by selective attrition because students who enter and subsequently leave charter schools are still counted among the winners, as are students who succeed in the lottery but never attend the charter schools. Nor are these studies distorted by population differences between those who attend or do not attend charter schools—for example in some districts, special-needs students and English learners are less prevalent in charter schools—because they focus on lottery winners and losers with the same population characteristics, not on comparisons of charter students to all noncharter students.

3. Davis and Raymond (2012) used the term "virtual control record" to describe their matching model.

4. For example, in 2013, the eighth-grade black–white test score gap in Boston was 31 points in reading and 38 points in math on the National Assessment of Educational Progress Trial Urban Assessment, as compared to standard deviations between 30 and 40 points; see nces.ed.gov/nationsreportcard/naepdata/dataset.aspx.

5. To address concerns with unmeasured selection into charter and traditional public high schools, Booker et al. (2011) implemented an instrumental variables selection model that relied on predictors of charter high school enrollment that did not affect attainment (except through charter high school enrollment), for example whether the charter school the student attended in eighth grade continued at least to ninth grade. The selection model worked well for the Florida data but not for the Chicago data, where the researchers found no indicators of charter high school enrollment that did not also affect attainment. Consequently, the model for Chicago was identified via the nonlinear functional form of the bivariate model, a weaker basis for identification.

REFERENCES

Abdulkadiroğlu, A., Angrist, J. D., Dynarski, S. M., Kane, T. J., & Pathak, P. A. (2011). Accountability and flexibility in public schools: Evidence from Boston's charters and pilots. *Quarterly Journal of Economics, 126*(2), 699–748.

Abdulkadiroğlu, A., Angrist, J. D., Hull, P. D., & Pathak, P. A. (2016). Charter schools without lotteries: Testing takeovers in New Orleans and Boston. *American Economic Review, 106*(7), 1878–1920.

Alexander, K., & Morgan, S. L. (2016). The Coleman Report at fifty: Its legacy and implications for future research on equality of opportunity. *RSF: The Russell Sage Journal of the Social Sciences, 2*(5), 1–16.

An, B. P., & Gamoran, A. (2009). Trends in school racial composition in the era of unitary status. In C. Smrekar & E. B. Goldring (Eds.), *From the courtroom to the classroom: The shifting landscape of school desegregation* (pp. 19–47). Cambridge, MA: Harvard Education Press.

Angrist, J. D., Cohodes, S. R., Dynarski, S. M., Pathak, P. A., & Walters, C. D. (2013). *Charter schools and the road to college readiness: The effects on college preparation, attendance and choice.* Boston, MA: Boston Foundation and New Schools Venture Fund.

Angrist, J. D., Pathak, P. A., & Walters, C. R. (2013). Explaining charter school effectiveness. *American Economic Journal: Applied Economics, 5*(4), 1–27.

Baker, B. (2016). *Exploring the consequences of charter school expansion in U.S. cities.* Washington, DC: Economic Policy Institute.

Baker, B. D., Farrie, D., & Sciarra, D. G. (2016). *Mind the gap: 20 years of progress and re-trenchment in school funding and achievement gaps* (ETS Research Report No. RR-16-15). Princeton, NJ: Educational Testing Service.

Ballou, D., Teasley, B., & Zeidner, T. (2007). Charter schools in Idaho. In M. Berends, M. G. Springer, & H. J. Walberg (Eds.), *Charter school outcomes* (pp. 221–241). New York, NY: Lawrence Erlbaum Associates.

Berends, M. (2015). Sociology and school choice: What we know after two decades of charter schools. *Annual Review of Sociology, 41*, 159–180.

Betts, J. R., & Tang, Y. E. (2014). *The effects of charter schools on student achievement: A meta-analysis*. Seattle, WA: Center on Reinventing Public Education. Retrieved from www.crpe.org/sites/default/files/CRPE_meta-analysis_charter-schools-effect-student-achievement_workingpaper.pdf

Bifulco, R., & Ladd, H. F. (2006). The impacts of charter schools on student achievement: Evidence from North Carolina. *Education Finance and Policy, 1*(1), 50–90.

Booker, K., Gill, B., Sass, T., & Zimmer, R. (2014). *Charter high schools' effects on educational attainment and earnings*. New York, NY: Mathematica Policy Research. Retrieved from www.mathematicampr.com/~/media/publications/PDFs/education/charter_long-term_wp.pdf

Booker, K., Sass, T., Gill, B., & Zimmer, R. (2011). The effects of charter high schools on educational attainment. *Journal of Labor Economics, 29*(2), 377–415.

Burdick-Will, J., Keels, M., & Schuble, T. (2013). Closing and opening schools: The association of neighborhood characteristics and the location of new educational opportunities in a large urban district. *Journal of Urban Affairs, 35*(1), 59–80.

Carlson, D., Lavery, L., & Witte, J. F. (2012). Charter school authorizers and student achievement. *Economics of Education Review, 31*(2), 254–267.

Center for Research on Education Outcomes. (2009). *Multiple choice: Charter school performance in 16 states*. Stanford, CA: Author.

Center for Research on Education Outcomes. (2013). *National charter school study*. Stanford, CA: Author.

Center for Research on Education Outcomes. (2015). *Urban charter school study report on 41 regions*. Stanford, CA: Author.

Chabrier, J., Cohodes, S., & Oreopoulos, P. (2016). What can we learn from charter school lotteries? *Journal of Economic Perspectives, 30*(3), 57–84.

Chingos, M. M., & West, M. R. (2015). The uneven performance of Arizona's charter schools. *Educational Evaluation and Policy Analysis, 37*(1S), 120S–134S.

Clark, M., Gleason, P. M., Tuttle, C. C., & Silverberg, M. K. (2015). Do charter schools improve student achievement? *Educational Evaluation and Policy Analysis, 37*(4), 419–436.

Coleman, J. S., Campbell, E. Q., Hobson, C. F., McPartland, J. M., Mood, A. M., Weinfeld, F. D., & York, R. L. (1966). *Equality of educational opportunity*. Washington, DC: U.S. Government Printing Office.

Davis, D., & Raymond, M. (2012). Choices for studying choice: Assessing charter school effectiveness using two quasi-experimental methods. *Economics of Education Review, 31*(2), 225–236.

Denice, P., & Gross, B. (2016). Choice, preferences, and constraints: Evidence from public school applications in Denver. *Sociology of Education, 89*(4), 300–320.

Dobbie, W., & Fryer, R. G., Jr. (2011). Are high-quality schools enough to increase achievement among the poor? Evidence from the Harlem Children's Zone. *American Econom-

ic Journal: Applied Economics, 3, 158–187.

Dobbie, W., & Fryer, R. G., Jr. (2013). Getting beneath the veil of effective schools: Evidence from New York City. *American Economic Journal: Applied Economics, 5*(4), 28–60.

Dobbie, W., & Fryer, R. G., Jr. (2014). *The medium-term impacts of high-achieving charter schools.* Cambridge, MA: Harvard University.

Downey, D. B., & Condron, D. J. (2016). Fifty years since the Coleman Report: Rethinking the relationship between schools and inequality. *Sociology of Education, 89*(3), 207–220.

Edmonds, R. R. (1979). Effective schools for the urban poor. *Educational Leadership, 37*(1), 15–27.

Edmonds, R. R. (1982). Programs of school improvement: An overview. *Educational Leadership, 40*(3), 4–11.

Epple, D., Romano, R., & Zimmer, R. (2015). *Charter schools: A survey of research on their characteristics and effectiveness* [NBER Working Paper No. 21256]. Cambridge, MA: National Bureau of Economic Research.

Furgeson, J., Gill, B., Haimson, J., Killewald, A., McCullough, M., Nichols-Barrer, I., & Lake, R. (2012). *Charter-school management organizations: Diverse strategies and diverse student impacts.* Cambridge, MA: Mathematica Policy Research.

Gamoran, A. (2016). Gamoran comment on Downey and Condron. *Sociology of Education, 89*(3), 231–233.

Gamoran, A., & An, B. P. (2016). Effects of school segregation and school resources in a changing policy context. *Educational Evaluation and Policy Analysis, 38*(1), 43–64.

Glazer, J., Massell, D., & Malone, M. (2015). *Research into Tennessee's Achievement School District: Autonomy, incentives, and guidance for providers.* Nashville, TN: Tennessee Consortium on Research, Evaluation, and Development.

Gleason, P., Clark, M., Tuttle, C. C., & Dwoyer, E. (2010). *The evaluation of charter school impacts: Final report* (NCEE 2010-4029). Washington, DC: U.S. Department of Education, Institute of Education Sciences, National Center for Education Evaluation and Regional Assistance.

Hanushek, E. A., Kain, J. F., Rivkin, S. G., & Branch, G. F. (2007). Charter school quality and parental decision making with school choice. *Journal of Public Economics, 91*(5–6), 823–848.

Harris, D. N., & Larsen, M. (2016). *The effects of the New Orleans post-Katrina school reforms on student academic outcomes.* New Orleans, LA: Research Alliance for New Orleans. Retrieved from educationresearchalliancenola.org/files/publications/The-Effects-of-the-New-Orleans-Post-Katrina-School-Reforms-on-Student-Academic-Outcomes.pdf

Hoxby, C. M., Murarka, S., & Kang, J. (2009). *How New York City's charter schools affect achievement.* Cambridge, MA: New York City Charter Schools Evaluation Project. Retrieved from users.nber.org/~schools/charterschoolseval/how_NYC_charter_schools_affect_achievement_sept2009.pdf

Hoxby, C. M., & Rockoff, J. (2005). Findings from the city of big shoulders. *Education Next, 5*(4), 52–58.

Imberman, S. A. (2011). Achievement and behavior in charter schools: Drawing a more complete picture. *Review of Economics and Statistics, 93*(2), 416–435.

Jackson, C. K., Johnson, R. C., & Persico, C. (2015). The effects of school spending on educational and economic outcomes: Evidence from school finance reforms. *Quarterly Journal of Economics, 131*(1), 157–218.

Ladd, H. F., Clotfelter, C. T., & Holbein, J. B. (2015). *The growing segmentation of the charter school sector in North Carolina.* Washington, DC: National Center for Analysis of Longitudinal Data in Education Research.

Lafortune, J., Rothstein, J., & Schanzenbach, D. W. (2016). *School finance reform and the distribution of student achievement* [NBER Working Paper No. 22011]. Cambridge, MA: National Bureau of Economic Research.

Massell, D., Glazer, J. L., & Malone, M. (2016). *"This is the big leagues": Charter-led turnaround in a non-charter world.* Nashville, TN: Tennessee Consortium on Research, Evaluation, and Development.

Mills, J. N. (2013). The achievement impacts of Arkansas open-enrollment charter schools. *Journal of Education Finance, 38*(4), 320–342.

Ni, Y., & Rorrer, A. K. (2012). Twice considered: Charter schools and student achievement in Utah. *Economics of Education Review, 31*(5), 835–849.

Nisar, H. (2012). *Do charter schools improve student achievement?* [NCSPE Working Paper]. New York, NY: National Center for the Study of Privatization in Education. Retrieved from ncspe.tc.columbia.edu/working-papers/OP216.pdf

Office of English Language Acquisition, U.S. Department of Education. (2015). *English learners and charter schools.* Washington, DC: Author. Retrieved from www2.ed.gov/about/offices/list/oela/fast-facts/elcs.pdf

Sass, T. (2006). Charter schools and student achievement in Florida. *Education Finance and Policy, 1,* 91–122. Retrieved from www.mitpressjournals.org/doi/pdf/10.1162/edfp.2006.1.1.91

Sass, T. R., Zimmer, R. W., Gill, B. P., & Booker, T. K. (2016). Charter high schools' effect on long-term attainment and earnings. *Journal of Policy Analysis and Management, 35*(3), 683–706.

Thernstrom, A., & Thernstrom, S. (2003). *No excuses: Closing the racial achievement gap.* New York, NY: Simon and Schuster.

Tuttle, C. C., Gill, B., Gleason, P., Knechtel, V., Nichols-Barrer, I., & Resch, A. (2013). *KIPP middle schools: Impacts on achievement and other outcomes.* Washington, DC: Mathematica Policy Research.

Tuttle, C. C., Gleason, P., Knechtel, V., Nichols-Barrer, I., Booker, K., Chojnacki, G., Coen, T., & Goblel, L. (2015). *Understanding the effect of KIPP as it scales: Volume 1, impacts on achievement and other outcomes.* Washington, DC: Mathematica Policy Research.

Whitehurst, G. J., Reeves, R. V., & Rodrigue, E. (2016). *Segregation, race, and charter schools: What do we know?* Washington, DC: Center on Children and Families at Brookings. Retrieved from www.brookings.edu/wp-content/uploads/2016/10/ccf_20161021segregation_version-10_211.pdf

Winters, M. (2013). *Why the gap? Special education and New York City charter schools.* Seattle, WA: Center for Reinventing Public Schools.

Witte, J., Weimer, D., Shober, A., & Schlomer, P. (2007). The performance of charter schools in Wisconsin. *Journal of Policy Analysis and Management, 26,* 557–573.

Zimmer, R., Gill, B., Booker, K., Lavertu, S., & Witte, J. (2012). Examining charter school achievement in seven states. *Economics of Education Review, 31*(2), 213–224.

Zimmer, R., Kho, A., Henry, G., & Viano, S. (2015). *Evaluation of the effect of Tennessee's Achievement School District on student test scores.* Nashville, TN: Tennessee Consortium on Research, Evaluation, and Development.

CHAPTER 10

Civil Rights Protections for Students Enrolled in Charter Schools

Brenda Shum

In recognizing the humanity of our fellow beings, we pay ourselves the highest tribute.

—Thurgood Marshall, *Furman v. Georgia*

From their inception, charter schools have raised concerns about access and equity. Many of these concerns are linked to market incentives that require and reward positive student outcomes—even if those outcomes are achieved by excluding some of the most difficult to educate students (Vasquez Heilig, Holme, LeClair, Redd, & Ward, 2016). Indeed, studies reveal that charter schools enroll disproportionately fewer English-language learners (ELLs), students with disabilities, and low-income students (Vasquez Heilig et al., 2016). The reasons for this may vary, but often include restrictive enrollment and recruitment practices, the failure to provide necessary services and supports, and discipline policies that push out at-risk students.

Yet, charter schools are public and remain subject to all of the civil rights and special education laws, regulations, and guidelines that apply to other public schools.[1] These obligations apply to all aspects and operations of a charter school, including recruitment, admissions, academics, educational services and testing, school climate, discipline, athletics and nonacademic programs, and facilities and technology (Lhamon, 2014). This chapter addresses some of the challenges frequently observed in charter schools in terms of compliance with antidiscrimination provisions, the delivery of special education services, and adherence to due process protections and nondiscrimination requirements in school discipline.

LEGAL PROTECTIONS FOR STUDENTS IN CHARTER SCHOOLS

A number of federal statutes protect students against discrimination in all public school settings, including charter schools. These include Title VI of the Civil

Rights Act of 1964 (Title VI; 42 U.S.C. Sec. 2000[d] et seq.; 34 C.F.R. Part 100), which prohibits discrimination on the basis of race, color, or national origin; Title IX of the Education Amendments of 1972 (Title IX; 20 U.S.C. Sec. 1681 et seq.; 34 C.F.R. Part 106), which prohibits discrimination on the basis of sex; and Section 504 of the Rehabilitation Act of 1973 (Section 504; 29 U.S.C. Sec. 794; 34 C.F.R. Part 104) and Title II of the Americans with Disabilities Act of 1990 (Title II; 42 U.S.C. Sec. 12131 et seq.; 28 C.F.R. Part 35), which prohibit discrimination on the basis of disability. The Equal Educational Opportunities Act of 1974 also requires state and local education agencies to take affirmative action to overcome language barriers that prevent ELLs from equal participation in instructional programs (20 U.S.C. Sec. 1703). In addition to these antidiscrimination provisions, charter schools must also comply with a school's obligations under the Individuals with Disabilities Education Act (IDEA) and its implementing regulations, as well as the due process procedures required by the Fourteenth Amendment of the U.S. Constitution. Together, these federal provisions provide fundamental protections to students, whether in traditional or charter public schools.

Avoiding Discrimination in Admissions

While charter schools may set specific enrollment criteria, they may not discriminate in admissions on the basis of race, color, national origin, or disability (34 C.F.R. Section 100.3[b][1] [Title VI]; 104.4[b] [Section 504]). Eligibility criteria must be nondiscriminatory on their face and must also be applied in a nondiscriminatory manner. Charter schools may not use admissions criteria that have the effect of excluding students on the basis of their protected status without justification (34 C.F.R. Sec. 100.3[b][2], 100.3[b][6]). Similarly, charter schools may not categorically deny admission to students on the basis of disability or discourage students from applying to their school because they do not have the capacity to serve students with disabilities (34 C.F.R. Sec. 104[b]; 34 C.F.R Sec. 104.33–104.36). Further, like all public schools, charter schools must also ensure that students have access, regardless of immigration status or documentation. Because charter schools are schools of choice, it is important to ensure that recruitment is conducted in a way that does not, even unintentionally, exclude certain parents or students. For example, it is important for charter schools to consider different strategies to ensure that outreach is conducted in different languages or is accessible to parents with disabilities (Lhamon, 2014).

Ensuring Access and Due Process for Students with Disabilities

Federal and state laws establish the rights of students with disabilities. The federal statutes that protect students with disabilities include IDEA (20 U.S.C. Sec. 1400 et seq., 34 C.F.R. 300 et seq.), Section 504 of the Rehabilitation Act (29 U.S.C. Sec. 792, 34 C.F.R. 104), and Title II of the Americans with Disabilities Act (42 U.S.C. Sec. 12101 et seq., 34 C.F.R. 104) and their implementing regulations. However, state laws typically allocate the authority for the supervision and monitoring of the implementation of these laws to charter schools. While some charter schools operate as their own local education agency (LEA), others are within the jurisdiction of an LEA. States may also establish a charter board or independent authorizer to oversee the charter schools within that jurisdiction. Whatever the governance structure, the LEA remains primarily responsible for ensuring that special education services are provided and that students are offered a full spectrum of services and placement options, even if an individual charter is functioning as its own LEA.

However, charter schools enroll fewer students with disabilities and have not consistently invested adequate resources in developing programs for those students (Morando Rhim, Gumz, & Henderson, 2015).[2] Some students with disabilities are denied enrollment, do not receive legally required specialized education, and are illegally suspended or expelled. However, the law is clear that students with disabilities enrolled in charter schools retain all of the same rights and protections as those attending traditional public schools (34 C.F.R. 300.209[a]).[3]

Many charter schools are unaware that their obligation to serve students with disabilities is triggered even prior to a student's actual enrollment. Prospective students are entitled to nondiscrimination on the basis of disability in recruitment, application, and admission.[4] Recruitment efforts must not signal that a charter school will refuse admission to applicants with a disability or a specific type of disability (34 C.F.R. 104.4[a], [b][1][i]-[v], [4]).[5] For example, charter schools may not notify applicants that they are unable to serve students who have intellectual disabilities or who require sign language interpreters, and they may not steer those students to other schools. In addition, charter schools may not use admissions criteria that may appear objective but discourage students with disabilities from applying to that school—for example, a requirement that students attend a minimum number of days each year, without accounting for the need to accommodate students who may have a disability that impedes their ability to comply. Charter schools are also subject to Child Find, which requires that state and local education agencies have policies and procedures to ensure that all children with disabilities in need of special education or related services are "identified, located, and evaluated" regardless of the severity of the disability. Child Find also applies to students who are passing from grade to grade but still may have a qualifying disability requiring specialized instruction (34 C.F.R. 300.101[c]).

Charter schools must provide students with disabilities with a free appropriate public education as required by law.[6] Under IDEA, all children with disabilities enrolled in charter schools must receive special education and related services in accordance with their individualized education plan (IEP). Charter schools are therefore responsible for complying with all of the procedural requirements and timelines outlined in the law with respect to the development and reevaluation of that IEP (34 C.F.R. Sec. 300.323). They may not unilaterally limit the amount or types of special education or related services provided to children with disabilities at their schools (34 C.F.R. Sec. 300.209[a]). In addition, charter schools must immediately implement the IEP of students who transfer from another school, and revisions to the services provided for by that IEP must comply with the procedural requirements outlined by law (34 C.F.R. Sec. 300.320–300.324). This includes the provision of transportation services required by a child's IEP, regardless of whether the charter school provides transportation to its general education students (34 C.F.R. Sec. 300.34[a] and [c][16]). Charter schools must also educate students with disabilities in the least restrictive environment with their nondisabled peers to the maximum extent appropriate (34 C.F.R. Sec. 300.114[a][1] and 300.201).[7] While charter schools tend to place more students with disabilities in inclusive settings than traditional public schools (Morando Rhim et al., 2015), they must ensure those students receive appropriate services while there. Most placement challenges arise for charter schools that function as an independent LEA where the school is unable to offer the appropriate placement.

Charter schools may not impermissibly suspend or expel students with disabilities for the failure to meet certain school requirements. If a charter school believes that a student's behavior impedes the child's learning or that of others and seeks a change in placement, the IEP team must consider the extent to which the IEP includes behavioral interventions and supports that would address that behavior (34 C.F.R. Sec. 300.324[a][2], 34 C.F.R. Sec. 300.324[b][2], 34 C.F.R. Sec. 300.320[a][4]). Changes in placement must be recommended by the placement team and cannot be unilaterally determined by the charter school without complying with IDEA's procedural protections and due process requirements (34. C.F.R. Sec. 300.116[a][1]). Parents must receive prior written notice that a charter school intends to recommend a change in the child's educational setting (34 C.F.R. Sec. 300.503[b]–[c]).[8] More importantly, should parents disagree with that recommendation, they may invoke their right to "stay put," which freezes the child's placement until an administrative or judicial proceeding can be held and the placement can be resolved (34 C.F.R. Sec. 300.518).[9] Although charter schools may implement their own discipline policies and procedures, they must comply with a student's rights and protections under IDEA and avoid discrimination in the administration of school discipline (34 C.F.R. Sec. 300.209[a]).

Many charter schools are located in nontraditional spaces that have been adapted for an educational purpose. Charter schools are often unaware that Section 504 requires programs and facilities to be accessible (34 C.F.R. Sec. 104.21–104.23).[10] All public schools must ensure that students and parents with disabilities are not denied access to programs or services because of inaccessible facilities, academic buildings, walkways, restrooms, athletic facilities, or parking. This may require a charter school to reassign classroom space or relocate other services to accessible areas of the facility, alter current facilities, or construct new facilities that comply with accessibility requirements. When selecting facilities, a charter school may not choose facilities that would deny persons with disabilities the benefits of the school program or substantially impair the ability of those with a disability to receive the benefits of the program. These obligations extend to charter schools regardless of whether their facilities are owned or rented (U.S. Department of Education, 2016).

Ensuring Educational Opportunity for English-Language Learners

ELLs constitute one of the fastest-growing demographic groups among schoolchildren in this country. Charter schools must comply with federal laws to ensure that ELLs can participate meaningfully in educational programs. More specifically, the 1974 Supreme Court decision in *Lau v. Nichols* held that school districts must take affirmative steps to address language deficiencies that prevent ELLs from effectively participating in educational programs (414 U.S. 563 [1974]). The Equal Educational Opportunities Act of 1974 later codified that ruling and requires state and local education agencies to address language barriers that prevent ELLs from equal participation in instructional programs (National Charter School Resource Center, 2014). School districts, including charter schools that function as their own LEAs, must have procedures to accurately and timely identify potential ELLs using home language surveys and valid, reliable tests of English proficiency in speaking, listening, reading, and writing. They must also exit ELLs from language acquisition programs once those students are proficient in English. Charter schools may not exclude ELLs from participation in educational programs (including special education or gifted programs) because of language barriers or limited English proficiency, but ELLs should also not be inappropriately designated as disabled due to limited English proficiency.

Schools, including charters, may not segregate students on the basis of national origin or ELL status.[11] Although certain ELL programs may be designed to provide ELLs with separate instruction for a limited portion of the day or period of time, schools are expected to implement their ELL programs in a way that has the least segregative impact. This applies to both academic and nonacademic programs, such as pre-K, recess, physical education, magnet programs, or career education. Similarly, charter schools must avoid maintaining students in an alternative language program for longer than necessary. Many of the protections for ELLs also apply to their parents, in that charter schools should communicate meaningfully with parents who are nonnative English speakers or who have limited English proficiency. Written or oral translations of important school information should be provided to parents and guardians in a language that they can understand (National Charter School Resource Center, 2014).

Charter schools must also comply with state laws that address the educational needs of ELLs. Many laws provide dedicated funding for the education of ELLs, establish accountability guidelines for the academic performance of those students, and require schools and districts to address the needs of ELLs in school improvement plans. State law may also mandate certain practices related to the education of ELLs. In general, however, charter schools will be subject to the same accountability provisions as all public schools as they relate to ELLs, although states may exempt charter schools or permit charter schools to seek a waiver from compliance in some cases.

Due Process and Nondiscrimination in the Administration of School Discipline

Anecdotal evidence and available data suggest problems with the discipline of students in some charter schools (Moyer, 2015), which might be related, in part, to the less restrictive system of oversight used for charter schools as compared to traditional public schools. Charter schools suspend students with disabilities at a higher rate than noncharters. Students, particularly students of color, are often disciplined for minor or subjective infractions of school discipline policies. However, charter schools do not consistently suspend more students than traditional public schools for each racial group at each grade configuration (Losen, Keith, Hodson, & Martinez, 2016, pp. 2–3). In other words, there is variation in terms of the excessive or disparate impact of school discipline on certain groups of students. This issue appears to be systemic for some charter schools, but not a universal problem for all charter schools.[12]

Under *Goss v. Lopez*, all children educated in public schools have baseline constitutional rights (419 U.S. 565 [1975]). Students have a legitimate property interest in a public education that is legally protected by the due process clause. As a result, the right to education cannot be denied for misconduct without adhering to the minimum requirements of due process, which apply whenever students are facing suspension or expulsion. These due process protections include, at a minimum, prior notice of the alleged violation and proposed consequences, as well as a fair hearing (419 U.S. 565, 582–83 [1975]). Although these protections also apply to charter school students, evidence demonstrates that these students may be disparately affected by legally deficient disciplinary practices.

Titles IV and VI of the Civil Rights Act of 1964 also protect students from discrimination in discipline. These statutes cover charter schools, as well as those a charter relies on to administer discipline, such as school resource officers, counselors, administrators, and staff. Moreover, these provisions protect students at every stage of the disciplinary process, from behavior management within the classroom, to referrals, to final resolution of the incident. In addition to subjecting students to different treatment on the basis of race, even racially neutral discipline policies may subject students to impermissible discrimination as demonstrated by disparate impact on a legally protected class of students.

NEW ORLEANS: A CASE STUDY AND CAUTIONARY TALE

Prior to Hurricane Katrina, New Orleans consistently ranked among the worst-performing school systems in the country. The state legislature responded by creating the Recovery School District (RSD) and authorizing it to take over schools in academic crisis. After Katrina, the RSD assumed control of nearly all of the public schools in New Orleans and replaced many schools with charter schools. What emerged was a wholly decentralized system of education whereby no single administrative entity retained direct control or supervision of the public schools operating within the city. The state had essentially created what amounted to over 60 distinct LEAs managing over 90 schools, most of them charters. Within 5 years, almost 80% of the city's public school students were educated in those charter schools (Heilman, 2013). While many hailed this transformation as a success for school choice, the restructured system raised significant concerns that the educational needs and legal rights of many students were being ignored.

In many respects, New Orleans serves as a cautionary tale of the dangers associated with enacting reforms rooted in market-based principles without considering their effect on legally protected rights. There are many lessons to be learned from the district's rapid transformation into the first school system relying almost exclusively on charter schools to educate its students. Several of the legal violations discussed earlier in this chapter quickly surfaced once the RSD began to charter all of the schools within its jurisdiction without monitoring their capacity to comply with the law.[13] Many charter schools with limited institutional capacity or expertise in federal education and civil rights law found themselves unprepared to satisfy their obligations to students with disabilities. As a result, some of the city's most vulnerable students were denied their substantive and procedural rights and subjected to impermissible discrimination.

In the post-Katrina education system, students in New Orleans were not assigned to a particular neighborhood school and were instead required to apply to multiple schools. However, not all families had access to information about the special education services or accommodations available at individual schools. This not only placed a tremendous burden on parents, but also explicitly or implicitly discouraged certain students from applying to certain schools. In the end, many children with disabilities were denied access to schools in violation of laws requiring that open-admission schools serve all students. Implementation of a common enrollment process offered limited relief. Through the OneApp system, families were allowed to rank their schools of choice. While no students were guaranteed their preferred school, the goal was to ensure that all students had an opportunity to be matched with a school on their list (Heilman, 2013).

In addition, it was almost impossible to comply with the obligation under Child Find to identify and evaluate students in accordance with state and federal law in a district with over 60 schools functioning as their own LEAs. By virtue of its unusually decentralized system, New Orleans became the only jurisdiction within Louisiana where a school's Child Find obligations would not be triggered until after a student had enrolled in that school. Without a centralized entity managing Child Find across the system, many students in between schools found themselves without a school obligated to identify or evaluate those suspected of having a qualifying disability (Heilman, 2013). Many of these challenges were exacerbated by the highly mobile student population produced by Hurricane Katrina.

Moreover, evidence indicated that many of the charter schools lacked the capacity or commitment to provide services for students with disabilities in the least restrictive environment. Individual charter schools frequently lacked the staff and expertise to provide students with the array of specially designed instructional and related services. Moreover, most of the charter schools were unable to benefit from the economies of scale enjoyed by larger school districts. Consequently, many offered students a "one-size-fits-all" approach to services inconsistent with an individualized determination of a student's unique needs. Charter schools also had limited access to the continuum of placement options necessary to serve students in the least restrictive environment. Many students were included in the general education setting, but without necessary services to succeed in a whole-class environment (Heilman, 2013). As a result, these students were denied the specially designed instruction in appropriate educational placements, in direct violation of the law.

Overreliance on exclusionary disciplinary practices for students with disabilities was another troublesome practice observed in post-Katrina New Orleans. Children with disabilities were punished and excluded from the classroom at rates among the highest in the state. Several of the charter schools had rigid codes of conduct and behavior-management policies. Many students with disabilities struggled to conform to expectations, and many charter schools operated outside of state laws and regulations regarding school discipline. Evidence showed that many school administrators lacked the technical knowledge of IDEA's requirements related to due process for students with disabilities, contributing to the pushout of those students. Between the 2009–2010 and 2012–2013 school years, both the RSD's traditional schools and charter schools were cited for noncompliance with IDEA's discipline requirements (Heilman, 2013).

Today, New Orleans has become a nearly all-charter district that offers "universal choice," where parents may choose which school their child will attend. Some reforms have been implemented: The district established a common application process and a centralized hearing office for school discipline matters, and the state became more active in closing underperforming charter schools. Research shows that the RSD made achievement gains when compared with results before the post-Katrina reforms (Gamoran & Fernandez, 2018). However, the charter system remains highly segregated by race and socioeconomic status, and selective schools continue to operate their own admission processes, which reinforce segregation (Vanacore, 2017).

CONCLUSION

Charter schools are continuing to play an increasingly important role in educating public school students across the country. Moving forward, it is essential to ensure that they have the capacity, commitment, and expertise necessary to comply with the applicable federal civil rights and education laws. Charter laws and regulations should include incentives for compliance and provide for appropriate monitoring and supervision. Charter schools should be administered in a way that ensures access in recruitment, admission, and enrollment and does not further the disadvantages high-poverty families face in navigating the system.

NOTES

1. Charter schools that receive federal funds directly or indirectly through a grant program are also subject to all of the requirements of that program. In addition, charter schools must comply with all of the applicable state laws related to the protection of students, which are not discussed here.

2. In 2012, the Government Accountability Office also determined that charter schools enroll a lower percentage of students with disabilities than traditional LEAs.

3. Protections against disability discrimination include the right to equal treatment in terms of the ability to participate in nonacademic and extracurricular programs (34 C.F.R. Sec. 104.37[a]–[c]).

4. Under Section 504, schools are generally not permitted to ask whether a prospective student has a disability or counsel that student against applying to a charter school (34 C.F.R. Sec. 104.4[b][1]).

5. These requirements apply to information posted on a charter school website, included in application materials, shared during recruitment meetings, or in response to family inquiries about the school.

6. Free appropriate public education includes special education and related services provided at public expense, under public supervision and direction, and without charge, that meet the standards of the state education agency and are provided in conformity with the child's IEP (34 C.F.R. Sec. 300.320 to 300.324).

7. Special or separate classrooms or removal from regular education can occur only if the nature of the disability is such that education within the mainstream education environment with the use of supplementary aids and services cannot be satisfactorily achieved (34 C.F.R. Sec. 300.114[a][2]).

8. Prior written notice must be provided in the parent's native language or mode of communication.

9. Many states may also offer alternative dispute resolution or mediation procedures.

10. Section 504 addresses accessibility of facilities constructed or altered after 1977. Title II incorporates accessibility requirements for facilities constructed or altered after 1992.

11. While ELLs are entitled to services, these are voluntary and parents may opt out of language acquisition programs.

12. In addition, many of these due process concerns are also observed in traditional public schools.

13. The Lawyers' Committee for Civil Rights Under Law and Southern Poverty Law Center filed litigation against the Louisiana State Department of Education on behalf of a number of students with disabilities in New Orleans alleging violations of IDEA, Title II, and Section 504. See *PB v. White*, No. 2:10-cv-04049 (E.D. La. Oct. 26, 2010).

REFERENCES

Gamoran, A., & Fernandez, C. M. (2018). Do charter schools strengthen education in high-poverty urban districts? In I. C. Rotberg & J. L. Glazer (Eds.), *Choosing charters: Better schools or more segregation?* (pp. 133–152). New York, NY: Teachers College Press.

Heilman, E. B. (2013). Stranger than fiction: The experiences of students with disabilities in the post-Katrina New Orleans school system. *Loyola Law Review, 59*, 355–380.

Lhamon, C. E. (2014, May 14). *Dear colleague letter on charter schools.* Washington, DC: U.S. Department of Education. Retrieved from www2.ed.gov/about/offices/list/ocr/letters/colleague-201405-charter.pdf

Losen, D. J., Keith, M. A., II, Hodson, C. L., & Martinez, T. E. (2016, March). *Charter schools, civil rights, and school discipline: A comprehensive review.* Los Angeles, CA: The Civil Rights Project.

Marshall, T. (1972). *Furman v. Georgia.* Retrieved from documents.routledge-interactive.s3.amazonaws.com/9780415506434/document9.pdf

Morando Rhim, L., Gumz, J., & Henderson, K. (2015, October). *Key trends in special education in charter schools: A secondary analysis of the civil rights data collection 2011–2012.* New York, NY: National Center for Special Education in Charter Schools.

Moyer, K. C. (2015, January 15). *Due process rights in charter schools* [Webinar, Children's Rights Litigation, American Bar Association]. Retrieved from apps.americanbar.org/litigation/committees/childrights/content/articles/winter2015-0115-due-process-rights-in-charter-schools.html

National Charter School Resource Center. (2014). *Legal guidelines for educating English learners in charter schools.* Houston, TX: Author.

U.S. Department of Education. (2016, December 28). *Frequently asked questions about the rights of students with disabilities in public charter schools under Section 504 of the Rehabilitation Act of 1973.* Retrieved from www2.ed.gov/about/offices/list/ocr/docs/dcl-faq-201612-504-charter-school.pdf

Vanacore, A. (2017, January 7). What New Orleans can teach Betsy DeVos about charter schools. *Politico.* Retrieved from www.politico.com/magazine/story/2017/01/what-new-orleans-can-teach-betsy-devos-about-charter-schools-214610

Vasquez Heilig, J., Holme, J. J., LeClair, A. V., Redd, L. D., & Ward, D. (2016). Separate and unequal? The problematic segregation of special populations in charter schools relative to traditional public schools. *Stanford Law & Policy Review, 27*(2), 251–293.

CHAPTER 11

Church-State Entanglement Within Charter Schools

Suzanne Eckes, Nina K. Buchanan, and Robert A. Fox

The society that loses its grip on the past is in danger, for it produces men who know nothing but the present, and who are not aware that life had been, and could be, different from what it is.

—Trevor Saunders, Introduction, *The Politics by Aristotle*

The advent of charter schools as a genuine public school alternative has generated new challenges related to the First Amendment and the church-school wall. Can charter schools choose to teach creationism in science courses or allow teachers to lead the students in prayer without running afoul of the First Amendment? Is it possible to locate a charter school in a current church facility? Can a religious denomination legally convert its schools into charter schools? Can an ethnocentric niche charter school, which claims to be focused on Hawaiian or Native American culture or on Hebrew or Arabic language, really claim to be secular?

Charter schools' straddling of the church-school wall was an unexpected consequence that came with charter legislation. In this chapter, we examine how charter schools sometimes contribute to a blurring of the traditional separation of religion and education. After a brief overview, we begin by citing some of the key legal cases related to religion in public schools to set the context. We follow this with some examples of a few ways in which charter schools can encourage this blurring: the establishment of ethnocentric niche charter schools and charter schools operating in religious-affiliated buildings.

OVERVIEW

As Ray Budde (1974) first conceived of charter schools in the 1970s, Albert Shanker (1988) advocated for them before the National Press Club in the 1980s, and the first one was founded in Minnesota in 1992, they offered a number of promises.

These promises included (1) greater freedom for teachers; (2) independence from excessive regulation; (3) improved student performance; (4) decreased educational costs; and (5) more equal distribution of quality education. In 1988 Budde suggested that small groups of teachers be given contracts or "charters" by their local school boards to explore new approaches to instruction and school governance (Budde, 1988; Kahlenberg, 2008; Kolderie, 2005). This chartering strategy was to have been bottom-up, empowering those closest to the students at the level of the school to take charge of their education.

But critics feared that chartered schools would become a new vehicle for white flight from desegregated schools or that they would create ethnic enclaves. In response, some states required charter school developers to include information on how they would achieve a racial balance (Green, 2001). Despite the legislative attempts to create racial and socioeconomic status balance, ethnic diversity in many charter schools is now at a lower level than it was 25 years ago (see Finley, 2015, for a detailed analysis of the growth of segregation).

Educational researchers have assumed that, in every case, schools with diverse and inclusive student bodies are better for all students, especially for minority students (Cobb & Glass, 2009; Orfield & Lee, 2004). However, today this belief is not universally held. During the past 25 years, one can identify many examples of minority groups that do not view diverse schools as good for them (see Fox & Buchanan, 2014). As a result, parents and communities have been able to create charter schools with curricula that they believe better meet the native language and cultural needs of their children (Fox & Buchanan, 2014). In the process of connecting students to their culture, the lines between culture *and religion* can easily become blurred. In some cases, charter schools have even been housed in religious-affiliated buildings. It is not surprising that legal issues have arisen in cases like this (see *ACLU of Minnesota v. Tarek ibn Ziyad Academy*, 2009a, 2009b, 2009c, 2009d, 2010, 2011).

RELIGION IN PUBLIC SCHOOLS

While it is illegal for school officials to promote or endorse religion in public schools, including charter schools, it is sometimes unclear how much religion-related material and practices are constitutionally permissible. The earlier litigation involving church–school relations equally affects both traditional public schools and charter schools. Some legal challenges relate to state claims, but more involve federal constitutional allegations. With regard to state claims, several states have laws that prohibit government aid to educational institutions that have religious affiliations (Becket Fund for Religious Liberty, n.d.; Pew Research Center, 2008)—often referred to as Blaine amendments (Pew Research Center, 2003). Some state laws are more restrictive than others.

Similarly, the First Amendment prohibits public schools from endorsing religion. The First Amendment states:

Congress shall make no law respecting an *establishment* of religion, or prohibiting the *free exercise* thereof; or abridging the freedom of speech, or of the press; or the right of the people peaceably to assemble, and to petition the government for a redress of grievances. (U.S. Constitution, Amendment I, 1791; emphasis added)

The first of these phrases is known as the Establishment Clause and the second as the Free Exercise Clause. At the federal level, these tend to be the bases of arguments that blurring of education and religion is unconstitutional. This amendment, which actually refers only to the federal government, applies to the states through the incorporation of the Fourteenth Amendment.

Establishing Religion in Schools

Just as in traditional public schools, teachers in charter schools have been accused of impermissibly leading prayer in class (*Daugherty v. Vanguard Charter School Academy*, 2000; Scott, 2015; Svokos, 2014) or promoting religion in other ways (see *ACLU of Minnesota v. Tarek ibn Ziyad Academy*, 2009a, 2009b, 2009c, 2009d; Kopplin, 2014; *Nampa Classical Academy v. Goesling*, 2010). Although to date no U.S. Supreme Court cases have addressed such questions specifically in charter schools, the Court has examined these issues within the traditional public school context. Because charter schools are public schools, the same laws regarding religion apply.

When courts examine whether a school policy or activity violates the Establishment Clause, they typically utilize one of three tests. The *Lemon* test was the first test developed by the U.S. Supreme Court; under this test, a school policy violates the Establishment Clause if it does not have a secular purpose; its principal or primary effect either advances or inhibits religion; or there is excessive government entanglement with religion (*Lemon v. Kurtzman*, 1971). The Court subsequently created an alternative to *Lemon* in the "endorsement test," another analytic wherein a school's policy will be struck down if the Court finds a reasonable person would perceive the policy as endorsing or disapproving of religion (*County of Allegheny v. ACLU*, 1989). Further, under the Court's "coercion test," public school students must not be directly or indirectly coerced to profess a faith. For example, if a teacher wanted to proselytize by reading the Koran to her 5th-graders each morning, the action would violate all three: the *Lemon*, endorsement, and coercion tests (see Eckes & Fetter-Harrott, 2014).

Prohibition of religion-related activities in public school settings has evolved over time. When interpreting the Establishment Clause, the Supreme Court held that school-sponsored prayer in the classroom is unconstitutional (*Engel v. Vitale*, 1962). One year later, the Court ruled that required reading or recitation of the Bible in public schools violated the First Amendment (*School District of Abington Township, Pennsylvania v. Schempp*, 1963). Several years later, a student successfully challenged a school practice of inviting clergy to give graduation invocations, finding that a principal's invitation to a rabbi to read a nonsectarian prayer constituted school sponsorship of religion (*Lee v. Weisman*, 1992). In another case involving school prayer, the Court asserted that a district policy that permitted school prayer at public high school football games (even if student-led and student-initiated) was unconstitutional (*Santa Fe Independent School District v. Doe*, 2000). The Court reasoned that the prayer appeared to be school sponsored because it was delivered over the school's intercom and was under the supervision of school personnel and because the school's policy encouraged prayer. The U.S. Department of Education has interpreted these earlier decisions with very distinct guidelines about when prayer is constitutionally permissible (U.S. Department of Education, 2003).

The controversies are related not only to prayer. Some charter schools have been accused of teaching creationism in science courses (Kopplin, 2014). The controversy related to teaching creationism is puzzling on many fronts because the law is quite settled in this area. For example, in *Epperson v. Arkansas* (1968), the Supreme Court rejected a state law that banned the teaching of evolution in favor of teaching creationism in public school classrooms because it violated the Establishment Clause. Likewise, in 1987, the Court struck down a Louisiana law that required teachers to deliver instruction on "creation science" when teaching about evolution in science courses (*Edwards v. Aguillard*, 1987).

In other cases, charter schools have been suspected of impermissibly using religious texts or promoting religion through the curriculum in class. For example, litigation was threatened in Mesa, Arizona, when the Heritage Academy Charter School was accused of using religious texts in its history courses (Creno, 2014). Also, a federal district court in Idaho ruled against a charter school that alleged that the state was unlawfully prohibiting charter school personnel from using religious texts in the curriculum (*Nampa Classical Academy v. Goesling*, 2010). Finally, a charter school in Florida was rumored to have promoted Scientology throughout its curriculum and raised legal concerns (Americans United for Separation of Church and State, 2012).

But some aspects of religion in public schools remain. The Court has also ruled that public schools are permitted to release their students during noninstructional time in order to attend off-campus religious instruction (*Zorach v. Clauson*, 1952). In *Zorach*, the Court observed that such policies merely accommodated students and that there was no religious favoritism involved. Also, public schools can implement a moment of silence each day if it is genuinely neutral toward religion; when the state of Alabama tried to require a moment of silence for "meditation or voluntary prayer" in public schools, it was found to be unconstitutional by the U.S. Supreme Court because it appeared that the state was promoting prayer (*Wallace v. Jaffree*, 1985). In some situations, no Supreme Court decisions have addressed an issue to provide guidance. In these instances, charter school officials might look to lower federal courts and state courts for guidance. These federal court decisions would be binding only within specific jurisdictions.

For example, in one federal appellate court case, a student claimed that the school district violated the Establishment Clause when her music teacher allegedly promoted religion by requiring her to perform religious songs at religious sites (*Bauchman v. West High School*, 1997). Upholding the district court decision to dismiss the case, the Tenth Circuit Court of Appeals did note that the student failed to allege facts indicating that the teacher had a clearly religious purpose in choosing the songs and the religious venues. This decision is binding only within the Tenth Circuit, and other circuits may take a different approach to this issue.

For a counterexample, a different federal appellate court held that a public school cannot hold school graduation in a church because it violates the Establishment Clause (*Doe v. Elmbrook School District*, 2012). In this case, a group of parents and students sued the school district alleging that holding high school graduation and other school-related events in a church violated the Establishment Clause. The Seventh Circuit found that the 15- to 20-foot cross in the sanctuary, the religious materials in the lobby, the Bibles in the pews, and the religious literature distributed to attendees created a pervasively Christian environment.

Although some of these legal cases involved traditional public schools, these court decisions are equally informative for charter schools. Specifically, because charter schools are public schools, the law is equally applicable.

Accommodating Religious Beliefs

The First Amendment does not prohibit all religion from charter schools (Mullally, 2011). To the contrary, under the Free Exercise Clause, public schools, including charter schools, would generally need to have a compelling reason to burden substantially a student's sincerely held and constitutionally protected religious practice. A Free Exercise violation might occur, for example, if school personnel prohibited a charter school student from reading his Torah during study hall. From decisions like these, it is clear that charter schools must allow students to engage in private, student-initiated prayer or religious reading during noninstructional times under some circumstances.

But in many instances, schools or states accommodate students' religious requests with little controversy. In several parts of the country, parents made requests for schools to accommodate their family's religious beliefs. In response to some requests, a bill was introduced in the 2015–2016 session of the New York State Assembly to require schools in large cities to provide halal food at no cost upon request. San Diego Unified School District has expanded its halal lunch program (Burks, 2015). The federal government subsidizes halal meals in several school districts (Markind, 2015). Kosher school lunches are available in such widely separated places as Beverly Hills, California, and Great Neck, New York.

Sometimes legal controversies arise involving student attire in charter schools that are related to religious practice. To illustrate, in a Minnesota charter school, the majority of the students wore a hijab in the school (Kersten, 2008). According to the American Civil Liberties Union (ACLU, n.d.), "Students may wear religious attire, such as yarmulkes and head scarves, and they may not be forced to wear gym clothes that they regard, on *religious* grounds, as immodest" (emphasis added; n.p.).

As such, charter school officials must require that students receive reasonable religious accommodations unless a compelling reason exists not to do so.

Parental Rights

The U.S. Supreme Court has also addressed the rights of parents to make educational choices for their children that are applicable to the charter context. For example, the Court held that a state law banning foreign languages as a medium of instruction in a private school was unconstitutional because it violated parents' liberty rights guaranteed by the Fourteenth Amendment (*Meyer v. Nebraska*, 1923). This decision paved the way for schools in which the subject or the medium of instruction was Hebrew, Hawaiian, Spanish, Native American, Aleut, or other languages.

Two years later, in *Pierce v. Society of Sisters* (1925), the Court established the legal basis on which, in many respects, religious schools have been allowed to exist at all. In this case, the Court examined Oregon's compulsory education law, which required students to attend public school. The Court found that this law infringed upon parents' right to direct their children's religious upbringing. While religious schools could not receive public funds, they could teach students. In *Wisconsin v. Yoder* (1972), the Supreme Court went further and determined that parental religious rights superseded state compulsory school attendance laws when a group of Amish parents were granted the right to pull their children out of school. The Court found that the First Amendment Free Exercise right outweighed the state's interest in compelling school past the 8th grade. Both of these rulings contributed to the concept that the bar on religion as it relates to public education is not as absolute as some would believe.

School personnel walk a fine line in attempting to balance parents' interests in directing their children's religious upbringing against the concept of church–state separation. Several federal courts have addressed these issues. For example, the Second Circuit Court of Appeals rejected a parent's request that his son be allowed to opt out of the district's mandatory health course in *Leebaert v. Harrington* (2003). In *Leebaert*, the parent had alleged that some parts of the class, such as discussions related to drugs and alcohol, conflicted with his sincerely held religious beliefs. The court reasoned that the course did not violate the family's Free Exercise rights because, unlike what occurred in *Yoder*, the health class did not threaten his faith's "entire way of life." In a similar federal case, the First Circuit Court of Appeals reasoned that the *Meyer* and *Pierce* decisions do not give parents wide latitude to restrict the flow of information provided in the public schools (*Brown v. Hot, Sexy and Safer Productions, Inc.*, 1995). Although these cases highlight parental rights to decide some educational matters, they also demonstrate that these rights are not absolute.

ETHNOCENTRIC CHARTER SCHOOLS
AND THE BLURRING OF RELIGIOUS LINES

As noted, some charter schools are designed around a specific culture and/or language, the very existence of which sometimes leads to the blurring of religious lines. We begin by profiling ethnocentric schools for Native Hawaiians to demonstrate some of the complex issues involved. Buchanan and Fox (2003, 2005) and Fox and Buchanan (2014) in collaboration with Native Hawaiian educators, have been reporting on the school choice landscape in Hawaii from the point of view of the indigenous Hawaiian people. Before enabling legislation for charter schools was enacted in Hawaii in 1999, Native Hawaiian students interested in a "Hawaiian experience" were limited to applying to attend Kamehameha Schools, a privately funded school system with substantial tuition costs. One huge obstacle was that it was located on Oahu, many miles and a plane trip away from any other island in the state. If a student met the entry requirements, parents were faced with the difficult task of sending their young child off to the school as a boarder and, in many instances, of paying substantial tuition. The only other alternative was to remain in their assigned public school and receive minimal instruction in Hawaiian culture and language within the statewide Department of Education. According to some parents, traditional public schools were not meeting the Hawaiian students' need to either attend highly effective schools or to participate in cultural and language learning to become grounded in their indigenous culture (Kamehameha Schools & Bernice Pauahi Bishop Estate, 1983).

Within 2 years after charter school legislation empowered charter schools in Hawaii, half of the chartered schools were focused on Hawaiian culture or Hawaiian language immersion. Hawaiians expressed their dissatisfaction with data that identified Hawaiian students as the lowest achieving group in the traditional Hawaii Department of Education schools and as the group most identified for special education services. The adults were proud of their culture and thought their children deserved better, so were able to create schools based on Hawaiian culture or language that were designed to teach in ways they believed Hawaiian students learned best: using hands-on activities in outdoor settings. The motivating factor was not the level of integration or segregation in Hawaii Department of Education schools; it was the lack of culturally appropriate education and role models. Native Hawaiian students had been trapped in a system that did not work for them; they were overrepresented in compensatory education and had the lowest health and employment rates (see Harvard University Native American Program, n.d.; Takayama, 2008).

Hawaiian culturally focused and language charter schools begin the school day with an entrance protocol such as *Oli Kāhea* that students must memorize and be able to chant in the appropriate context using correct pronunciation (Kamehameha Schools, n.d.). According to Ohukaniohia Gon (2007), such a protocol focuses students' attention on the school; demonstrates respect for the land, school, and teachers; prepares students to engage seriously in their work; socially unifies students; and creates a mood that transports students from the mundane to a higher purpose. This sense of a spiritual connection to the land and each other is as highly significant in the Hawaiian culture as is the ability to *pule* or pray (Kamehameha Schools, 2016). Some charter schools in Hawaii require students to chant *meles* which, while characterized as representative of Hawaiian culture, contain much overt religious significance. Native American charter schools are another example of charters that often engage in extensive cultural activities that are hard to distinguish from the spiritual (Fox & Buchanan, 2014). Should Hawaiian spirituality be considered a religion? Should indigenous practices be exempt from the separation of church and state? In 2015, a complaint was filed with the Hawaiian Civil Rights Commission challenging the religious practice of prayer in Native Hawaiian charter schools (Terrell, 2015). At this writing, the commission has not posted a decision.

The current situation in Hawaii is not unique. A growing number of ethnic groups in addition to indigenous peoples are willing to sacrifice diversity and inclusion for other values (Fox & Buchanan, 2014). For example, at the country's first English-Hebrew charter school, the Ben Gamla Charter School seeks to provide what it claims is a bilingual and bicultural curriculum to students. Ben Gamla is run by a rabbi and was founded by an orthodox Jew; many students left private Jewish day schools to attend this charter (Siracusa Hillman, 2008). One report suggests that 80% of the school's students are Jewish (see Americans United for Separation of Church and State, 2012). In some instances, schools like this may attract large populations of Jewish students, resulting in segregated ethnic enclaves, but this is not always the case (see Medina, 2010). Nevertheless, these schools have been subject to scrutiny, and some have questioned whether the schools are secular. According to Diane Ravitch, "It violates the long-established principle of separation of church and state to spend public funds on an institution that promotes religion" (Cohen, 2013, p. 1). She also posits that the Hebrew-centric charter schools are "essentially religious" (p. 1).

Other ethnocentric charter schools have been criticized for being too homogeneous and/or too connected to religion. Tarek ibn Ziyad Academy (TiZA) in Minnesota focused on Muslim culture as well as the Arabic language. The principal was a local imam and a founding member of the Muslim American Society of Minnesota; this organization shared a building with TiZA, and the vast majority of students enrolled were Muslim. The school was eventually sued by the ACLU because it was alleged that the school promoted religion (*ACLU v. Tarek ibn Ziyad Academy*, 2009a, 2009b, 2009c, 2009d, 2010, 2011; Mulvey, Cooper, & Maloney, 2010; Weinberg & Cooper, 2007). The legal concerns raised with TiZA included organized prayer time after school and buses that ran only after the prayer was completed (Kersten, 2008). In this case, the school eventually closed.

Some Turkish charter schools have been suspected of promoting Islam as well. Critics have contended that the curricular focus is on Islam. There are more than 150 charter schools in the United States founded by Turkish immigrants, some of whom follow Fethullah Gulen, who has been characterized as a moderate Sufi Islamic leader. Almost all of the teachers are recruited from Turkey. The *New York Times* raised the question about whether tax dollars are being used to fund the Gulen movement (Saul, 2011). Similar criticisms arose when an Hellenic, or Greek-focused, charter school opened in a New York Greek Orthodox church. Unsurprisingly, these schools contend that language and culture are integrated into their curriculum, but assert that they refrain from endorsing religion.

CHARTER SCHOOL FACILITIES IN RELIGIOUS-AFFILIATED BUILDINGS

Unlike traditional public schools, a new charter school often must find and fund its own facility because charter school sponsors typically do not provide a building (see National Alliance for Public Charter Schools, 2013). Currently, only 13 states and Washington, DC, provide charter schools with funding for their facilities (Batdorff et al., 2014). Some states have taken different approaches to assist charter school organizers with facilities. For example, the state might require school districts to allow charter schools to be housed in public schools if there is unused space or the state may provide some funding toward facilities.

In addition to the facility concerns noted above with TiZA and the Hellenic charter schools, this issue received national attention in 2008 when several financially strapped Catholic schools in Washington, DC, were converted to charter schools (Sanchez, 2008). In fact, in many inner cities, Catholic schools have closed because of low enrollment and funding issues (National Catholic Education Association, 2016) with the result that charter school organizers, at least in some cases, have chosen to locate their schools there. In addition to Catholic schools, other private Christian schools have converted to charters for financial reasons (Clawson, 2011). Although this practice might be entirely related to wise budgeting, some have raised concerns about religious influences in the charter schools when they are housed in religious-affiliated institutions (see Decker & Carr, 2015; Eckes, Fox, & Buchanan, 2011; Fox, Buchanan, Eckes, & Basford, 2012; Saiger, 2013; Scruggs, 2015; Siracusa-Hillman, 2008). This has led to some charter schools being sued because they hold classes in religious-affiliated buildings, which some argue violates the Establishment Clause (*Porta v. Klagholz*, 1998).

In some instances, religious groups have been accused of benefiting from taxpayer money or influencing the curriculum. Smith (2013) found that between 2010 and 2013, 16 of the 23 charter contracts that the state of Texas awarded went to entities with religious ties. Smith wrote that auditors for the Texas Education Agency found inappropriate use of state money in some cases. For example, in one charter school in San Antonio, the school's leader used school funds to buy a former church and then leased the church to the charter school. The U.S. Department of Education's (2014) nonregulatory guidance on this topic requires that, with regard to facilities, charter school organizers "may lease space from a religious organization so long as the charter school remains non-religious in all its programs and operations" (p. 23). The *Bauchman* (1997) and *Elmbrook* (2012) decisions discussed earlier provide some guidance, but as noted the U.S. Supreme Court has not yet addressed this issue.

The law is clear that, similar to traditional public schools, a charter school must not get entangled with religion. To be legal, charter schools must be secular and, if a faith-based organization owns the property where the charter school is housed or a religious figure runs the school, there must be no control over the school's program. For example, there should be no signs or symbols directly related to the religion.

CONCLUSION

Similar to traditional public schools, charter schools will attract additional scrutiny if they promote religion. This chapter highlighted how charter schools have raised legal concerns or have been sued when they have been viewed as promoting religion through curricular decisions or by leading prayer in school. Ethnocentric charter schools, such as the Hebrew-centric charters discussed, present related challenges, as a student's culture is often intertwined with spiritual beliefs. Likewise, charter schools that choose to locate in religious-affiliated buildings or private religious schools that have converted to charter status for financial reasons have experienced increased attention due to Establishment Clause concerns. Whether in an ethnocentric charter school or a Catholic-conversion charter school, charter school leaders must not promote or endorse one religion over another.

Although no U.S. Supreme Court cases specifically involve charter schools on this matter, the earlier Supreme Court cases involving traditional public schools are applicable to charter schools. As noted, charter schools are public schools, and federal and state laws related to establishing religion apply. As the charter school movement continues to expand, legal issues will likely continue to arise in this area. By considering court precedent and applying the balancing tests and analytical frameworks articulated by the courts, charter leaders can make reasoned decisions that support conscience, education, and the Constitution.

REFERENCES

ACLU. (n.d.). *Joint statement of current law of religion in the public schools.* Retrieved from www.aclu.org/joint-statement-current-law-religion-public-schools

ACLU Minn. v. Tarek ibn Ziyad Acad., Civil No. 09-138, Memorandum Opinion & Order, July 21, 2009(a).

ACLU Minn. v. Tarek ibn Ziyad Acad., 2009 U.S. Dist. LEXIS 62567 (D. Minn. July 21, 2009b).

ACLU Minn. v. Tarek ibn Ziyad Acad., 2009 U.S. Dist. LEXIS 88425 (D. Minn. Sept. 24, 2009c).

ACLU Minn. v. Tarek ibn Ziyad Acad., 2009 U.S. Dist. LEXIS 114738 (D. Minn. 2009d).

ACLU Minn. v. Tarek ibn Ziyad Acad., 2010 U.S. Dist. LEXIS 44818 (D. Minn. 2010).

ACLU Minn. v. Tarek ibn Ziyad Acad., 643 F.3d 1088 (8th Cir. Minn. 2011).

Americans United for Separation of Church and State. (2012, June). *Charter for controversy*. Retrieved from www.au.org/church-state/june-2012-church-state/featured/charter-for-controversy

Batdorff, M., Maloney, L, May, J., Speakman, S., Wolf, P., & Cheng, A. (2014). *Charter school funding: Inequity expands*. Fayetteville, AR: University of Arkansas.

Bauchman v. West High Sch., 132 F.3d 542 (10th Cir. 1997).

Becket Fund for Religious Liberty. (n.d.). *Text of the federal Blaine Amendment (1875)*. Retrieved from web.archive.org/web/20021008090825/http://www.blaineamendments.org:80/background/BAtext-US.html

Brown v. Hot, Sexy and Safer Prods., 68 F.3d 525 (1st Cir. 1995).

Buchanan, N. K., & Fox, R. A. (2003). To learn and to belong: A case study of emerging ethnocentric charter schools in Hawaii. *Educational Policy Analysis Archives, 11*(8) [online]. Retrieved from epaa.asu.edu/ojs/article/download/236/362

Buchanan, N. K., & Fox, R. A. (2005). Back to the future: Ethnocentric charter schools in Hawaii. In E. Rofes & L. M. Stulberg (Eds.), *The emancipatory promise of charter schools: Towards a progressive politics of school choice* (pp. 77–106). New York, NY: State University of New York Press.

Budde, R. (1974). *Education by charter*. Andover, MA: Regional Laboratory for Educational Improvement of the Northeast and Islands.

Budde, R. (1988). *Education by charter: Restructuring school districts*. San Francisco, CA: WestEd.

Burks, M. (2015). San Diego Unified expands halal school lunch program. *KPBS*. Retrieved from www.kpbs.org/news/2015/nov/11/san-diego-unified-expands-halal-school-lunch-progr/

Clawson, C. (2011, August 9). Florida Christian school magically becomes public charter school. *Daily Kos*. Retrieved from www.dailykos.com/story/2011/8/9/1004935/-

Cobb, C. D., & Glass, G. V. (2009). School choice in a post-desegregation world. *Peabody Journal of Education, 84*(2), 262–278.

Cohen, R. (2013, August 5). Are Hebrew language charter schools really religious schools? *Nonprofit Quarterly*. Retrieved from nonprofitquarterly.org/2013/08/05/are-hebrew-language-charter-schools-really-jewish-religious-schools/

County of Allegheny v. ACLU, 492 U.S. 573 (1989). [cf. supreme.justia.com/cases/federal/us/492/573]

Creno, C. (2014, July 14). Mesa charter school teaches religion, group says. *Arizona Republic*. Retrieved from www.azcentral.com/story/news/local/mesa/2014/07/14/mesa-charter-school-religion/12615041

Daugherty v. Vanguard Charter Sch. Acad., 116 F.Supp.2d 897 (W.D. Mich. 2000).

Decker, J. R., & Carr, K. (2015). Church state entanglement at religiously affiliated charter schools. *Brigham Young University Education & Law Journal, 2015*(1), 77–105.

Doe v. Elmbrook Sch. Dist., 687 F.3d 840 (7th Cir. 2012).

Eckes, S., & Fetter-Harrott, A. (2014). Religion and the public school curriculum. In C. J. Russo (Ed.), *International perspectives on education, religion and law* (pp. 28–41). New York, NY: Routledge.

Eckes, S., Fox, R., & Buchanan, N. (2011). Legal and policy issues regarding niche charter schools: Race, religion, culture and the law. *Journal of School Choice, 5*(1), 85–110.

Edwards v. Aguillard, 482 U.S 578 (1987).

Engel v. Vitale, 379 U.S. 421 (1962).

Epperson v. Arkansas, 393 U.S. 97 (1968).

Finley, B. (2015). Growing charter school segregation. *San Diego Law Review, 52*(1), 933–949.

Fox, R. A., & Buchanan, N. K. (Eds.). (2014). *Proud to be different: Ethnocentric niche charter schools in America.* New York, NY: Rowman & Littlefield.

Fox, R., Buchanan, N., Eckes, S., & Basford, L. (2012). The line between cultural education and religious education: Do ethnocentric niche charter schools have a prayer? *Review of Research in Education, 36*(1), 282–306.

Green, P. C., III. (2001). Racial balance provisions and charter schools: Are charter schools out on a constitutional limb? *Brigham Young University Education & Law Journal, 2001*(1), 65–85.

Harvard University Native American Program. (n.d.). *Native Hawaiian statistics.* Retrieved from www.hunapstatisticsproject.info/NativeHawaiianCategory/NativeHawaiian Employment.htm

Kahlenberg, R. D. (2008, March 25). The charter school idea turns 20: A history of the evolution and role reversals. *Education Week.* Retrieved from www.edweek.org/ew/articles/2008/03/26/29kahlenberg_ep.h27.html

Kamehameha Schools. (2016). *Living Hawaiian culture: Kumukahi. Kahuna.* Retrieved from www.kumukahi.org/units/na_kanaka/kaiaulu/kahuna

Kamehameha Schools. (n.d.). *Learning place, protocol for each chant.* Retrieved from apps.ksbe.edu/olelo/learning-place/chant/foundational/recite-memorized-chants

Kamehameha Schools & Bernice Pauahi Bishop Estate. (1983). *Native Hawaiian educational assessment project.* Retrieved from www.ksbe.edu/_assets/spi/pdfs/kh/NHEA_1983. pdf

Kersten, K. (2008, September 11). Storm brewing between state officials and TiZA school. *Star Tribune.* Retrieved from www.startribune.com/katherine-kersten-storm-brewing-between-state-officials-and-tiza-school/28117969

Kolderie, T. (2005). Ray Budde and the origins of the "charter concept." *Education Evolving.* Retrieved from www.educationevolving.org/pdf/Ray-Budde-Origins-Of-Chartering. pdf

Kopplin, Z. (2014, January 16). Texas public schools are teaching creationism. *Slate. com.* Retrieved from www.slate.com/articles/health_and_science/science/2014/01/creationism_in_texas_public_schools_undermining_the_charter_movement.html

Lee v. Weisman, 505 U.S. 577 (1992).

Leebaert v. Harrington, 332 F.3d 134 (2d Cir. 2003).

Lemon v. Kurtzman, 403 U.S. 602 (1971).

Markind, J. (2015). Federal government subsidizes halal food in public schools. *PJ Media.* Retrieved from pjmedia.com/blog/federal-government-subsidizes-halal-food-in-public-schools

Medina, J. (2010, June 24). Success and scrutiny at Hebrew charter school. *New York Times.* Retrieved from www.nytimes.com/2010/06/25/nyregion/25hebrew.html?_r=0

Meyer v. Nebraska, 263 U.S. 390 (1923).

Mullally, C. (2011, September 16). Free-Exercise Clause overview. *First Amendment Center.* Retrieved from www.firstamendmentcenter.org/free-exercise-clause

Mulvey, J. D., Cooper, B. S., & Maloney, A. T. (2010). *Blurring the lines: Charter, public, private, religious schools come together.* Charlotte, NC: Information Age.

Nampa Classical Acad. v. Goesling, 714 F. Supp. 2d 1079 (D. Idaho 2010).

National Alliance for Public Charter Schools. (2013). *Public charter school facilities: Results from the NAPCS national charter school survey, school year 2011–2012.* Washington DC: Author.

National Catholic Education Association. (2016). *United States Catholic elementary and secondary schools 2015–2016: The annual statistical report on schools, enrollment, and staffing.* Retrieved from www.ncea.org/NCEA/Proclaim/Catholic_School_Data/ NCEA/Proclaim/Catholic_School_Data/Catholic_School_Data.aspx?hkey=8e90e-6aa-b9c4-456b-a488-6397f3640f05

New York State Assembly. (2015). *Regular sessions, A00695.* Retrieved from assembly.state. ny.us/leg/?default_fld=&bn=A00695&term=2015&Summary=Y&Text=Y

Ohukaniohia Gon, S. M., III. (2007). *What is Hana Kupono (Hawaiian Protocol)?* Retrieved from www.mgf-hawaii.org/HTML/Hula/hula_hawaiian_protocol.htm

Orfield, G., & Lee, C. (2004, January). Brown *at 50: King's dream or Plessy's nightmare?* Cambridge, MA: Civil Rights Project, Harvard University. Retrieved from www. civilrightsproject.ucla.edu/research/k-12-education/integration-and-diversity/brown-at-50-king2019s-dream-or-plessy2019s-nightmare/orfield-brown-50-2004.pdf

Pew Research Center. (2003). *Separation of church and states.* Retrieved from www. pewforum.org/2003/03/28/separation-of-church-and-states-an-examina-tion-of-state-constitutional-limits-on-government-funding-for-religious-institutions

Pew Research Center. (2008, July 24). *The Blaine game: Controversy over the Blaine amendments and public funding of religion.* Retrieved from www.pewforum.org/2008/07/24/ the-blaine-game-controversy-over-the-blaine-amendments-and-public-funding-of-religion

Pierce v. Society of Sisters, 268 U.S. 510 (1925).

Porta v. Klagholz, 19 F. Supp. 2d 290 (D.N.J. 1998).

Saiger, A. (2013). Charter schools, the Establishment Clause, and the neoliberal turn in public education. *Cardozo Law Review, 34*(4), 1163–1226.

Sanchez, C. (2008, September 16). To remain open, Catholic schools become charters. *National Public Radio.* Retrieved from www.npr.org/templates/story/story.php?story-Id=94680744

Santa Fe Indep. Sch. Dist. v. Doe, 530 U.S. 290 (2000).

Saul, S. (2011, June 6). Charter schools tied to Turkey grow in Texas. *New York Times.* Retrieved from www.nytimes.com/2011/06/07/education/07charter.html?_r=0

Saunders, T. (1981). Reviser's introduction. In *The politics by Aristotle* (pp. 29–44). New York, NY: Penguin.

School Dist. of Abington Township, Penn. v. Schempp, 374 U.S. 203 (1963).

Scott, M. (2015, September 30). Civil rights complaint forces school to change role in religious ceremony. *Michigan Live.* Retrieved from www.mlive.com/news/grand-rapids/ index.ssf/2015/09/complaint_causes_school_distri.html

Scruggs, L. (2015). *Separation of church and school: Guidance for public charter schools using religious facilities.* Washington, DC: National Alliance for Public Charter Schools.

Shanker, A. (1988). National press club speech, Washington, DC. Retrieved from reuther. wayne.edu/files/64.43.pdf

Siracusa-Hillman, B. (2008). Is there a place for religious charter schools? *Yale Law Journal, 118*(3), 554–599.

Smith, M. (2013, August 10). When charter schools are in churches, conflict is in the air. *New York Times.* Retrieved from www.nytimes.com/2013/08/11/us/when-charter-schools-are-in-churches-conflict-is-in-the-air.html

Svokos, A. (2014, November 21). North Carolina charter school updates religion policy after teacher's prayer in class. *Huffington Post*. Retrieved from www.huffingtonpost.com/2014/11/21/charter-school-classroom-prayer_n_6201594.html

Takayama, B. (2008). Academic achievement across school types in Hawaii: Outcomes for Hawaiian and non-Hawaiian students in conventional public schools, western focused charters, and Hawaiian language and culture-based schools. *Hūlili: Multidisciplinary Research on Hawaiian Well-Being, 5*, 245–283.

Terrell, J. (2015, June 29). Is school prayer crossing a line at some Hawaii charter schools? *Honolulu Civil Beat*. Retrieved from www.civilbeat.org/2015/06/is-school-prayer-crossing-a-line-at-some-hawaii-charter-schools

U.S. Constitution, Amendment I. (1791). Retrieved from www.archives.gov/exhibits/charters/bill_of_rights_transcript.html

U.S. Department of Education. (2003). *Guidance on constitutionally protected prayer in public elementary and secondary schools.* Retrieved from www2.ed.gov/policy/gen/guid/religionandschools/prayer_guidance.html

U.S. Department of Education. (2014). *Charter schools program, Title V, Part B of the ESEA, Nonregulatory guidance.* Washington, DC: Author. Retrieved from www2.ed.gov/programs/charter/fy14cspnonregguidance.doc

Wallace v. Jaffree, 472 U.S. 38 (1985).

Weinberg, L. D., & Cooper, B. S. (2007, June 18). What about religious charter schools? *Education Week*. Retrieved from www.edweek.org/ew/articles/2007/06/20/42cooper.h26.html

Wisconsin v. Yoder, 406 U.S. 205 (1972).

Zorach v. Clauson, 342 U.S. 306 (1952).

CHAPTER 12

How the Design of School Choice Can Further Integration

Jennifer B. Ayscue and Erica Frankenberg

Separate educational facilities are inherently unequal.

—Earl Warren, *Brown v. Board of Education*

The United States' increasingly diverse public school enrollment provides opportunities for creating racially desegregated schools. However, since the peak of desegregation in the 1980s, school segregation has been intensifying in many districts (Orfield & Frankenberg, 2014).[1] This trend is cause for concern because segregation is systematically related to unequal educational opportunities and outcomes, while integration is related to numerous academic, social, and economic benefits for students and communities (Linn & Welner, 2007; Mickelson & Nkomo, 2012). As the education landscape has shifted its focus from equity and access to competition and accountability, choice has also expanded (Petrovich & Wells, 2005) and is likely to continue to grow. Choice can support desegregation because it breaks the link between school and residential segregation, allowing students and families to choose schools outside of their neighborhoods and allowing schools to draw from a more diverse set of students than those typically residing in close proximity to one another. However, if not regulated with diversity as a goal, choice can segregate and further stratify students. The purpose of this chapter is to identify how the design of choice can further integration by learning from history and the various forms of choice that have existed in the educational landscape.

School choice encompasses a broad umbrella of different types of policy design, with different theoretical assumptions, primarily in terms of importance given to individual preferences as compared to community goals. These differences hold even when examining only charter schools. The market theory of school choice presumes that choice is beneficial because it creates a marketplace that will produce better results than government as schools respond to the choices made by families. For charter schools specifically, flexibility was provided so that the schools would be able to experiment, parents would choose the best schools, and the strongest schools would survive while those not chosen would be forced either to transform or close. However, critics question the assumptions of the market theory, arguing that schooling might be too complex for families to understand what types of choices are best for their child, assuming they have full knowledge of all options and the ability to choose (e.g., Orfield, 2013). Moreover, research on charter school choices continues to illustrate the extent to which racial composition influences choices made (Frankenberg, Kotok, Schafft, & Mann, 2017; Weiher & Tedin, 2002) and that some charter schools have requirements that limit entry for all. By contrast, the integration theory of school choice places more priority on group preferences, thereby giving a larger role to the government in terms of whether families' choices are granted if the result of the choices would conflict with a community's goal of diversity; in some instances, this requires denying some families' choices and, in other cases, welcoming more students of color to largely white, affluent schools.

A school choice system, such as charter schools, designed based on the market theory of choice is not likely to facilitate integration and, more often, leads to increased segregation. However, by examining research about school choice systems such as magnet schools and districtwide controlled choice plans, it is possible to identify policies and practices that could transform the design of charter schools so that they further integration.

HISTORY OF CHOICE AND DESEGREGATION

Resisting Desegregation with Freedom of Choice, Vouchers, and Open-Enrollment Plans

In the 1954 *Brown v. Board of Education* decision, the Supreme Court unanimously decided that segregated schools were "inherently unequal" but did not specify the means by which desegregation must be achieved. Without the weight of enforcement in the ruling, many Southern states adopted freedom-of-choice plans, which were intended to minimize the impact of desegregation by permitting students to select their schools. White students continued to attend formerly white schools, while black students had to apply for transfers to white schools. Often accompanied by a burdensome process and threats from the white community, this early form of public school choice essentially allowed segregation to persist. It was not until 1968 with *Green v. New Kent County* that the Court required segregation to be dismantled "root and branch," specified the factors that must be addressed, and forbade the district's use of a freedom-of-choice plan because it had done little to achieve desegregation, placing the responsibility for desegregation on individual students of color without a systemic effort to address segregation. In such instances—then and now—choice is likely to have limited, if any, impact on integration.

Mounting a campaign of massive resistance, the state of Virginia used a different form of choice—vouchers—to stall desegregation. The Virginia state legislature enacted a law that called for the closing of any school that began integration, and the governor closed schools in several districts rather than allow them to desegregate. In 1959, Prince Edward County, Virginia, closed its entire school system and instead provided tuition grants, or vouchers, for white students to attend new private white academies. Because there were no private schools for African American students, these students were left with no schooling options.

Unlike the 17 states in the South that had *de jure* segregation, cities in the North maintained segregated schools by linking schools to segregated housing patterns, changing school boundary lines as neighborhoods changed. As nonwhite populations grew, some white families remained in predominantly minority neighborhoods and schools. To allow these white students to attend white schools, many cities created optional attendance zones and adopted open-enrollment policies that allowed families to transfer schools, thereby maintaining a system of racially segregated schools (Orfield, 2013).

Facilitating Desegregation with Transfers, Magnets, and Controlled Choice

The combination of the 1964 Civil Rights Act, which tied federal funding to desegregation efforts, and the *Green* decision meant that schools had to take more proactive steps toward actual desegregation rather than token desegregation. Subsequently, desegregation efforts often required the reassignment of students to different schools, which could include busing students to assigned schools in order to achieve desegregation. Later efforts included more voluntary measures based on an integration theory of choice; as such, these efforts, including transfers, magnet schools, and controlled choice, allowed for some family choice in order to achieve racial desegregation goals.

Beginning in the 1960s, many desegregation plans included a majority-to-minority transfer plan, which allowed students to transfer from a school in which they were part of the racial majority to a school in which they would be part of the racial minority. Transfer policies were typically within a district, but some popular examples of desegregation policies included between-district transfers. While they could enhance desegregation efforts, transfer plans often had a limited impact because rather than creating a system of magnet schools that had diversity goals or creating a districtwide controlled choice policy that involved all students, transfer plans relied on a subset of students making the choice to move from one school to another.

Magnet schools were created in the 1970s as a voluntary tool for desegregation, pioneered by leaders in Milwaukee, Cincinnati, and Buffalo. Often sited in schools that had been predominantly attended by students of color, magnets were intended to attract diverse groups of students through the use of innovative themes and curricula coupled with active recruitment. Historically, magnets often had diversity guidelines and free transportation to facilitate desegregation; however, magnets currently vary in their commitment to this goal. As part of the *Sheff v. O'Neill* mandate, Connecticut operates a system of interdistrict magnet schools (54 schools in 2007), which are intended to reduce, eliminate, or prevent racial, ethnic, or economic isolation. These interdistrict magnets have been successful in providing less segregated learning environments—including having higher percentages of white students and lower percentages of free lunch–eligible students—for minority students coming from the most isolated central cities as well as for white students from suburban districts (Cobb, Bifulco, & Bell, 2011). A study of eight interdistrict magnet programs found that in addition to less segregation, they also resulted in higher student achievement, better racial attitudes, growing acceptance across races, and improved long-term outcomes, such as higher graduation and college-going rates as well as higher occupational aspirations and attainment (Wells, Warner, & Grzesikowski, 2013).

In 1981, Cambridge, Massachusetts, was the first district to implement a controlled choice student assignment plan. Districtwide controlled choice policies operate through a process in which families rank schools and the district assigns students to schools according to their choices in ways that are compatible with the district's diversity goals. In this situation, there are no zoned schools; instead, all the district's schools are choice schools. Berkeley, California, is well known for its controlled choice plan, which it modified in 2004 to employ a sophisticated analysis of neighborhood characteristics, including race and income, to maintain racial desegregation, grant families one of their top three choices, and withstand challenge in California's courts (Frankenberg, 2013). The use of a controlled choice plan in Jefferson County, Kentucky, has allowed the district to largely maintain integrated schools, resulting in lower levels of segregation than would exist in comparison to a simulated, non–integration-focused policy (Frankenberg, 2017). Other work has found that districts with a "strong" or more comprehensive use of diversity in student assignment policies—as is the case among controlled choice policies—are more racially diverse (Reardon & Rhodes, 2011).

Abandoning Diversity Goals, Embracing Charter Schools

Following the 1991 Supreme Court decision in *Board of Education v. Dowell*, numerous school districts were released from court-ordered desegregation. As court-ordered desegregation dwindled, the use of choice for voluntarily adopted integration efforts became even more important. In the 2007 *Parents Involved in Community Schools v. Seattle* decision, the Supreme Court decided that in voluntarily adopted integration plans, student assignment decisions could not be based solely on an individual student's race. Already, fewer districts were employing integration policies than during the era of court-ordered desegregation and, consequently, many districts either shifted their voluntary desegregation efforts to race-neutral diversity plans that considered socioeconomic status or abandoned diversity efforts altogether (Siegel-Hawley & Frankenberg, 2011b).

During the same time period, charter schools entered the educational landscape. However, unlike magnet schools, charter schools were not created with diversity goals; founded on the market theory of choice, charters were created to spur innovation and competition. Although early proponents hoped that charters might remedy segregation because they were not limited by district boundaries (Shanker, 1988; Wells, 1993), the more recent expansion of choice in the charter sector is largely unregulated with respect to diversity—as was the case with some earlier forms of choice—and, similarly, is linked to intensifying segregation (Frankenberg, Siegel-Hawley, & Wang, 2010; Ladd, Clotfelter, & Holbein, 2015).

HOW CHOICE CAN FACILITATE INTEGRATION

As our nation's educational history with school choice demonstrates, choice can either facilitate desegregation or exacerbate segregation. Understanding the ways in which regulated choice furthers integration can inform the design of current choice systems, including the segregated charter sector, so that they can become more equitable, accessible, and diverse.

Diversity Goals

First, diversity goals are an important foundation for creating lasting integration. As described above, some, although not all, magnet schools continue to pursue diversity goals, and those that have desegregation goals tend to be more diverse than those without such goals (Siegel-Hawley & Frankenberg, 2013). The federal Magnet School Assistance Program (MSAP) has required that grantees identify goals and strategies for addressing racial isolation.

While some charter schools have diversity goals, including those that are members of the National Coalition of Diverse Charter Schools, many charters have been designed to meet the needs of a particular homogeneous group of students, such as low-income students, immigrants, or racial minorities (Kahlenberg & Potter, 2014). This pattern could be due, in part, to the fact that some education policy and philanthropic communities have prioritized funding for charter schools that serve high concentrations of low-income and minority students (Scott, 2009). In about a dozen states, charter legislation prioritizes funding for charters that intend to serve large numbers of at-risk or low-income students (Kahlenberg & Potter, 2012); state laws might also make it difficult for charter schools to draw students across district boundary lines. Additionally, some federal funding programs give incentives for serving more low-income students. Taken together, along with the demographic overlap in economically and racially concentrated communities, these public and private forces provide disincentives for charter schools to achieve racial and socioeconomic diversity.

State charter laws vary considerably regarding the extent to which they require affirmative efforts to maintain diverse enrollments in charter schools, although a review of court challenges and administrative investigation found little evidence that such provisions are enforced (Siegel-Hawley & Frankenberg, 2011a). In fact, one state retained a "racial balance" provision in its charter school law while formally agreeing not to enforce it. The Obama administration incorporated some diversity preferences in competitive funding grants for charter schools in recent years (National Coalition on School Diversity, 2017). The most recent federal charter schools program funding cycle for state agencies included points based on whether they were "approving charter school petitions with design elements that incorporate evidence-based school models and practices, including, but not limited to, school models and practices that focus on racial and ethnic diversity in student bodies" (National Coalition on School Diversity, 2017, p. 9).

Having diversity goals is important, but schools and districts must also implement strategies to achieve their goals, a number of which—including outreach and recruitment, noncompetitive admissions criteria, weighted lotteries, and transportation—were recently promoted by the U.S. Department of Education (2017) as strategies to increase student diversity. The federal government also released guidance in 2014 about protecting the civil rights of all students in charter schools because of concerns about disproportionate access and retention for students from some historically disadvantaged backgrounds (U.S. Department of Education, 2014).

Outreach and Admissions

Ensuring that a diverse group of students and families is aware of the choices being offered is essential. Information is often shared informally through social networks, which tend to include people who are similar to one another (Holme, 2002; McPherson, Smith-Lovin, & Cook, 2001); thus, it is incumbent upon the school and/or district to provide information to diverse groups of families. To recruit a diverse student body, it is important to target a broad demographic by providing information in multiple forms, including online, in print, and by phone, as well as in languages other than English (Dougherty et al., 2013). In addition, the U.S. Department of Education (2017) recommends using an enrollment guide, school fairs or expos, and a single, universal application.

When demand for choice programs exceeds capacity, schools can use admissions criteria, lotteries, or open enrollment to admit students. A sample of 236 magnet programs indicated that magnets that used lotteries or open enrollment had the highest levels of desegregation (Siegel-Hawley & Frankenberg, 2013). Of the magnets that used admissions criteria, those that used competitive admissions criteria, including auditions, test scores, and grade point averages, were less likely to be desegregated than those that used more holistic approaches, such as interviews and essays. In addition, at least 11 of the nation's 165 competitive admissions exam schools that require students to take an exam as part of the entrance criteria—including all eight of New York City's specialized high schools (Adegbile et al., 2012) and two high schools in Buffalo (Orfield et al., 2015)—have been under civil rights investigation for racial disproportionality in admissions.

In many schools of choice, lotteries are held to select students randomly. This approach is seen as more equitable than allocating seats on a first-come, first-served basis, which might privilege more advantaged families. Most choice programs receiving federal funding are encouraged to use a lottery of some kind. In some cases, such as districtwide controlled choice plans, districts use lotteries for making all student assignments. In other cases, individual schools, such as magnets or charters, use lotteries to admit students to a single school.

Before conducting the lottery, the district or individual school sometimes assigns weights to students with specified characteristics so that they have an increased likelihood of being selected from the applicant pool. For example, siblings of current students, children of staff members, or children living within close proximity to the desired school often receive an extra weight. These types of weights will likely not contribute to creating diversity because they replicate existing enrollment patterns and, in the case of proximity weights, perpetuate the association between residential and school segregation. However, some districts or schools assign diversity-related weights. For example, low-income students or students from a designated area of the district in which there is a high percentage of students of color might receive a weight. Districts under court-ordered desegregation could use an individual student's race as a factor in weighted lotteries, but those implementing voluntary desegregation typically use a student's socioeconomic status (often based on whether a student qualifies for free or reduced-priced lunch) as a factor for the weighted lottery, or use the racial composition of a geographic area.[2] In controlled choice plans, weighted lotteries can help entire school districts achieve their diversity goals by employing algorithms that seek to admit students from different diversity categories into each school (Chavez & Frankenberg, 2009; Frankenberg, 2017).

MSAP includes a competitive priority for funding magnet schools that use lotteries as opposed to selective admissions criteria. Although no states explicitly prohibit the use of weighted lotteries in charter schools, only four expressly permit them. In other states with charter schools, laws related to the use of weighted lotteries are ambiguous (Baum, 2015). In 2014, federal guidance from the U.S. Department of Education expanded the circumstances in which charter schools receiving funding from the Charter Schools Program could use weighted lotteries (U.S. Department of Education, 2014). When consistent with state law, charters receiving Charter Schools Program funds can use weights for educationally disadvantaged students, including students who are economically disadvantaged, students with disabilities, migrant students, limited-English-proficient students, neglected or delinquent students, and homeless students. In a study of eight charter schools that have been able to create diverse student enrollments, providing weights for income or geographic areas was important for creating diversity in five of the eight schools (Kahlenberg & Potter, 2014).

Transportation and Location

Provision of transportation is essential to make school choice a realistic option for all families and not just those with the resources and flexibility to transport their children to school. Since 1965, the Department of Health, Education, and Welfare (and now the Department of Education) has recognized the need for transportation to support desegregation (Orfield, 1969), and for many years, the provision of transportation was a requirement for MSAP grantees. Although it is not currently mandatory, the 2017 grant cycle for the MSAP allows grantees to use grant funds for transportation costs as described in the Every Student Succeeds Act. Transportation requirements for charter schools vary according to state law. Not all charters are required to provide transportation (Siegel-Hawley & Frankenberg, 2011a). In 18 states and Washington, DC, charters are provided with transportation funding similar to the funding that district schools receive; in six additional states, charters receive some, although less, funding for transportation than district schools (Potter, 2015). Intentionally locating schools of choice in areas that are easily accessible by families of different racial and economic backgrounds, particularly when free transportation is not provided, is important for supporting integration efforts. Locating a school in a mixed-income neighborhood or selecting a location accessible to students from different communities can also be effective. With a substantial share of charter schools located in suburban settings (Frankenberg et al., 2011), it should be feasible to find a school location that is proximate to neighborhoods that contain both white families and families of color.

Interdistrict Choice

Interdistrict choice programs allow students to attend schools outside of their home school district. Because the majority of current segregation is due to segregation between school districts (Clotfelter, 2004; Reardon, Yun, & Eitle, 2000; Stroub & Richards, 2013), this metropolitan-wide approach to encouraging students to voluntarily cross district boundaries is an important way of creating more integrated learning environments. This approach is particularly important in places where school districts themselves are racially isolated, making integration efforts within the school district logistically challenging and sometimes not feasible. Where state charter school laws permit charter schools to draw students from multiple districts, interdistrict enrollment could help to create more diversity. Charter school laws in 11 states provide for transportation of students to charter schools in some circumstances beyond the district in which the student resides (Siegel-Hawley & Frankenberg, 2011a).

Currently, eight unique interdistrict transfer programs allow students from central-city schools, who tend to be low-income students of color, to transfer to suburban schools, which are likely to be more white and middle class (Wells et al., 2013). The Metropolitan Council for Educational Opportunity (METCO), which was established in 1966 and is the longest-running interdistrict transfer program, allows students from Boston to attend schools in more than 30 suburban districts. The program has proven educational and long-term benefits (Eaton, 2001). However, funding for METCO has been historically unstable, and demand for the program has exceeded its capacity (Eaton & Chirichigno, 2011). The success of METCO and other interdistrict transfer programs suggest that these programs could be successful models for creating diverse schools in other metropolitan areas.

Charter schools have a unique potential to draw students from across a broad geographic area, cutting across district boundary lines. In most cases, charter schools are not bound by school catchment zones, nor are they bound by district boundary lines. In 36 of the 43 states where charters currently exist, some charter schools do not have a required preference for in-district students (Potter, 2015). Therefore, the potential for interdistrict or regional charter schools exists in these 36 states. However, there are only a very few examples, including Blackstone Valley Prep Mayoral Academy in Rhode Island and the Interdistrict School for Arts and Communication in Connecticut, of intentionally creating regional charter schools. Blackstone Valley Prep Mayoral Academy serves students from four communities, two of which are higher-income suburban communities and two of which are lower-income urban communities, creating a racially and socioeconomically diverse student body (Potter, 2015). Maintaining diversity in charter schools by pulling from multiple public school districts may be especially difficult and require cooperation between charter school operators and relevant district administrators to achieve the charter school's goal. Federal and state policies could create incentives for charter schools to engage in interdistrict enrollment efforts that foster diversity.

In many ways, the charter school sector as a whole, with some exceptions of individual charter schools, has not embraced the potential of choice to support desegregation and is not using the strategies described above (Welner, 2013). Therefore, it is not surprising that charter schools, unlike other forms of regulated choice, tend to be more segregated (Frankenberg et al., 2011; Ladd et al., 2015).

PERSISTENCE IN THE FACE OF CHALLENGE

Efforts to pursue integration are often met with logistical challenges and political resistance. Logistically, residential segregation is a major impediment to desegregation efforts. The role of residential segregation in perpetuating school segregation highlights the need for coordination between housing agencies and education agencies in order to address segregation. In particular, as communities address the new housing regulations to affirmatively further fair housing and reduce the disparate impact of housing policies, the Departments of Housing and Urban Development, Education, and Transportation (2016) called on local leaders to work together across jurisdictions to break down impediments to accessing opportunity, including to diverse schools. School choice can be helpful for addressing segregation because it breaks the link between residential and school segregation by not relying on a system of assigning students to the school closest in proximity to their home.

Demographic change across the nation is altering the racial enrollment of public schools, creating a more multiracial enrollment that may make integration more feasible (Frey, 2014), particularly in suburban areas that have historically been more white and middle class (Frankenberg & Orfield, 2012). Gentrification in urban areas also offers an opportunity for creating diverse schools in areas that historically have been more segregated, presuming the middle-class households have school-aged children and enroll them in public schools and the communities of color are not displaced (Mordechay & Ayscue, 2017). By monitoring demographic data and adopting regulated choice systems with diversity goals and strategies to achieve those goals, school districts and charter schools can harness the potential of increased diversity to create more desegregated schools. However, if left unattended, as history has demonstrated, it is likely that segregation will persist, and perhaps even intensify, particularly if a school choice system is unregulated. Once achieved, school diversity can be difficult to sustain due to changing demographic and sociopolitical contexts, shifting priorities, or a sense that desegregation has been achieved and no longer needs attention.

In geographic areas with little racial diversity, a different challenge exists. For example, some areas have such a small share of white students that it is nearly impossible to create desegregation within the nearby area or school district. In such instances, other approaches that are more regional in nature, such as interdistrict transfers or regional charters or magnets, could be more effective than neighborhood or within-district options.

Developing the political will needed to support integration efforts through choice policies is also challenging, perhaps particularly so if they cross jurisdictions. Surveys of students and parents involved in desegregation efforts find that they favor diversity and continuing desegregation efforts (Orfield & Frankenberg, 2013). Some charter schools and intentionally diverse districts struggle to maintain racial and economic diversity because the diversity is so valued by white parents seeking diverse environments for their children that white families flood the diverse schools. In such cases, students of color, the very students who are providing the diversity that the white parents originally desired, are pushed out, resulting in a school that is no longer racially diverse. However, recent examples of districts working to expand access and diversity in their choice systems in Buffalo, New York (Orfield et al., 2015), Charlotte, North Carolina (Mickelson, Giersch, Hawn Nelson, & Bottia, 2018), and Montgomery County, Maryland (Ayscue, 2017) reveal that actually creating or changing a choice system so that it promotes diversity is often met with strong resistance by those who believe they are currently benefitting from it—white middle-class families—and who want to preserve the status quo.

Having strong community and business partnerships can be helpful for building support and political will. To enhance the curricular theme, magnet schools often have partnerships that can be beneficial for building community support of the magnet. In addition, business and military leaders filed briefs in recent cases in which the Supreme Court considered policies to promote diversity in K–12 and higher education. These leaders asserted that a diverse educational environment is important because the cross-cultural experience and understanding that students develop while attending racially diverse schools are necessary for our multiracial society and global marketplace.

CONCLUSION

Using choice to facilitate desegregation can be challenging, but ensuring that choice facilitates desegregation rather than exacerbates segregation is essential, particularly when public school enrollment is becoming majority nonwhite. Research continues to confirm the benefits of racially and economically diverse schools for all students. Desegregated schools are associated with improved academic achievement, enhanced intergroup relations, and positive long-term life outcomes (Linn & Welner, 2007; Mickelson & Nkomo, 2012). Students who attend desegregated schools achieve at higher levels and are less likely to drop out of high school (Balfanz & Legters, 2004; Hallinan, 1998; Swanson, 2004). Attending desegregated schools is also linked to lower prejudice, negative attitudes, and stereotypes, while also increasing friendships and comfort with peers of diverse backgrounds as well as critical thinking, communication, and problem solving (Allport, 1954; Kurlaender & Yun, 2001, 2005, 2007; Pettigrew & Tropp, 2006; Tropp & Prenevost, 2008). In the long term, desegregated schools are associated with increased educational and occupational attainment, higher college quality and adult earnings, reduced likelihood of incarceration, better health, and greater likelihood of living and working in diverse environments later in life (Braddock & McPartland, 1989; Johnson, 2011; Wells & Crain, 1994).

Therefore, understanding how various choice mechanisms can help districts and schools achieve diverse enrollments is critical. It is possible to identify the potential that charter schools have for facilitating or constraining diversity by examining research on a variety of forms of choice—those that have had some success in achieving desegregation, such as magnet schools and controlled choice, and those that have more often furthered segregation, such as freedom-of-choice plans, vouchers, and open enrollment.

NOTES

1. Trends in school segregation vary depending on the methods used to measure segregation (Orfield, Siegel-Hawley, & Kucsera, 2014; Reardon & Owens, 2014). Using two key measures of segregation—concentration and exposure/isolation—segregation has been intensifying (Orfield & Frankenberg, 2014). These patterns vary by racial group and region of the country.

2. In *Parents Involved in Community Schools v. Seattle* (2007), the Supreme Court ruled that school districts could not consider the race of an individual student as the deciding factor when assigning students to schools; however, school districts may consider the overall racial composition of a geographic area, such as a neighborhood, or use race as one of multiple factors in student assignment policies (U.S. Department of Justice & U.S. Department of Education, 2011).

REFERENCES

Adegbile, D. P., Boddie, E., Hewitt, D. T., Kleinman, R. M., Smith-Evans, L., . . . Gibbs, J. (2012, September 27). *The admissions process for New York City's elite public high schools violates Title VI of the Civil Rights Act of 1964 and its implementing regulations* [Letter to the New York Office, Office for Civil Rights, U.S. Department of Education]. Retrieved from www.naacpldf.org/files/case_issue/Specialized%20High%20 Schools%20Complaint.pdf

Allport, G. W. (1954). *The nature of prejudice.* Reading, MA: Addison Wesley.

Ayscue, J. B. (2017, February). *Reclaiming the potential for equity and diversity in Montgomery County's schools of choice.* Washington, DC: National Coalition on School Diversity.

Balfanz, R., & Legters, N. E. (2004). Locating the dropout crisis: Which high schools produce the nation's dropouts? In G. Orfield (Ed.), *Dropouts in America: Confronting the graduation crisis* (pp. 57–84). Cambridge, MA: Harvard Education Press.

Baum, L. E. (2015). *State laws on weighted lotteries and enrollment practices.* Washington, DC: National Alliance for Public Charter Schools.

Board of Education of Oklahoma v. Dowell, 498 U.S. 237 (1991).

Braddock, J. H., & McPartland, J. M. (1989). Social-psychological processes that perpetuate racial segregation: The relationship between school and employment desegregation. *Journal of Black Studies, 19*(3), 267–289.

Brown v. Board of Education of Topeka, 347 U.S. 483 (1954).

Chavez, L., & Frankenberg, E. (2009). *Integration defended: Berkeley Unified's strategy to maintain school diversity.* Berkeley, CA: The Chief Justice Earl Warren Institute on Race, Ethnicity & Diversity; Los Angeles, CA: Civil Rights Project.

Clotfelter, C. T. (2004). *After* Brown: *The rise and retreat of school desegregation.* Princeton, NJ: Princeton University Press.

Cobb, C. D., Bifulco, R., & Bell, C. (2011). Legally viable desegregation strategies: The case of Connecticut. In E. Frankenberg & E. DeBray (Eds.), *Integrating schools in a changing society: New policies and legal options for a multiracial generation* (pp. 131–150). Chapel Hill, NC: University of North Carolina Press.

Dougherty, J., Zannoni, D., Chowhan, M., Coyne, C., Dawson, B., Guruge, T., & Nukic, B. (2013). School information, parental decisions, and the digital divide. In G. Orfield, E. Frankenberg, & Associates (Eds.), *Educational delusions? Why choice can deepen inequality and how to make schools fair* (pp. 221–239). Berkeley, CA: University of California Press.

Eaton, S. (2001). *The other Boston busing story: What's won and lost across the boundary line.* New Haven, CT: Yale University Press.

Eaton, S., & Chirichigno, G. (2011). *METCO merits more: The history and status of METCO.* Boston, MA: Pioneer Institute.

Frankenberg, E. (2013). The promise of choice: Berkeley's innovative integration plan. In G. Orfield, E. Frankenberg, & Associates (Eds.), *Educational delusions? Why choice can deepen inequality and how to make schools fair* (pp. 69–88). Berkeley, CA: University of California Press.

Frankenberg, E. (2017). Assessing segregation under a new generation of controlled choice policies. *American Educational Research Journal, 54*(1), 219–250.

Frankenberg, E., Kotok, S., Schafft, K., & Mann, B. (2017). Exploring school choice and the consequences for student racial segregation within Pennsylvania's charter school transfers. *Education Policy Analysis Archives, 25*(22), 1–34.

Frankenberg, E., & Orfield, G. (2012). *The resegregation of suburban schools: A hidden crisis in American education.* Cambridge, MA: Harvard Education Press.

Frankenberg, E., Siegel-Hawley, G., & Wang, J. (2011). Choice without equity: Charter school segregation. *Education Policy Analysis Archives, 19*(1), 1–96.

Frey, W. H. (2014). *Diversity explosion: How new racial demographics are remaking America.* Washington, DC: The Brookings Institution.

Green v. County School Board of New Kent County, 391 U.S. 430 (1968).

Hallinan, M. (1998). Diversity effects on student outcomes: Social science evidence. *Ohio State Law Journal, 59*, 733–754.

Holme, J. J. (2002). Buying homes, buying schools: School choice and the social construction of school quality. *Harvard Educational Review, 72*(2), 177–206.

Johnson, R. C. (2011). *Long-run impacts of school desegregation and school quality on adult attainments* [NBER Working Paper Series]. Cambridge, MA: National Bureau of Economic Research.

Kahlenberg, R. D., & Potter, H. (2012). *Diverse charter schools: Can racial and socioeconomic integration promote better outcomes for students?* Washington, DC: Poverty & Race Research Action Council and The Century Foundation.

Kahlenberg, R. D., & Potter, H. (2014). *A smarter charter: Finding what works for charter schools and public education.* New York, NY: Teachers College Press.

Kurlaender, M., & Yun, J. (2001). Is diversity a compelling educational interest? Evidence from Louisville. In G. Orfield (Ed.), *Diversity challenged* (pp. 111–141). Cambridge, MA: Harvard Education Publishing Group.

Kurlaender, M., & Yun, J. (2005). Fifty years after *Brown:* New evidence of the impact of school racial composition on student outcomes. *International Journal of Educational Policy, Research and Practice, 6*(1), 51–78.

Kurlaender, M., & Yun, J. T. (2007). Measuring school racial composition and student outcomes in a multiracial society. *American Journal of Education, 113*(2), 213–242.

Ladd, H. F., Clotfelter, C. T., & Holbein, J. B. (2015). *The growing segmentation of the charter school sector in North Carolina.* Cambridge, MA: National Bureau of Economic Research.

Linn, R., & Welner, K. (2007). *Race-conscious policies for assigning students to schools: Social science research and the Supreme Court cases.* Washington, DC: National Academy of Education.

McPherson, M., Smith-Lovin, L., & Cook, J. M. (2001). Birds of a feather: Homophily in social networks. *Annual Review of Sociology, 27*, 415–444.

Mickelson, R. A., Giersch, J., Hawn Nelson, A., & Bottia, M. C. (2018). Do charter schools undermine efforts to create racially and socioeconomically diverse public schools? In I. C. Rotberg & J. L. Glazer (Eds.), *Choosing charters: Better schools or more segregation?* (pp. 116–132). New York, NY: Teachers College Press.

Mickelson, R. A., & Nkomo, M. (2012). Integrated schooling, life course outcomes, and social cohesion in multiethnic democratic societies. *Review of Research in Education, 36*, 197–238.

Mordechay, K., & Ayscue, J. (2017). *White growth, persistent segregation: Could gentrification become integration?* Los Angeles, CA: Civil Rights Project.

National Coalition on School Diversity. (2017). *Federal support for school integration: An Obama administration review* [Issue Brief 8]. Washington, DC: Author. Retrieved from school-diversity.org/pdf/DiversityIssueBriefNo8.pdf

Orfield, G. (1969). *The reconstruction of Southern education: The schools and the 1964 Civil Rights Act.* Hoboken, NJ: John Wiley & Sons.

Orfield, G. (2013). Choice and civil rights: Forgetting history, facing consequences. In G. Orfield & E. Frankenberg (Eds.), *Educational delusions? Why choice can deepen inequality and how to make schools fair* (pp. 3–35). Berkeley, CA: University of California Press.

Orfield, G., Ayscue, J., Ee, J., Frankenberg, E., Siegel-Hawley, G., Woodward, B., & Amlani, N. (2015). *Better choices for Buffalo's students: Expanding and reforming the criteria schools system.* Los Angeles, CA: Civil Rights Project.

Orfield, G., & Frankenberg, E. (2013). Experiencing integration in Louisville: Attitudes on choice and diversity in a changing legal landscape. In G. Orfield & E. Frankenberg (Eds.), *Educational delusions? Why choice can deepen inequality and how to make schools fair* (pp. 238–254). Berkeley, CA: University of California Press.

Orfield, G., & Frankenberg, E. (2014). *Brown at 60: Great progress, a long retreat, and an uncertain future.* Los Angeles, CA: Civil Rights Project.

Orfield, G., Siegel-Hawley, G., & Kucsera, J. (2014). *Sorting out deepening confusion on segregation trends.* Los Angeles, CA: Civil Rights Project.

Parents Involved in Community Schools v. Seattle School District No. 1, 551 U.S. 701 (2007).

Petrovich, J., & Wells, A. S. (Eds.). (2005). *Bringing equity back: Research for a new era in American educational policy.* New York, NY: Teachers College Press.

Pettigrew, T., & Tropp, L. (2006). A meta-analytic test of intergroup contact theory. *Journal of Personality and Social Psychology, 90*(5), 751–783.

Potter, H. (2015). *Charters without borders: Using inter-district charter schools as a tool for regional school integration.* Washington, DC: The Century Foundation.

Reardon, S. F., & Owens, A. (2014). 60 years after *Brown*: Trends and consequences of school segregation. *Annual Review of Sociology, 40,* 199–218.

Reardon, S. F., & Rhodes, L. (2011). The effects of socioeconomic integration policies on racial school desegregation. In E. Frankenberg & E. DeBray (Eds.), *Integrating schools in a changing society: New policies and legal options for a multiracial generation* (pp. 187–207). Chapel Hill, NC: University of North Carolina Press.

Reardon, S. F., Yun, J. T., & Eitle, T. M. (2000). The changing structure of school segregation: Measurement and evidence of multiracial metropolitan-area school segregation, 1989–1995. *Demography, 37*(2), 351–364.

Scott, J. (2009). The politics of venture philanthropy in charter school policy and advocacy. *Educational Policy, 23*(1), 106–136.

Shanker, A. (1988, March 31). *National Press Club speech.* Retrieved from reuther.wayne.edu/files/64.43.pdf

Siegel-Hawley, G., & Frankenberg, E. (2011a). Does law influence charter school diversity? An analysis of federal and state legislation. *Michigan Journal of Race and Law, 16*(2), 321–376.

Siegel-Hawley, G., & Frankenberg, E. (2011b). Redefining diversity: Political responses to the post-*PICS* environment. *Peabody Journal of Education, 86*(5), 529–552.

Siegel-Hawley, G., & Frankenberg, E. (2013). Designing choice: Magnet school structures and racial diversity. In G. Orfield & E. Frankenberg (Eds.), *Educational delusions? Why choice can deepen inequality and how to make schools fair* (pp. 107–128). Berkeley, CA: University of California Press.

Stroub, K. J., & Richards, M. P. (2013). From resegregation to reintegration: Trends in the racial/ethnic segregation of metropolitan public schools, 1993–2009. *American Educational Research Journal, 50*(3), 497–531.

Swanson, C. B. (2004). Sketching a portrait of public high school graduation: Who graduates? Who doesn't? In G. Orfield (Ed.), *Dropouts in America: Confronting the graduation rate crisis* (pp. 13–40). Cambridge, MA: Harvard Education Press.

Tropp, L. R., & Prenovost, M. A. (2008). The role of intergroup contact in predicting children's interethnic attitudes: Evidence from meta-analytic and field studies. In S. R. Levy & M. Killen (Eds.), *Intergroup attitudes and relations in childhood through adulthood* (pp. 236–248). New York, NY: Oxford University Press.

U.S. Department of Education. (2014). *Charter schools program, Title V, Part B of the ESEA, Nonregulatory guidance*. Washington, DC: Author. Retrieved from www2.ed.gov/programs/charter/fy14cspnonregguidance.doc

U.S. Department of Education. (2017). *Improving outcomes for all students: Strategies and considerations to increase student diversity*. Washington, DC: Author.

U.S. Department of Housing and Urban Development, U.S. Department of Education, & U.S. Department of Transportation. (2016). *Dear colleague letter*. Washington, DC: Authors. Retrieved from www2.ed.gov/documents/press-releases/06032016-dear-colleagues-letter.pdf

U.S. Department of Justice & U.S. Department of Education. (2011). *Guidance on the voluntary use of race to achieve diversity and avoid racial isolation in elementary and secondary schools*. Washington, DC: Author.

Warren, E. (1954). *Brown v. Board of Education*. Retrieved from landmarkcases.org/en/landmark/cases/brown_v_board_of_education

Wells, A. S. (1993). *Time to choose: America at the crossroads of school choice policy*. New York, NY: Hill and Wang.

Wells, A. S., & Crain, R. L. (1994). Perpetuation theory and the long-term effects of school desegregation. *Review of Educational Research, 64*(4), 531–555.

Wells, A. S., Warner, M., & Grzesikowski, C. (2013). The story of meaningful school choice: Lessons from interdistrict transfer plans. In G. Orfield & E. Frankenberg (Eds.), *Educational delusions? Why choice can deepen inequality and how to make schools fair* (pp. 187–218). Berkeley, CA: University of California Press.

Weiher, G. R., & Tedin, K. L. (2002). Does choice lead to racially distinctive schools? Charter schools and household preferences. *Journal of Policy Analysis and Management, 21*(1), 79–92.

Welner, K. G. (2013, April). The dirty dozen: How charter schools influence student enrollment. *Teachers College Record* [online], ID Number 17104. Retrieved from nepc.colorado.edu/publication/TCR-Dirty-Dozen

Part III

EDUCATION IN A PLURALISTIC SOCIETY

CHAPTER 13

Charter Schools
Rending or Mending the Nation

Henry M. Levin

The real safeguard of democracy is education.

—Franklin D. Roosevelt, "Message for American Education"

School choice has always had some appeal in the United States. We are a society based on freedom of belief and expression, and schools are an extension of that freedom to choose options for our offspring. To the degree that families want to mold their children to their own values and goals, the concept of school choice overlaps with family rights to child rearing. School choice enables families to use schools to achieve their private purposes. Of course, if school choice improves general schooling outcomes through matching educational needs or the effects of school competition, broad social benefits might also be achieved through better academic results for society. However, such a finding is not common in the research on charter schools and choice (Epple, Romano, & Zimmer, 2015; Urquiola, 2016), although some studies for particular localities have shown advantages in student achievement for certain types of charter schools (Angrist, Pathak, & Walters, 2013).

Beyond the private purpose of education, schools also have a more universal, public purpose, one that accounts for their rapid historical adoption by governments and the establishment of compulsory education laws. That purpose is to prepare students to participate in and reproduce the very institutions and practices that enable our freedoms (Callan, 1997; Gutmann, 1986).

In this chapter we discuss both private and public purposes of education in the context of charter schools, highlighting the challenges and possible ways forward.

PUBLIC VERSUS PRIVATE PURPOSES OF EDUCATION

Public education stands at the intersection of two legitimate rights (Levin, 1987). The first is the right of a democratic society to assure its reproduction and continuous democratic functioning through preparation of all of its members to understand and accept a common set of values and knowledge required for societal equity and cohesion. The second involves the rights of families to decide the manner in which their children will be guided and molded and the types of influences to which their children will be exposed. To the degree that families have different personal, political, social, philosophical, and religious beliefs and values, a basic incompatibility might exist between their private concerns and the public functions of schooling.

In terms of private benefits, it has long been known that schooling enhances individual productivity and earnings (Becker, 1962). In addition, schooling contributes to the trainability of workers, enhanced health, efficiency in consumption, access to information, and a wide variety of other private results (Lochner, 2011). School-based education also contributes to greater personal efficacy in political participation and the inculcation of civic values. Finally, schooling can contribute to social status, technical and cultural literacy, and promotion of personal values.

Schooling also serves the nation, region, and community by creating an institutional and legal environment that provides opportunities and protections. To develop democratic participation, schools must prepare the young to understand and participate effectively in their social, economic, and political institutions. In this respect, schools are charged with contributing to the formation of an equitable and stable society. Empirical research demonstrates that educational attainment can increase voter participation and support for free speech and increase civic knowledge (Dee, 2004; Niemi & Junn, 2005). In the aggregate, schools contribute to society in many broader ways (McMahon, 2004), including economic growth and employment for the country and its regions. Schooling is also viewed as developing the skills for cultural and scientific advances in discovering and developing latent talents that benefit all of society.

Government funding of education is mainly justified by its public benefits. Even Milton Friedman, the foremost champion of using private markets to increase school choice, argued that schooling serves a public function that justifies funding by government: "A stable and democratic society is impossible without a minimum degree of literacy and knowledge on the part of most citizens and without widespread acceptance of some common set of values" (Friedman, 1982, p. 75). He was also concerned that some parents could not afford to pay for the schooling of their children, so the public pursuit of equity also depends upon government funding. He concluded that the government role was to provide funding for every child to obtain a minimum level of schooling in a school that met the approved requirements for democratic preparation.

A nation must reconcile the differences between private and public benefits, providing a common framework to prepare the young for their public roles in their overall political, economic, and social context along with the freedom to pursue individual goals. To some degree, public and private goals of schooling can be reinforcing. For example, worker productivity and wages are higher for less-educated workers in enterprises and regions that have higher *average* worker education (Moretti, 2004). But, the private goals of families might also undermine public goals such as social cohesion and civic collaboration if the education that is sought seeks political, religious, and philosophical exclusion rather than an embrace of democratic processes in addressing social needs and addressing social differences.

THE CASE OF CHARTER SCHOOLS

The concept of charter schools is one that combines the public sponsorship of schools and the promotion of private differences that correspond to family preferences and perceived educational needs. Although funding and regulation of charter schools are subject to government authority, these schools are awarded considerable autonomy with the waiver of many laws and regulations that constrain traditional public schools.

A note of caution is warranted about overly generalizing the specific features of charter schools (National Alliance for Public Charter Schools, 2016), since their operations have been defined under the authorities of different laws in each of the 43 states and the District of Columbia that sponsor them. States have employed widely different requirements for establishment, funding, waivers from existing state and local requirements, and sponsorship. There are almost 7,000 charter schools, attended by 3.1 million students, constituting an enormous variety of educational situations. What gives charter schools a common theme is the overall frame of governance conferred by their states, not the specific organizational forms, goals, or activities that they sponsor. These schools vary from sponsorship of traditional educational practices with a centralized curriculum and teaching methods to highly experimental institutions with considerable teacher and student voice. They can employ unionized teaching staffs with considerable employment protection or nonunionized teachers on annual contracts or even teacher-managed schools. They can adopt traditional curricula from commercial publishers or teacher-developed curricula or embrace student participation in the establishment and implementation of learning activities. They can take the form of virtual learning institutions with heavy use of technology or even schools where all instruction is done exclusively through the Internet with little teacher guidance or student accountability. They can embrace a student body representative of the diversity in a geographical area or limit their appeal to a particular demographic. Some states permit a wide choice of sponsorship and organizational approaches, while other states are more restrictive. At the heart of all of these schools is a focus on attracting families with distinct educational preferences.

Clearly, a tension can arise in school policies that focus on choices emphasizing family beliefs and values at the expense of a more common set of practices

that prepare all children for a unified democratic society. Even when schools focus on the perceived educational demands of democracy, the translation of these
principles into school practices can differ immensely. Differences can be further
exacerbated by student and family perspectives that are reinforced by the ubiqui-
tous reliance for information on social media that reflect a restricted perspective
on social issues. Any political solution is always temporal, as the forces that push
for greater choice and those that push for greater cohesion and solidarity are potentially in conflict, sometimes at an ideological level (Belfield & Levin, 2005). The
search for balance between choice and uniformity in charter schools has constituted a part of a larger historical struggle in U.S. education between public and
private goals.

At each point in history, the search for educational reforms has yielded primacy
to one side or the other, but the underlying determinants of the struggle do not
evaporate and play themselves out as long as the political tensions between public
and private goals are still present (Carnoy & Levin, 1985). In the rural America
of the 19th century, schools were village or community based and premised on
local values (Katz, 1968; Tyack, 1974). With the increasingly urban consolidation
of the nation in the 19th century, accompanied by massive waves of immigration, school organization and governance became more centralized, with powerful
political pressures for a more universal experience to unify educational practices
for national cohesion. This was followed by the struggle for increased equity and
social cohesion in schools throughout the 20th century, with a push for racial integration, school finance equalization, gender equity, and educational rights for
students with disabilities.

By the end of the 20th century, political forces had risen to challenge educational uniformity and standardization, with calls for radical decentralization,
deregulation of schooling practices, and the expansion of school choice. The establishment of charter schools and school vouchers was the leading edge of this
movement, promoting an education that could differ substantially from school to
school according to family preferences. These historical shifts can best be understood by the continuing struggles between forces favoring the public or private
purposes of education.

In the case of charter schools, the shift from public to private purposes of education has taken two forms that have increasingly threatened to undermine the
public goal of democratic preparation. The first is that as charter schools take different approaches to education, there is less of a common focus on preparing students for a shared democratic experience. Second, the charter mechanism has led
to increasing stratification of school populations, reducing exposure of students
to children from different social classes, races, values, disabilities, and cultures.
This is true even when comparing charter school enrollments to those in existing public schools in the same neighborhoods (Whitehurst, Reeves, & Rodrigue,
2016). Exposure to peers with different backgrounds, races, and educational needs
is considered to represent an important part of preparation for democracy (Gurin,
Nagda, & Lopez, 2004).

Stratification is not a stated purpose of charter schools as much as a collateral impact of choice. Studies of parental preference show that distance from home is negatively related to selection of a school, so that schools have an incentive to locate near the types of families that match their appeals (Glazerman & Dotter, 2016). Further, parents tend to choose schools for their offspring with students of a preferred social class and race. Thus, it is no surprise that charter schools have been found to be more racially and economically segregated than traditional public schools (Whitehurst et al., 2016). Charter schools also commonly have fewer English-language learners or students with disabilities, particularly severe disabilities.

THE CHALLENGE

The challenge is how to accommodate diverse choices that parents may seek for the education of their own children with an educational experience that serves to prepare all the young for a common set of social, political, and economic institutions. As stated earlier, we can expect a tension between these two goals because they are not fully compatible. When societies are highly homogeneous, there can be considerable consensus on the common educational experience with only minor adjustments to embrace educational choice, but when large differences in the religious, political, cultural, and philosophical beliefs of populations lead to substantial differences in educational accommodations (Wilson, 2017), educational choice can conflict with the inculcation of common values and beliefs required for democratic functioning. The risk is that if charter schools are designed to affirm the specific beliefs of the families they serve, their educational programs are unlikely to reflect the diverse views of a pluralistic society.

Further challenges relate to the degree that major public goals of education include equity across populations and social cohesion. Parents are motivated to give their children a unique advantage for success in life, and the right school might offer educational advantages that they do not wish to share with others. These motives can exist even in a traditional system, where higher income provides greater access to neighborhoods with preferred schools. Even if a family is also committed to the democratic goals of equity and social cohesion, those goals are not readily attainable by an individual family, but are the products of public policy and government action. Such families must work through collective, political solutions, which require strong social involvement and substantial time and effort in a complex political environment. Thus, school choice through charter schools favors private preferences relative to educational needs for creating a society in which democratic participation is enhanced.

As an advocate of choice, Milton Friedman confronted the challenge of how to obtain democratic and public benefits under a framework of parental choice of schools. He proposed a voucher system that would encompass—at least theoretically—both sets of goals. Although the main mechanism would be a voucher system of payments to parents that could be used for educational choice, he would require all schools to meet minimal government regulations that would ensure the values and behaviors necessary for democracy. His analogy was deceptively simple: "The role of the government would be limited to insuring that the schools met certain minimum standards such as the inclusion of a minimum common content in their programs as it now inspects restaurants to ensure that they maintain minimum sanitary standards" (Friedman, 1982, p. 78). This is an inappropriate analogy, as it compares the substance of education not to a restaurant's product but only to basic hygienic standards. Further, a restaurant meal can be judged more easily and quickly than the quality of an education. In many cases, quality can be ascertained only after a lengthy educational experience, months or years, in a specific school.

Unlike hygienic practices, training for democracy requires substantive effort to ensure preparation of the young with a common educational experience for a productive and sustaining role in a democratic society. This education entails not only the obvious focus on knowledge of political institutions and processes, market and government roles in the economy, and social institutions and conventions, but also the social and emotional capacities required to support civic and economic participation (Levin, 2012b). Even the knowledge requirements of democratic participation are formidable, such as serving on a jury of peers in which intricacies of law and evidence must be understood and interpreted in a legal context. A civic response might be required for major public controversies, such as the challenge of global warming. Many economic issues require complex insights, such as the controversy over the establishment and magnitude of a minimum wage, subsidized health care, and the employment implications of automation. In addition, citizens need some understanding of the complications of threats to national security and the defense of the nation to make intelligent choices in these domains.

Various divisive forces—such as populism, identity politics, religious conflict, and even strident differences in conventional political and philosophic views on education and other issues—can interfere with rational and productive democratic interactions. The public goal of education must focus on sustaining an accepted political process that transcends issues so that members of society can work together productively, despite their private differences. How does one reconcile the different privately held views that motivate family educational choice with the public requirements for sustaining a democracy? How can schools serve to address ideological and public policy differences in a manner that is productive and sustains a harmonious contribution to social stability while honoring educational preferences? Clearly, we must find a way of reconciling educational choice and education for the effective functioning of a democratic society.

In an age of social media, civic participation has grown more challenging (Sunstein, 2017). One might argue that with so many political and public policy news sources available online, our young are exposed to a richer and more variegated flow of information than in the past. Within easy reach are explanations and evidence on different sides of the issues. However, the reality is the opposite: Users are informed by sources that customize the messages reaching them to mirror the patterns of search and utilization reflected in previous usage. This exposure provides a confirmatory bias to their beliefs and understandings (Lee, Choi, Kim, & Kim, 2014). Such channels of information do not seek balance among competing views, but serve to reinforce the worldview of their audiences, creating "alternative facts" as needed to suit the claim. Students are vulnerable to these trends (Domonoske, 2016). If the choice of schools is just a reinforcement of partisan views of the world already held by families, the role of schools will circumvent the informed decisionmaking required for democratic governance.

A further challenge to U.S. democracy is the very steep rise in economic inequality combined with the impact of unlimited funding of political candidates by wealthy families and corporate entities. Recent historical study suggests that massive wealth accumulation combined with poverty and deterioration of the middle class have not been arbitrated effectively by democratic processes. Such extremes have led to war, authoritarian rule, and street-level conflict and violence, precisely the opposite of the purposes of the democratic process (Sitaraman, 2017).

CONCLUSIONS

The public and the private goals of education as accounted for by charter schools are not fully compatible. An increase in the number of charter schools is likely to increase choice but diminish the unifying influence of schools for creating the common values and knowledge required for effective participation in a democracy. In some cases, there has already been a movement toward charter school districts, where every school is a charter school competing for the district's students (Levin, 2012a).

The tension between choice and uniformity is at the heart of charter school policy in the United States. Charter schools must meet specific family preferences while molding the young for a common society for which all members are held accountable. Charter schools may lead to greater parental satisfaction with schools in addressing their private goals and values, but they may also lead to greater segregation of students and a tattering of the social fabric of preparation for democratic and civic participation.

Charter schools have a strong incentive to "differentiate their product" to create a competitive edge to attract students. This appeal is in conflict with the goal of creating a common public purpose to education among schools that will promote the public interest in preparing the young for civic participation. If charter schools attract more students by emphasizing narrow political and philosophic values and ideologies, they will have a disassembling effect on preparing students for democracy.

Recommendations. No simple solution can resolve this conflict. To the degree that charter schools are authorized by state and local legal provisions, the degree of commonality in teaching and learning can be addressed, at least theoretically, to increase the public benefits. For example, the Netherlands has embraced full school choice for a century, but has employed a strong regulatory function on curriculum, testing, admissions, and other important features that have buttressed choice with common goals and accountability (Levin, Cornelisz, & Hanisch-Cerda, 2013). Yet, states have taken very different stances on how much regulation is desirable, and substantial differences of opinion exist in the charter community on whether charter schools should be regulated at all, despite their public funding. For example, the Center for Education Reform (2017) ranks state charter school legislation as strongest when little or no regulation or oversight by authorities interferes with charter school autonomy. Although some individual charter schools may place very high value on what they consider to be the public goals of education, others see their competitive advantages as appealing to and serving narrower family preferences and values only.

A further complication is that laws on teaching for democracy are difficult to enforce or to translate into meaningful action. Purposeful education requires not only procedural compliance with laws, but their extension to the educational process and content. Often schools view such requirements as a checklist requiring only mechanical obeisance without fully accepting or honoring their educational purpose. It is not course names or their putative content that is important, but how the topics are taught and applied (Kahne & Bowyer, 2017; Westheimer, 2015).

One potential direction is to establish a curriculum among the grades that culminates in service learning, the experience of applying knowledge to political, social, and economic challenges faced by the communities in which they live (Morgan & Streb, 2001). As a beginning, it would be encouraging for charter school organizations and schools to collaborate to develop such a plan.

The goal is not complete uniformity and rigidity in educational approaches. Some differentiation among schools can be valuable and lead to new approaches for addressing particular learning objectives of civic education. However, educational authorities will need to ensure that schools will address the requirements for civic education that fully encompass the learning needs of all students in a world in which democratic knowledge, participation, and behavior have become more complex and rising inequality is a major challenge. We cannot ignore this priority by leaving it to charter schools to decide idiosyncratically what to do. Democratic preparation of the young is a precursor to the kind of society that makes choice possible by creating an institutional environment that can sustain differences within a common political framework.

REFERENCES

Angrist, J. D., Pathak, P. A., & Walters, C. R. (2013). Explaining charter school effectiveness. *American Economic Journal: Applied Economics, 5*(4), 1–27.

Becker, G. S. (1962). Investment in human capital: A theoretical analysis. *Journal of Political Economy*, *70*(5, Part 2), 9–49.

Belfield, C., & Levin, H. M. (2005). Vouchers and public policy: When ideology trumps evidence. *American Journal of Education*, *111*(4), 548–567.

Callan, E. (1997). *Creating citizens: Political education and liberal democracy*. Oxford, UK: Oxford University Press.

Carnoy, M., & Levin, H. M. (1985). *Schooling and work in the democratic state*. Stanford, CA: Stanford University Press.

Center for Education Reform. (2017). *National charter school law ranking & scorecard*. Washington, DC: Author. Retrieved from www.edreform.com/2017/03/national-charter-school-law-rankings-scorecard

Dee, T. (2004). Are there civic returns to education? *Journal of Public Economics*, *88*(9–10), 1697–1720.

Domonoske, C. (2016, November 23). Students have dismaying inability to tell fake news from real, study finds. *National Public Radio*. Retrieved from www.npr.org/sections/thetwo-way/2016/11/23/503129818/study-finds-students-have-dismaying-inability-to-tell-fake-news-from-real

Epple, D., Romano, R., & Zimmer, R. (2015). *Charter schools: A survey of research on their characteristics and effectiveness* [NBER Working Paper No. 21256]. Cambridge, MA: National Bureau of Economic Research. Retrieved from www.nber.org/papers/w21256

Friedman, M. (1982). The role of government in education. In *Capitalism and freedom* (pp. 85–107). Chicago, IL: University of Chicago Press.

Glazerman, S., & Dotter, D. (2016). *How do DC parents rank schools and what does it mean for policy?* [Policy Brief]. Washington, DC: Mathematica Policy Research.

Gurin, P., Nagda, B. R. A., & Lopez, G. E. (2004). The benefits of diversity in education for democratic citizenship. *Journal of Social Issues*, *60*(1), 17–34.

Gutmann, A. (1986). *Democratic education*. Princeton, NJ: Princeton University Press.

Kahne, J., & Bowyer, B. (2017). Education for democracy in a partisan age: Confronting the challenges of motivated reasoning and misinformation. *American Educational Research Journal*, *54*(1), 3–34.

Katz, M. B. (1968). *The irony of early school reform*. Cambridge, MA: Harvard University Press.

Lee, J. K., Choi, J., Kim, C., & Kim, Y. (2014). Social media, network heterogeneity, and opinion polarization. *Journal of Communication*, *64*(4), 702–722.

Levin, H. M. (1987). Education as a public and private good. *Journal of Policy Management and Analysis*, *6*(4), 628–641.

Levin, H. M. (2012a). Some economic guidelines for design of a charter school district. *Economics of Education Review*, *31*(2), 331–343.

Levin, H. M. (2012b). More than just test scores. *Prospects*, *42*(3), 269–284.

Levin, H. M., Cornelisz, I., & Hanisch-Cerda, B. (2013). Does educational privatisation promote social justice? *Oxford Review of Education*, *39*(4), 514–532.

Lochner, L. (2011). *Non-production benefits of education: Crime, health, and good citizenship* [NBER Working Paper No. 16722]. Cambridge, MA: National Bureau of Economic Research. Retrieved from www.nber.org/papers/w16722.ack

McMahon, W. (2004). The social and external benefits of education. In G. Johnes & J. Johnes (Eds.), *International handbook on economics of education* (pp. 211–259). Northampton, MA: Edward Elgar.

Moretti, E. (2004). Workers' education, spillovers, and productivity: Evidence from plant-level production functions. *American Economic Review, 94*(3), 656–690.

Morgan, W., & Streb, M. (2001). Building citizenship: How student voice in service-learning develops civic values. *Social Science Quarterly, 82*(1), 154–169.

National Alliance for Public Charter Schools. (2016). *A closer look at the charter school movement.* Washington, DC: Author. Retrieved from www.publiccharters.org/wp-content/uploads/2016/02/New-Closed-2016.pdf

Niemi, R. G., & Junn, J. (2005). *Civic education: What makes students learn.* New Haven, CT: Yale University Press.

Roosevelt, F. D. (1938, September 27). Message for American education. Retrieved from www.presidency.ucsb.edu/ws/?pid=15545

Sitaraman, G. (2017). *The crisis of the middle-class constitution: Why economic inequality threatens our republic.* New York, NY: Random House.

Sunstein, C. (2017). *#Republic: Divided democracy in the age of social media.* Princeton, NJ: Princeton University Press.

Tyack, D. B. (1974). *The one best system: A history of American urban education* (Vol. 95). Cambridge, MA: Harvard University Press.

Urquiola, M. (2016). Competition among schools: Traditional public and private schools. In E. Hanushek, S. Machin, & L. Woessman (Eds.), *Handbook of the economics of education* (Vol. 5, pp. 209–237). Oxford, UK: Elsevier.

Westheimer, J. (2015). *What kind of citizen? Educating our children for the common good.* New York, NY: Teachers College Press.

Whitehurst, G. J., Reeves, R. V., & Rodrigue, E. (2016). *Segregation, race, & charter schools: What do we know?* Washington, DC: Center on Children and Families at Brookings.

Wilson, T. (2017). Philosophical understanding of American school choice. In R. Fox & N. Buchanan (Eds.), *The Wiley handbook of school choice* (pp. 81–95). Malden, MA: John Wiley & Sons.

CHAPTER 14

The Problem We All Still Live With

Neo-Plessyism and School Choice Policies in the Post-Obama Era

Janelle Scott

Despite what appears impossible at present, we can, with determination and perseverance, still achieve the kind of America we dream of.

—Julius Chambers, "Great Lives in the Law"

Race and racism are central issues in the history of public education and in American social life. The *Plessy vs. Ferguson* decision of 1896 established the doctrine of "separate but equal" in public schools, transportation, and society more broadly. State-mandated segregation and the achievement of equality, however, proved impossible to reconcile. America's public schools and schooling systems remained racially segregated *and* woefully unequal. Despite the obvious failure to live up to its political tenets, the separate but equal doctrine stood as the nation's operating principle until the *Brown v. Board of Education* ruling of 1954 and subsequent civil rights laws upended it. Yet, due in part to widespread and sustained resistance on the part of policymakers, leaders, parents, and teachers to fully dismantle dual systems of schooling, the realization of equitable and full integration has been elusive in the United States (Aggerwaal & Mayoraga, 2016; Roda, 2015; Wells, Holme, Revilla, & Atanda, 2009).

While the implementation of *Brown* was not what advocates and educators had hoped for, the decision was the result of decades of organizing and advocacy. School desegregation was a prime policy goal during the midcentury civil rights movement. Parents, educators, and legal advocates who pushed for school desegregation litigation and laws to dismantle separate and unequal schooling did so because they believed that equal and integrated education was essential for the achievement of civil rights, along with other protections in labor, housing, and justice policies. These advocates began to experience favorable judicial rulings beginning with the *Brown* decision of 1954, with courts finding that policymakers had harmed Black children by ensuring separate and unequal schooling. Because of massive White resistance, state-sponsored voucher programs were established to enable White families to avoid desegregation mandates, and in Virginia public schools were closed for several years. While African American families had long engaged in alternative institution building due to their exclusion from public education opportunities (Forman, 2005), the establishment of vouchers, one of the first state-sponsored school choice policies, was inextricably tied to racism and racial exclusion (Lassiter & Davis, 1998). And efforts to desegregate schools were often met with violence from White people. Such violence was immortalized in Norman Rockwell's painting depicting Ruby Bridges, "The Problem We All Live With" in 1964 (see Figure 14.1b).

The "problem we all live with" of racial segregation extends to contemporary school choice policies. Beginning in the early 1990s, advocates pushed for the legislative adoption and expansion of charter schools for a variety of reasons that included civil rights and education. For example, some advocates argued that charter schools would disrupt the connection between where students lived and where they attended school and, as such, would create more racial and ethnic diversity than was possible under neighborhood zoned schools. Other advocates posited that charter schools would give parents of color greater choice and voice and thereby power over their children's schooling. Yet these civil rights and empowerment commitments were distinct and, in many ways, contradictory from those of charter advocates who shared greater commitments to deregulation, competition, and privatization of public services. Now in its third decade, the charter school policy and advocacy sector continues to be characterized by these factions, raising tensions about the role of charter schools in increasing or redressing racial segregation within and across school districts.

The political tensions that shape charter school policies in the United States are informed by a history in which policymakers have deployed forms of school choice to enhance or to restrict equitable access and democratic participation. For example, racial exclusion and Native American genocide were part of the foundations of American public and private education systems (Anderson, 1988; Donato, 1997; Telles & Ortiz, 2008). When the United States began developing its state systems of public education, African American, Latinx,[1] Native American, and Asian American children were often excluded from the schooling opportunities afforded to most White children, or offered woefully substandard versions of the ones provided to White children (Tyack, 2001). Parents, advocates, and community leaders pursued a range of strategies to pressure national, state, and local officials and agencies to deliver schooling that was high quality, equitable, and that honored the linguistic, cultural, and other strengths of children in order to realize the elusive potential of public education in a democratic, multiracial society (Perlstein, 2004; Walker, 2013).

This chapter considers the popular assertion that education is the last remaining civil right to be secured and that charter schools and school choice policies are the most powerful manifestation of that right. This assertion is considered in light of the Trump administration's push for an expansion of school choice and a rollback of civil rights enforcement (Huseman & Waldman, 2017). Civil rights enforcement in the post-Obama era has shifted radically from the state regulating and enforcing equality for all. In this context, the expansion of school choice policies that further remove the regulatory power of state agencies to ensure equitable practices could stand to make already vulnerable children and families more vulnerable to the whims of market forces. The chapter also examines how school choice supporters, critics, and opponents articulate their visions and preferences for civil rights in the face of an increasingly segregated and unequal public school and societal context and in light of evidence of the effects of school choice expansion on the racial composition of schools.

THE SYMBOLIC IMPORTANCE OF
BROWN VS. BOARD OF EDUCATION IN THE AMERICAN IMAGINATION

Each year, Americans commemorate the anniversary of the May 1954 *Brown v. Board of Education* decision, which invalidated the 1896 *Plessy v. Ferguson* doctrine of "separate but equal" that had governed segregation and racial hierarchies in America (Chapman, 2005). While schooling systems were slow to implement *Brown*, even when subjected to court orders or consent decrees, school desegregation, at its peak, contributed greatly to disrupting housing segregation and its effects on racially isolated schools (Clotfelter, 2004). As desegregation orders were challenged and vacated when districts argued they had met judicial standards of desegregating their systems, schools and school systems rapidly resegregated, after adopting choice plans (Mickelson, 2001).

Racial, linguistic, and socioeconomic segregation now characterizes American public, private, and charter schooling systems. Similarly, in the last days of the Obama presidency, 19 schools around the country were named in his honor, and nearly all were racially homogenous (Mitchell & Harwin, 2017). A number of factors have contributed to the segregation of American schools. First, the granting of unitary status to districts around the country, coupled with Supreme Court rulings that have limited the ability of districts to use race in student assignment, enabled district leaders to cease their affirmative efforts to desegregate schools. Second, the rapid expansion of school choice policies that lack regulatory mandates for racial, ethnic, and linguistic diversity, such as charter schools and vouchers, have heightened already existing patterns of segregation. Third, shifts in the political economy of regions, the redevelopment of cities, and rising economic inequality have resulted in displacement and migration of particular groups of people (Scott & Holme, 2016).

Some researchers and advocates have argued that school choice is a more "natural" mechanism for integrating schools given urban-suburban demographics, because it is the most expedient means for integration across city and suburban lines without mandates. Yet many of these diagnoses gloss over the racist roots of neighborhood segregation that have shaped possibilities for integrated housing and schooling in traditional and school choice settings. For example, Rothstein (2017) argued that segregation and multigenerational denial of wealth accumulation through the ability to purchase a home in a desired neighborhood is an example of *de jure* and not *de facto* segregation and, therefore, requires state remedies beyond the movement of children from one school to another. The Public Works Administration, the Federal Housing Administration, the Supreme Court, banks, real estate agents, neighborhood associations, police forces, individual citizens—all were complicit in reifying segregation in housing and education and, perhaps most importantly, in creating residential segregation where none had existed previously. This was often accomplished through the demolition of integrated housing and the construction of segregated housing developments. Given these geographic limitations, researchers have found that without regulations or incentives, a negative relationship exists between school choice policies and racial diversity, and that school choice policies tend to further sort and segregate students by race, socioeconomic status, language, and academic performance unless these policies provide clear frameworks, regulations, and incentives for ensuring that they produce diverse and equitable schooling (Scott & Wells, 2013).

Efforts to desegregate housing as part of the civil rights movement were met with massive resistance that included violent protests and attacks on Black families who attempted to move into predominantly White neighborhoods and prosecution of White families who sold their homes to Black families in violation of racially restrictive covenants. Similarly, almost immediately after the *Brown* rulings, legal remedies to integrating schooling were resisted around the country. Yet, many communities struggled to make desegregation—if not integration—a reality. School choice has played a complicated role in the politics of school integration. In its numerous forms, school choice has provided White and middle-class families with a means to opt out of public school desegregation plans through the southern academies and suburban development that sprouted in the post-*Brown* years, while also providing a means to limited racial stability in schooling through magnet schools, transfer programs, and open enrollment plans.

Many funders and advocates locate their efforts to expand school choice for Black and Latinx families in the realm of civil rights and educational opportunity. The claims that educational policies are generating empowerment for otherwise powerless parents are being articulated against a contemporary and historical backdrop of racial segregation and income inequality, where the state has been a regulator and enforcer of efforts to make schools more equitable and has also been complicit in maintaining inequality through a range of policy levers that have kept many urban, suburban, and rural schools segregated and under-resourced (Orfield, 2001). Thus, even as the nation celebrates the Supreme Court's affirmation of desegregation, schools and communities find themselves negotiating school choice options against a complicated history of racial and social class exclusion in cities, suburbs, and rural areas, and the rise of neoliberal ideology, which holds that the state should provide optimal opportunities for nonstate actors to shape schooling options. Moreover, many of the signature civil rights era legislative efforts that followed the *Brown* decision have been weakened or vacated, and in the aftermath of the 2008 global financial crisis, many states continue to struggle with adequate and equitable funding for schools and social services. This has left school choice as the primary prism through which market actors view civil rights in education.

Schools in the United States are more diverse in their overall populations, with students of color comprising the majority of students in many school districts and some states, like California. Nevertheless, schools are also deeply segregated and stratified by race, poverty, and language (Fiel, 2013; McArdle, Osypuk, & Acevedo-Garcia, 2010; Orfield, Frankenberg, Ee, & Kuscera, 2014; Reardon & Owens, 2014). Because students are learning in segregated learning environments within and across district boundaries, school choice can exacerbate such inequities.

While the Obama administration's educational policy approach did not emphasize school desegregation until the end of his term, it maintained funding to the federal Magnet Schools Assistance Program and created the "Opening Doors, Expanding Opportunities" (ODEO) grant program (U.S. Department of Education, 2016), which provided school districts that aimed to affirmatively develop diversity plans with planning and implementation funding. In addition, under President Obama, the Department of Education's Office for Civil Rights, in collaboration with the Department of Justice, became a much more active force in civil rights complaints and investigation than in the Bush and Clinton administrations, particularly in investigating and responding to racial disproportionality in school discipline and suspensions (Murphy, 2017). In 2017, however, Secretary of Education Betsy DeVos announced the elimination of the ODEO program, and the proposed 2018 budget will cut Department of Education funding by 13%, making civil rights enforcement and oversight more vulnerable and constrained (Wall, 2017).

SCHOOL CHOICE AS A CIVIL RIGHT AND THE RISE OF NEO-PLESSYISM

Many educational policies fail to address housing segregation and stratification beyond very limited school desegregation plans. Instead, they accept this segregation and approach schooling improvement with what Amy Stuart Wells and I have called "neo-Plessyism." This ideal, often articulated by conservatives and many progressives, states that we can achieve separate but equal schooling with the right policies, and that school choice is central to that achievement because it reduces the role of the state and elevates the power of parents to choose schools that are higher quality, thereby placing consumer pressure on schools and school systems to meet their needs (Scott & Wells, 2013).

In the last two decades, through the advocacy for and the adoption of market-oriented school choice policies, advocates from multiple ideological standpoints have come to embrace a form of neo-Plessyism, harkening to the logic that held that racial segregation was permissible, provided the separate spaces were equal. With charter schools, this rationale is increasingly articulated in the context of high-performing charter schools serving students of color and the need for the replication and expansion of these schools (Barrone & Lombardo, 2016). While some high-profile charter networks have achieved impressive outcomes as measured by test scores, graduation rates, or enrollment in colleges and universities, these data must be examined in light of patterns of selectivity, attrition, and exclusion. Such data reveal that many charter schools underenroll students with disabilities and lose large numbers of low-achieving students through suspension, expulsion, or attrition. For example, the Civil Rights Project at the University of California at Los Angeles found that racially homogenous charter schools had out-of-school suspension rates of more than 25% of the student body and that hundreds of charter schools suspended 50% of their special education populations (Losen, Keith, Hodson, & Martinez, 2016).

Despite these patterns, for conservative and neoliberal adherents, realizing a vision of school choice with minimal state regulation means dismantling state systems of public education and removing teachers' unions in favor of portfolio models that allow for innovation, experimentation, and more responsive schooling that gives parents the power to vote with their feet. For example, former Ohio Secretary of State Ken Blackwell (2007) argued:

> Today, our nation is a testament to both Rev. King's accomplishments and those of whom he inspired. African-Americans hold positions of power and influence at the highest levels of government and industry. Progress has been made on the old civil rights battlefronts. But new fronts have opened.
>
> The battle over school choice is one. In fact, school choice programs—developed to free poor urban and rural children from failing public schools—represent this century's defining civil rights issue. . . .
>
> In the 1960's, Rev. King fought segregationists who put up barriers to basic human rights and denied African-Americans the civil rights each of our nation's citizens are guaranteed. Today, we fight entrenched bureaucracy, greedy teachers' unions and their politician allies. Their hearts may be different, but their desired result is the same. They seek to deny poor children a fundamental civil right—equal access to a quality education. (paras. 3, 4, 20)

Adherents of differing ideological and partisan perspectives have often asserted that school choice is a civil right (Scott, 2011). This claim was invoked during the 2016 U.S. presidential campaign with (then Republican candidate) Donald Trump, who often lamented the "hell" in which "inner-city" families lived, with "failing" schools. Consistent with many Republicans and neoliberal Democrats, Trump regularly critiqued teachers' unions as causing educational harm to Black students and expressed his opposition to unions and support for charter schools and vouchers, even as he vowed to restore "law and order" through increased policing of these same communities and engaged in racist and xenophobic rhetoric on the campaign trail and at rallies in which people of color were often beaten by his supporters. Furthermore, he appointed Senator Jeff Sessions as attorney general, a choice widely criticized due to Sessions's history of prosecuting African Americans seeking to register to vote. Because of this history of explicit racism and his use of the law to block voting rights, Coretta Scott King opposed his 1986 nomination for a federal judgeship. In her letter to Congress she argued, "I believe his confirmation would have a devastating effect on not only the judicial system in Alabama, but also on the progress we have made toward fulfilling my husband's dream."

Given Sessions' appointment, and the current majority on the Supreme Court, school choice policies operate without a robust federal framework of civil rights beyond the ability of parents to choose schools. Yet, school choice policies are growing in number and scope. There are charter school laws in 43 states and the District of Columbia, with roughly 3.1 million children enrolled in them (National Alliance for Public Charter Schools, 2017). Charters are authorized by districts, counties, or states, but operate as autonomous schools. While charters exist in urban and suburban settings, they are often concentrated in urban districts that predominantly serve students of color. As the numbers of charter schools have grown, some urban districts have experienced financial strain caused by a loss of students to charter schools, leading to school closures, consolidations, and teacher and staff layoffs.

School choice policies that emanated from the school desegregation era include magnet schools and inter- and intradistrict choice plans, and these persist, despite a constrained funding environment. Yet there are a number of other choice forms that reduce the role of the state, not only in the area of civil rights, but also in accountability, teaching and learning, and personnel. For example, there are 17 publicly funded school voucher plans, which allow families to receive what often amounts to partial tuition from the state to pay for private school tuition. There are over 40 tuition tax credit plans, which allow parents to deduct the cost of private school tuition on their state tax forms. Roughly 2 million children are being homeschooled. Private charter school management organizations and online and blended learning companies have also altered how schools are operated and governed in urban school districts. Together, these choice policies have promised to remove the barriers to schooling borne out of the tradition of zoning children to attend schools based on their residential location.

In education reform, it has become fashionable to dismiss the importance of zip code. A Google search of "quality education no matter a child's zip code" resulted in roughly 1.25 million hits. An example of this argument comes from Secretary of Education DeVos, who said in 2016, "I believe every child, no matter their zip code or their parents' jobs, deserves access to a quality education." We hear this argument from Democrats, Republicans, and from those at all points on the ideological spectrum. But rather than examining how zip codes came to be racially identifiable and marked by multigenerational stratification (Sharkey, 2013), many education reformers assert educational policies for students living in zip codes that were constructed through state policies and processes that intentionally segregated Black families. Moreover, there tends not to be serious policy consideration of requiring wealthy school districts to open their schools to families seeking access to them. Secretary of Education DeVos has ushered in a revitalized era of neo-Plessyism in her embrace of market-driven choice policy without civil rights protections necessary to protect against further segregation or discrimination against families.

SECRETARY DeVOS AND INDIVIDUALISM AS FEDERAL POLICY

The Senate narrowly confirmed Betsy DeVos as the nation's secretary of education in a contentious hearing that required an unprecedented tiebreaker vote from Vice President Pence after key Republicans opposed her confirmation. President Trump's appointment of Secretary DeVos was significant for several reasons. DeVos, a wealthy Republican philanthropist, had invested significant resources and effort to enact and broaden market-oriented school choice policies in Michigan, including vouchers, charter schools, and for-profit supplemental service provision. Her family foundation contributed $35 million to educational organizations and education reform (Dick and Betsy DeVos Family Foundation, 2015). Yet she lacked any formal experience working in schools, school systems, or state departments of education. Her ascendance to lead the Department of Education signaled the rise of venture philanthropy, a form of philanthropy that is modeled after venture capitalist strategies, into the highest levels of educational policymaking (Scott, 2009).

Her nomination was met with disapproval from a number of constituencies. Over 600 educational researchers signed a letter to the Senate HELP committee voicing opposition to her appointment (Abes et al., 2017).[2] This letter not only criticized Secretary DeVos's lack of experience and knowledge, but also found fault with her vision for the department in relation to its civil rights history:

> Throughout her hearing, Mrs. DeVos backed away from recognizing the Department of Education's responsibility to ensure the provision of equal opportunities for all students. But this responsibility would be central to her role in the Department. More than any other law, the Elementary and Secondary Education Act of 1965 is the origin of the federal role in American schools. This law is, as our colleague Bob Pianta notes, "at its heart a civil rights law." We believe that a qualified nominee for Secretary of Education must commit to the mission of equal opportunity and safety for all American students—including students with disabilities, students of color, English language learners, gay and lesbian students, and student survivors of campus rape. To back away from that role would be a mistake. (Abes et al., 2017, para. 6)

DeVos's longstanding commitment to expanding market-oriented choice in Michigan is well documented. Less understood is her focus on parents as the primary drivers of what counts as quality schooling and her desire for government to cede to localities to meet parental desires. This individualism philosophy is cloaked in a radical redefinition of the purpose and promise of education and a co-optation of what counts as equity and civil rights. Secretary DeVos (2017a) explained at a school choice event at the Brookings Institution:

> Our nation's commitment is to provide a quality education to every child to serve the greater public, common good. Accordingly, we must shift the paradigm to think about education funding as investments made in individual children, not in institutions or buildings.
>
> Let me say that again: we must change the way we think about funding education and invest in children, not in buildings. (paras. 9–10)

In this passage, DeVos begins by locating quality, equitable education as a public and common good, but concludes that the investment for securing such an education should be directed to children, and not institutions or buildings. It is clear that this rationale, despite being initially framed as a concern for the common good, is rather a promise to deliver a national school voucher program. And Secretary DeVos has made no commitment to ensure that the federal investments in "children" will assist in desegregating schools. In fact, at a February 2017 White House meeting with leaders of historically Black colleges and universities (HBCUs), Secretary DeVos (2017b) connected a history of exclusion from higher education for Black people and the subsequent founding of HBCUs with school choice and praised the founding of segregated colleges and universities as examples of freedom and equality:

> [HBCUs] started from the fact that there were too many students in America who did not have equal access to education. They saw that the system wasn't working, that there was an absence of opportunity, so they took it upon themselves to provide the solution.
>
> HBCUs are real pioneers when it comes to school choice. They are living proof that when more options are provided to students, they are afforded greater access and greater quality. (paras. 3–4)

In Secretary DeVos's analysis of the creation of HBCUs, the role of the state is left ambiguous. She lauds the founders of these institutions for taking things into their own hands, but leaves out the state's role in failing to provide equal access to elementary schools, high schools, and colleges for Black people. Yet, federal, state, and local policymakers engaged in *de jure* efforts to keep schooling inaccessible for Black children for most of this nation's history (Anderson, 1988; Jabbar, 2015). DeVos, neglecting the role of the state, turns to an elusive entity that might provide more options to students, and indicates that such provision results in access and quality. As the nation's leading educational policymaker, Secretary DeVos's advocacy for charter schools and vouchers, critique of teachers' unions, and vision that would remove state responsibility for ensuring access and equity signal a radical shift in how the nation's leading public policymaker imagines schools.

In February 2017, just after Secretary DeVos received Senate confirmation and was sworn in as secretary of education, she attempted to visit Jefferson Mid-

Figure 14.1. "Trashing Betsy DeVos" cartoon, by Glenn McCoy, which appeared in the *Belleville* [IL] *News-Democrat* on February 14, 2017 (top). The cartoon mirrored Norman Rockwell's 1964 painting of Ruby Bridges, *The Problem We All Live With* (bottom).

GLENN MCCOY © 2017 *Belleville News-Democrat*. Dist. by ANDREWS MCMEEL SYNDICATION. Reprinted with permission. All rights reserved.

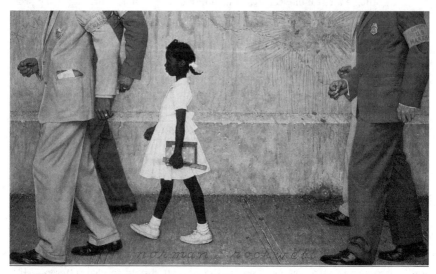

Artwork courtesy of the Norman Rockwell Family Agency.

dle School Academy in Washington, DC, a traditional public school. Parents and community protesters barred the doors and would not allow her and her staff entry due to their opposition to her stances on public education. While she was able to gain entry to the school later that day, many spoke critically about the incident on social media, insisting that the protesters were wrong for blocking her way. An Illinois political cartoonist, however, framed the critique over Secretary DeVos's treatment in a controversial image that compared her to Ruby Bridges, a 6-year-old Black girl attending a desegregated public school in New Orleans, protected by federal agents after being met with violent mobs protesting her access (Figure 14.1). Where Ruby Bridges walks in front of a wall with an ugly racist slur scrawled on it, Secretary DeVos is shown with the word "conservative" scribed on the wall, seemingly by the National Education Association, as if conservative were comparable to a racial slur aimed at a child. This image, in deriving a false equivalency between the violation of a child's constitutional right to attend public school and Secretary DeVos, makes a vivid assertion that DeVos, a school choice champion, is having her constitutional rights violated by parents and community members opposed to her desire to privatize public schools through vouchers and other mechanisms of choice. It has been shown that despite hopes that charter schools would help to diversify otherwise segregated public schools and allow parents freedom, they are as segregated as, and in some instances more segregated than, the school districts students attending them have left behind.

LOOKING FORWARD: PROSPECTS FOR CHARTER SCHOOLS TO CONTRIBUTE TO QUALITY, INTEGRATED SCHOOLING

In many urban school districts, school choice is the dominant policy, and charter schools are the primary example of school choice options. For example, in New Orleans, 92% of students enrolled in public schools attend charter schools (National Alliance for Public Charter Schools, 2016). This transformation of New Orleans public schooling also radically altered the demographics of the teaching force, with most Black teachers fired after the devastation of Hurricane Katrina in 2005 (Dixson, Buras, & Jeffers, 2015). In New Orleans, as well as in other regions where charter schools have proliferated, patterns of selectivity and discrimination against students with disabilities have also emerged (Welner, 2013).

Charter schools now account for 30% or more of public school students in 17 U.S. school districts (National Alliance for Public Charter Schools, 2016). Many of these schools are managed by charter school management organizations and tend to be racially homogenous. Because they are popular with the parents who are able to enroll and keep their children there, advocates argue that they should be allowed to grow to serve even more children (Barrone & Lombardo, 2016). Parents of color are often supportive of school choice policies such as charter schools, given their dissatisfaction with traditional public schools, particularly in an era of fiscal austerity for many urban school districts (Villavicencio, 2013), but their participation in charter school reform under the Obama administration operated under a revitalized federal civil rights policy framework. Absent such oversight, it remains to be seen how charter schools will operate in relation to desegregation or diversity.

Another related issue that researchers have examined is that charter schools are not only deepening racial and linguistic segregation, they are also increasingly notable for financial malfeasance. Some estimates give evidence of $200 million in charter school fraud in 15 states (Green, Baker, Oluwole, & Mead, 2016). These costs are absorbed by school districts, further challenging their ability to serve their students well. When considered against the evidence that some charter schools' admissions, expulsion, and discipline policies result in high numbers of students unable to access the promise of charter schools, or unable to stay there once accepted, this financial issue becomes even more important to examine (Jabbar, 2015; Jennings, 2010; Vasquez Heilig, Williams, McNeil, & Lee, 2011). Parents navigate these dynamics in ways that can advantage some children over others within the same community (Pattillo, 2015; Pattillo, Delale-O'Connor, & Butts, 2014). Those children left behind are often in districts under threat of state receivership (Holme, Finnigan, & Diem, 2016). In addition, efforts for school district secession are growing, with majority White and middle-class portions of school districts electing to partition themselves off from Black and Latinx neighborhoods and create new school districts (Sibilia, 2017).

As a result of these and other dynamics, the expansion of charter schools has often resulted in a destabilization of traditional public schools in districts that cannot afford to keep schools open amidst declining enrollment (Pappas, 2012). School closures have disproportionately affected Black and Latinx students and their families in districts such as Chicago, New York, and Philadelphia, often resulting in protests and a division of communities of color over the issue of charter schools (Lipman, 2002; Otterman, 2011; Persson, 2015).

The future patterns of neo-Plessyism in the context of charter schools need not be foreordained by these current dynamics, however, especially in view of the robust research literature on the long-term positive effects of school desegregation for all students. This literature also highlights pitfalls of desegregation efforts when they are focused only on numbers or percentages of different racial/ethnic groups in schools and not also on the equitable conditions of learning in ways that support and sustain all students (Walker, 2009).

Increasingly, charter schools are being founded with a goal of creating and sustaining racially, socioeconomically, and linguistically diverse student populations (Kahlenberg & Potter, 2012; Beabout, Nelson, & Rivera, 2017). Lessons from these "diverse by design" charter schools can help to provide best practices for the sector, particularly from those charter schools and charter school networks willing to share their approach to equitable access and sustained diversity over time. Leaders interested in creating and sustaining diverse charter schools would be remiss if they did not avail themselves of the lessons from researchers about the pedagogies and policy components that contribute to equitable schooling within diverse school settings, which include affirmative efforts to recruit and retain teachers of color and to honor the social, cultural, and linguistic strengths of all students.

While the federal climate might be hostile to these efforts, there is a role for state and local officials to provide incentives and support for diverse, truly integrated charter schools, much in the way that they have provided support for many successful inter- and intradistrict school choice plans (Wells, Warner, & Grzesikowski, 2013). The long-term evidence on desegregated schooling yoked with advancements in broader civil rights is strong and positive for all racial and ethnic groups (Braddock, Crain, & McPartland, 1984; Braddock & McPartland, 1988).

The evidence is clear, however, that expanding choice without a commitment to equity, desegregation, and diversity is almost certain to create more segregated and unequal schooling, just as it did during the nearly 60 years between *Plessy* and *Brown* (Mickelson, 2001). Yet in an era of limited federal oversight on matters of educational and social justice and civil rights, these patterns point to a renewed role for local and state governments and for the philanthropic sector to help realize the ideals of the ongoing movement for civil rights in an increasingly segregated and unequal country.

NOTES

1. The term "Latinx" provides for gender neutrality.
2. The author signed this letter.

REFERENCES

Abes, E. S., Abowitz, K. K., Albers, M., Alvermann, D., Anders, P., Aronson, B., . . . Kraft, M. A. (2017, January 30). *An open letter to the U.S. Senate HELP committee.* Retrieved from docs.google.com/document/u/1/d/1m7bkR-j1jxAxKW_aDfBWaw5YGCY-Hl-D-Sqe293Laas/pub

Aggerwaal, U. & Mayoraga, E. (2016). From forgotten to fought over: Neoliberal restructuring, public schools, and urban space. *The Scholar and Feminist Online, 13*(2).

Anderson, J. (1988). *The education of Blacks in the South, 1860–1935.* Chapel Hill, NC: University of North Carolina Press.

Barrone, C., & Lombardo, M. (2016). *A Democratic guide to public charter schools.* Washington, DC: Education Reform Now. Retrieved from edreformnow.org/wp-content/uploads/2016/10/A-Democratic-Guide-to-Public-Charter-Schools.final_.10.19.16.pdf

Beabout, B., Nelson, S., & Rivera, L. (2017). A demographic paradox: How public school students have become more racially integrated and isolated since Hurricane Katrina. *Education and Urban Society.* doi: 10.1177/0013124517714310

Blackwell, K. (2007). School choice and civil rights. *Townhall.* Retrieved from townhall.com/columnists/kenblackwell/2007/04/06/school-choice-and-civil-rights-n1083857

Braddock, J. H., II, Crain, R. L., & McPartland, J. M. (1984). A long-term view of school desegregation: Some recent studies of graduates as adults. *Phi Delta Kappan, 66*(4), 259–264.

Braddock, J. H., II, & McPartland, J. M. (1988). The social and academic consequences of school desegregation. *Equity and Choice, 4*(2), 5–10, 63–73.

Brown v. Board of Education of Topeka, 347 U.S. 483 (1954).

Chambers, J. (2002, October 22). Great Lives in the Law lecture, Duke University.

Chapman, T. (2005). Peddling backwards: Reflections of *Plessy and Brown* in the Rockford public schools de jure desegregation efforts. *Race Ethnicity and Education, 8*(1), 29–44. doi:10.1080/1361332052000340980

Clotfelter, C. T. (2004). *After Brown: The rise and retreat of school desegregation.* Princeton, NJ: Princeton University Press.

DeVos, B. (2017a, March 29). *U.S. Secretary of Education Betsy DeVos' prepared remarks to the Brookings Institution.* Retrieved from www.ed.gov/news/speeches/us-secretary-education-betsy-devos-prepared-remarks-brookings-institution

DeVos, B. (2017b, February 28). Statement from Secretary of Education Betsy DeVos following listening session with historically Black college and university leaders. Retrieved from www.ed.gov/news/press-releases/statement-secretary-education-betsy-devos-following-listening-session-historically-black-college-and-university-leaders

Dick and Betsy DeVos Family Foundation. (2015). *A year of charitable giving: 2015.* Grand Rapids, MI: Author.

Dixson, A., Buras, K., & Jeffers, E. (2015). The color of reform: Race, education reform, and charter schools in post-Katrina New Orleans. *Qualitative Inquiry, 21*(3), 288–299.

Donato, R. (1997). *The other struggle for equal schools: Mexican Americans during the civil rights era.* Albany, NY: State University of New York Press.

Fiel, J. E. (2013, October). Decomposing school resegregation: Social closure, racial imbalance, and racial isolation. *American Sociological Review, 78*(5), 828–848.

Forman, J. J. (2005). The secret history of school choice: How progressives got there first. *Georgetown Law Journal, 93,* 1287–1319.

Green, P., Baker, B., Oluwole, J., & Mead, J. (2016). Are we heading toward a charter school bubble? Lessons from the subprime mortgage crisis. *University of Richmond Law Review, 50,* 783. Retrieved from papers.ssrn.com/sol3/papers.cfm?abstract_id=2704305

Holme, J. J., Finnigan, K. S., & Diem, S. L. (2016). Challenging boundaries, changing fate? Metropolitan inequality and the legacy of Milliken. *Teachers College Record, 118*(3), 1–40.

Huseman, J., & Waldman, A. (2017). Trump Administration quietly rolls back civil rights efforts across federal government. *Mother Jones.* Retrieved from www.motherjones.com/politics/2017/06/trump-administration-quietly-rolls-back-civil-rights-efforts-across-federal-government

Jabbar, H. (2015). "Every kid is money": Market-like competition and school leader strategies in New Orleans. *Educational Evaluation and Policy Analysis, 37*(4), 638–659.doi: 10.3102/0162373715577447

Jennings, J. L. (2010). School choice or schools' choice? Managing in an era of accountability. *Sociology of Education, 83*(3), 227–247.

Kahlenberg, R. D., & Potter, H. (2012). *Diverse charter schools: Can racial and socioeconomic integration promote better outcomes for students?* Washington, DC: Poverty & Race Research Action Council and The Century Foundation.

Lassiter, M. D., & Davis, A. B. (1998). Massive resistance revisited: Virginia's White moderates and the Byrd Organization. In M. D. Lassiter & A. B. Davis (Eds.), *The moderates' dilemma: Massive resistance to school desegregation in Virginia* (pp. 1–21). Charlottesville, VA: University of Virginia Press.

Lipman, P. (2002). Making the global city, making inequality: The political economy and cultural politics of Chicago school policy. *American Educational Research Journal, 39,* 379–419.

Losen, D. J., Keith, M. A., II, Hodson, C. L., & Martinez, T. E. (2016, March). *Charter schools, civil rights, and school discipline: A comprehensive review.* Los Angeles, CA: The Civil Rights Project.

McArdle, N., Osypuk, T., & Acevedo-Garcia, D. (2010). Segregation and exposure to high-poverty schools in large metropolitan areas: 2008–9. *Poverty & Race, 19*(6), 6–8.

Mickelson, R. (2001). Subverting Swann: First- and second generation segregation in the Charlotte-Mecklenburg schools. *American Education Research Journal, 38*(2), 215–252.

Mitchell, C., & Harwin, A. (2017, January 17). 19 schools are named for the Obamas. Most of them are segregated. *Education Week.* Retrieved from www.edweek.org/ew/articles/2017/01/18/19-schools-are-named-for-the-obamas.html

Murphy, J. (2017, March 13). The Office for Civil Rights's volatile power. *The Atlantic.* Retrieved from www.theatlantic.com/education/archive/2017/03/the-office-for-civil-rights-volatile-power/519072

National Alliance for Public Charter Schools. (2016). *A growing movement: America's largest charter school communities.* Washington, DC: Author. Retrieved from www.public-charters.org/wp-content/uploads/2015/11/enrollmentshare_web.pdf

National Alliance for Public Charter Schools. (2017). *Estimated charter public school enrollment, 2016–2017.* Washington, DC: Author. Retrieved from www.publiccharters.org/wp-content/uploads/2017/01/EER_Report_V5.pdf

Orfield, G. (2001). *Schools more separate: Consequences of a decade of resegregation.* Cambridge, MA: Harvard Civil Rights Project.

Orfield, G., Frankenberg, E., Ee, J., & Kuscera, J. (2014). Brown *at 60: Great progress, a long retreat and an uncertain future.* Los Angeles, CA: Civil Rights Project.

Otterman, S. (2011, February 3). Protesting school closings, in a noisy annual ritual. *New York Times,* p. 18. Retrieved from www.nytimes.com/2011/02/04/nyregion/04panel.html

Pappas, L. (2012). School closings and parent engagement. *Peace and Conflict: Journal of Peace Psychology, 18*(2), 165–172.

Pattillo, M. (2015). Everyday politics of school choice in the Black community. *DuBois Review: Social Science Research on Race, 12*(1), 41–71.

Pattillo, M., Delale-O'Connor, L., & Butts, F. (2014). High stakes choosing: How parents navigate Chicago Public Schools. In A. Lareau & K. Goyette (Eds.), *Choosing homes, choosing schools* (pp. 237–267). New York, NY: Russell Sage Foundation.

Perlstein, D. (2004). *Justice, justice: School politics and the eclipse of liberalism.* New York, NY: Peter Lang.

Persson, J. (2015, September 22). *CMD publishes full list of 2,500 closed charter schools (with interactive map).* Madison, WI: Center for Media and Democracy. Retrieved from www.prwatch.org/news/2015/09/12936/cmd-publishes-full-list-2500-closed-charter-schools

Plessy v. Ferguson, 163 U.S. 537 (1896).

Reardon, S., & Owens, A. (2014). 60 years after *Brown*: Trends and consequences of school segregation. *Annual Review of Sociology, 40,* 199–218.

Roda, A. (2015). *Inequality in gifted and talented programs: Parental choices about status, school opportunities, and second-generation segregation.* New York, NY: Palgrave Macmillan.

Rothstein, R. (2017). *The color of law: A forgotten history of how our government segregated America.* New York, NY: Liveright.

Scott, J. (2009). The politics of venture philanthropy in charter school policy and advocacy. *Educational Policy, 23*(1), 106–136.

Scott, J. (2011). Market-driven education reform and the racial politics of advocacy. *Peabody Journal of Education, 86*(5), 580–599.

Scott, J., & Holme, J. J. (2016). The political economy of market-based educational policies: Race and reform in urban school districts, 1915 to 2016. *Review of Research in Education, 40*(1), 250–295.

Scott, J., & Wells, A. S. (2013). A more perfect union: Reconciling school choice policies with equality of opportunity goals. In K. Welner & P. Carter (Eds.), *The opportunity gap: What we must do to give every child a chance* (pp. 123–140). Oxford, UK: Oxford University Press.

Sharkey, P. (2013). *Stuck in place: Urban neighborhoods and the end of progress toward racial equality.* Chicago, IL: University of Chicago Press.

Sibilia, R. (2017). *Fractured: The breakdown of America's school districts.* Jersey City, NJ: EdBuild. Retrieved from edbuild.org/content/fractured/fractured-full-report.pdf

Spencer, K. (2015, May 18). Can you steal an education? Wealthy school districts are cracking down on "education thieves." *Hechinger Report.* Retrieved from hechingerreport. org/can-you-steal-an-education

Telles, E. M., & Ortiz, V. (2008). *Generations of exclusion: Mexican-Americans, assimilation, and race.* New York, NY: Russell Sage Foundation.

Tyack, D. (2001). *School: The story of American public education.* Boston, MA: Beacon.

U.S. Department of Education. (2016). *U.S. Education Secretary announces grant competitions to encourage diverse schools.* Retrieved from www.ed.gov/news/press-releases/ us-education-secretary-announces-grant-competitions-encourage-diverse-schools

Vasquez Heilig, J., Williams, A., McNeil, L. M., & Lee, C. (2011). Is choice a panacea? An analysis of Black secondary student attrition from KIPP, other private charters, and urban districts. *Berkeley Review of Education, 2*(2), 153–178.

Villavicencio, A. (2013). "It's our best choice right now": Exploring how charter school parents choose. *Education Policy Analysis Archives, 21*(81). Retrieved from epaa.asu.edu/ ojs/article/view/1274

Walker, V. S. (2009). Second-class integration: A historical perspective for a contemporary agenda. *Harvard Educational Review, 79*(2), 269–283.

Walker, V. S. (2013). Black educators as educational advocates in the decades before *Brown v. Board of Education. Educational Researcher, 42*(4), 207–222.

Wall, P. (2017, March 20). How Betsy DeVos could end the school-integration comeback. *The Atlantic.* Retrieved from www.theatlantic.com/education/archive/2017/03/how-betsy-devos-could-end-the-school-integration-comeback/520113

Wells, A. S., Holme, J. J., Revilla, A. T., & Atanda, A. K. (2009). *Both sides now: The story of school desegregation's graduates.* Berkeley, CA: University of California Press.

Wells, A. S., Warner, M., & Grzesikowski, C. (2013). The story of meaningful school choice: Lessons from interdistrict transfer plans. In G. Orfield & E. Frankenberg (Eds.), *Educational delusions? Why choice can deepen inequality and how to make schools fair* (pp. 187–218). Los Angeles, CA: University of California Press.

Welner, K. G. (2013, April). The dirty dozen: How charter schools influence student enrollment. *Teachers College Record* [online], ID Number 17104.

CHAPTER 15

Concluding Thoughts on Choice and Segregation

Iris C. Rotberg and Joshua L. Glazer

> The great achievement of liberal democracy is that it manages to *combine* the two distinct sets of core aims held by liberalism and democracy—the protections of personal freedoms and the maximisation of popular sovereignty—into a system which tries to avoid the worst excesses of each. . . . But the relative success of this achievement does not alter the fact that these are, at root, two contradictory sets of tendencies.
>
> —Jeremy Gilbert, "Liberalism Does Not Imply Democracy"

In the words and between the lines of this book lies a great American dilemma—choice versus the public good, liberalism versus democracy. The current debate over school choice has brought this dilemma to the forefront. Traditions of liberalism emphasize the right of individuals to make choices that they believe will enable personal advancement, whereas commitments to a democratic society favor policies that focus on advancing the public good.

Historian David Labaree (2010) has argued that nowhere is the internal contradiction between liberalism and democracy more visible than in the system of public schooling. He wrote: "In contrast to reformers, individual consumers of education have seen schools less as a way to pursue grand social designs than as a way to pursue intensely personal dreams of a good job and a good life" (p. 2). An amendment to Labaree's argument might be that nowhere is the tension between liberalism and democracy more visible than in controversies over the impact of charter schools on American education. The chapters of this book bring this point into sharp relief.

Charter schools unquestionably expand opportunities for personal choice, and to date approximately 3.1 million students have availed themselves of that choice. Given the wide variation in the quality of both charter and traditional public schools, we can expect some of the students who attend charter schools to have stronger, and others weaker, educational experiences than they otherwise would have had; for many, it will make little difference. But this analysis speaks only to the impact on individual families. It does not consider the social implications of the growth of charter schools. What do charter schools mean for Americans' ability to pursue a collective agenda and to live together in an increasingly diverse society? Several authors in this book argue, either directly or implicitly, that in tipping the scales in the direction of choice and the individual returns of education, charter schools have moved the country farther away from the collective and democratic goals of education.

Among the most important social costs of choice is increased segregation along racial and economic lines. The segregating effects of charter schools are particularly troublesome in light of the evidence that some of the schools establish policies that deliberately favor one population over another or are designed to appeal to one population while discouraging others, thereby seemingly contradicting their status as public institutions. Indeed, looking across the evidence, it is difficult to escape the conclusion that charter schools often exacerbate segregation in numerous and sometimes subtle ways. At the same time, charter schools have negative fiscal and social implications for the larger system of public education because they drain resources from traditional public schools and hamper efforts to integrate schools.

This analysis highlights the dilemma: Millions of children have enrolled in charter schools that offer some families educational experiences more aligned with their personal preferences, but the social costs of these schools are high. The dilemma is mirrored in the continuing controversies over charter schools, both in the communities that have high charter school enrollments and in the country more generally. Attempts have been made to mitigate the negative consequences, for example, by initiating regulated choice or regional integration plans. Although some of these efforts have strengthened school diversity, they are implemented infrequently. In this sense, the social costs of charter schools are largely a matter of our willingness to implement policies that seek a more equitable balance between individual choice and social good.

AN OVERVIEW OF THE MAIN THEMES OF THE BOOK

This section presents the main research findings of each of the book's chapters. No summary can do justice to the chapters' complexities and nuances. The chapters themselves give a much more comprehensive perspective on the impact of charter schools and the inevitable tradeoffs required in applying research findings to public policy decisions.

As policy analysts, our goal is to use research evidence to measure the effects of alternative public policies, and the field of school choice offers a large body of evidence from which to draw. To the extent possible, the conclusions in this book build on that evidence. However, these conclusions come with a caveat. As described above, there is a conflict between the freedom to choose and the social costs of increased segregation and inequality. Views of school choice are inevitably shaped by value judgments about the role of government and whether families' choices should be constrained by government policies. Research can show the consequences of alternative policy options, but the options ultimately chosen depend on value judgments about which goals are most important in a pluralistic society.

The conclusions drawn from the research findings are also influenced by underlying views about research methodology and education policy. For example, what criteria should be used to determine whether evidence is strong enough to inform policy? What constitutes a valid method for controlling for differences in student populations when comparing education programs? What outcome measures should be used to evaluate school quality? How much weight should be given to test score outcomes? To a broad-based educational experience? To considerations of equal access, diversity, and school climate? Our views and assumptions about these issues are inevitably reflected in the research topics we choose and the policy implications we draw from the findings.

This book demonstrates how charter school policies exacerbate segregation and how the increased segregation plays out in different situations and in different ways. Despite its segregating effects, school choice has expanded rapidly over the past 15 years. Both the Bush and Obama administrations strongly encouraged the expansion of charter schools. At the same time, an increasing number of states initiated voucher and tax benefit programs. The Trump administration is currently promoting vouchers and tax benefits, along with charter schools, and some states are considering increasing their own school choice options even before the administration's programs have been implemented.

Both families and schools make choices that contribute to segregation, which occurs in different ways in different contexts. In some districts, charter schools serve higher concentrations of minority students than traditional public schools; in others, they serve higher concentrations of white students or the charter schools themselves are divided by race, ethnicity, and income. Students with disabilities, especially severe disabilities, and English-language learners are often underrepresented in charter schools. The book's authors describe the large variation in charter schools and the contexts in which they operate. Some charter schools have little impact on segregation one way or the other. Others use their flexibility to draw students from across neighborhoods and take positive steps to increase access and diversity. However, without more policies that encourage charter schools to be diverse, the expansion of school choice will more typically exacerbate segregation.

Lotteries were intended to limit the participation of charter schools in the selection process but, as the chapter by Wagma Mommandi and Kevin Welner describes, many schools have strong incentives to make decisions that influence which students enroll and which remain in the school:

> Given that different students come with different financial costs, test scores, and behavior, they are differentially attractive as potential enrollees. To survive and to thrive,

charter schools must compete; they are successful when they enroll a sufficient number of students and when those students' outcomes allow the school to attract a new
group of students each year. Accordingly, success for a charter school depends on an
ongoing public perception as a successful school within a test-based accountability
system, and this reality creates strong incentives to attract and enroll students whose
behavior aligns with school philosophy, who have no expensive special needs, and who
have high test scores and fluency in English. (pp. 62–63)

A wide range of practices before, during, and after enrollment are used to
shape the student body; they include, for example, decisions about school location, marketing, curriculum, provision of special services, disciplinary practices,
"steering" families in the enrollment process, placing conditions on enrollment,
and "counseling out" students after enrollment. The chapter describes these practices as well as positive steps taken by some charter schools to increase access. The
authors conclude:

Because charter schools portray themselves as public schools, the barriers to access
that we discovered undermine fairness and wound our democracy. Because these
barriers distort enrollment, they also undermine attempts by researchers to compare
relative effectiveness of schools in the charter and noncharter sectors. And because
"creaming" practices depend on other schools to serve the students left behind, charter school reform cannot scale up if those schools are not broadly accessible. . . . As
research and policy both move forward, the future of charters—what role they play
within our democracy and our educational system—will crucially depend on levels of
actual access. (pp. 63, 77)

Charter schools also have an impact on districts' policies, as described by Roslyn Mickelson and her colleagues in their chapter on the Charlotte-Mecklenburg
Schools (CMS) in North Carolina. A combination of factors—reversion to neighborhood schools, greater diversity of the school-age population, and the availability of charter schools—have contributed to the resegregation of the district, which
had formerly been a national leader in desegregation. Drawing on results of their
case study, the authors write:

Charters and the district are becoming two parallel, unequal, and segregated sectors
of North Carolina public education. Increasingly, charters serve a bifurcated market,
with a smaller portion serving largely low-income black families and a larger portion
serving prosperous white families, some of whom are motivated, at least in part, by a
desire to avoid their racially and socioeconomically diverse traditional public schools.
(p. 127)

Moreover, the authors show that charter schools constrain the district's efforts
to create more diverse public schools:

The mere threat of charters luring students to enroll is an ever-present cloud hovering over the heads of Mecklenburg County's policy actors. This threat becomes part of the calculus of any reform strategy designed to reduce segregation in public schools and likely "puts the brakes" on considerations of bolder solutions. (p. 128)

The authors conclude: "Individual charters undoubtedly may offer equity and excellence to their students. Yet, given the sector's relationship to segregation, charter schools generally do not appear to advance racial or SES diversity in either traditional or charter schools" (p. 128).

The proliferation of charter schools and charter management organizations in high-poverty urban districts has led to another form of segregation as school districts and education programs that serve low-income and minority students have become quite different from those that serve the rest of the student population. Iris Rotberg's chapter describes how multiple competing school management systems in these districts have led to school finance constraints and inequities over and above those already existing. Moreover, competitive pressures have encouraged some charter schools to design instructional models specifically for students in high-poverty urban districts. The most controversial are the "no-excuses" models, which combine structured instructional methods and testing with highly prescriptive behavioral requirements and strict disciplinary practices. The large majority of students in no-excuses schools are low-income and minority; these schools are rarely found in more affluent communities. The chapter notes:

It is understandable given these inequities [between high-poverty and more affluent districts] that an alternative to traditional districts might seem attractive. However, the inequities . . . have not been mitigated by a transition to charter schools. Instead, the opposite has occurred. The transition has exacerbated those inequities. . . . In an attempt to reduce the achievement gap, it is important that we do not implement policies that risk further separating the educational experiences of students in high-poverty communities from those of their more affluent peers. (pp. 42, 54)

Drawing on a case study of Rocketship charter schools, Gordon Lafer's chapter describes the "blended learning" instructional model used by these schools, which, like the no-excuses model, is being promoted in high-poverty urban communities. Blended learning combines online learning with classroom instruction; it focuses on reading, math, and testing and reduces costs by replacing teachers with online learning for part of the school day and relying on younger, inexperienced, and, therefore, lower-cost teachers for classroom instruction. Lafer draws a distinction between the role of technology in the Rocketship model and its role in privileged schools:

Students in privileged schools often make extensive use of technology. But while these students are encouraged to be *active* users of technology—writing code, editing films, recording music, and designing graphics—Rocketship's students are *passive* users of technology, essentially plugged into video game–based applications designed to drill them for upcoming tests. (p. 88)

He concludes:

Decades of scholarly research aimed at defining what constitutes a "good school" point in part to the importance of small classes, experienced teachers, and broad curricula. But research aside, we can answer this question in a simple way: Look at where wealthy people send their own children. While these schools include technology, it is not used to substitute for teachers. . . . Some school districts might not be able to afford what wealthy children have, [but] we should not be confused by this into believing there are different definitions of good education for rich and poor children. (pp. 91, 92)

A recent development in the charter school sector is the establishment of school districts in which schools with low test scores are grouped into one district, irrespective of the geographical proximity of the schools. These high-poverty specially created districts raise questions with respect to the perpetuation of segregation, the boundaries between public and private, and the capacity of charter operators to run schools in an environment that severely limits their ability to shape the student body and to control their environment. The chapter by Joshua Glazer and his colleagues reports on the experience of charter operators in the Tennessee Achievement School District (ASD), which includes 20 of the lowest-scoring schools in the state. The authors illustrate the pressures that charter operators encountered when forced to educate all students—those with severe disabilities, those who do not speak English, those who enter midyear, those who have behavioral problems, and those who, for whatever reason, charter operators believe do not "fit" with the goals of the program. Charter operators found that their traditional strategies were ineffective and often incommensurate with the demands of an environment that departed from what they were accustomed to. The authors write:

We do not conclude from this that every school operator working in an ASD-like environment is destined to fail. In fact, we have encountered operators with sophisticated and thoughtful designs. We do contend, however, that re-creating charter-like flexibility inside state turnaround districts is more difficult than proponents might suppose, and that even charter organizations with a track record of success can be expected to encounter unfamiliar challenges that will require substantial adaptations. Those operators that do succeed will do so not because their status as charters provides advantages over traditional schools. They will do so because they have devised highly sophisticated school-level designs buttressed by extraordinary organizations capable of adapting to their complex institutional environments. (p. 112)

The challenges that extreme decentralization poses to charter operators working without a central office is further discussed in the chapter by Brenda Shum. The author describes the civil rights and other legal protections afforded students under a variety of federal statutes. These protections not only prohibit numerous forms of discrimination, but specify the complex obligations that all public schools, including charters, must comply with. The author notes: "These obligations apply to all aspects and operations of a charter school, including recruitment, admissions, academics, educational services and testing, school climate, discipline, athletics and nonacademic programs, and facilities and technology" (p. 153).

One point that emerges from Shum's account is that compliance with federal laws and regulations that protect students' rights is not just a matter of will, but in fact demands considerable organizational capacity and resources. Small charter operators who lack the requisite experience, and who cannot rely on a district office to perform these functions, are likely to struggle to meet the obligations and risk being noncompliant with the laws.

The chapter also shows how extreme decentralization at the city level can compromise oversight and enforcement of laws protecting students. Based on evidence from New Orleans, where post-Katrina reforms converted the vast majority of schools into independent charters, the author warns that in the absence of a centralized system, the rights and legal protections of the most vulnerable students are put at risk.

> In many respects, New Orleans serves as a cautionary tale of the dangers associated with enacting reforms rooted in market-based principles without considering their effect on legally protected rights. . . . Several of the legal violations . . . quickly surfaced once the RSD [Recovery School District] began to charter all of the schools within its jurisdiction without monitoring their capacity to comply with the law. (p. 159)

The chapter by Suzanne Eckes and her colleagues considers the constitutional issues that charter schools raise with respect to the separation of church and state.

> The advent of charter schools as a genuine public school alternative has generated new challenges related to the First Amendment and the church-school wall. Can charter schools choose to teach creationism in science courses or allow teachers to lead the students in prayer without running afoul of the First Amendment? Is it possible to locate a charter school in a current church facility? Can a religious denomination legally convert its schools into charter schools? Can an ethnocentric niche charter school, which claims to be focused on Hawaiian or Native American culture or on Hebrew or Arabic language, really claim to be secular? (p. 163)

The chapter gives examples of specific situations in which these church–state issues have been raised. It also describes issues of segregation that arise in the case of ethnocentric niche charter schools, which are designed to connect students with their culture and often attract homogeneous student populations.

Civil rights complaints and lawsuits have been brought on a number of the church–state issues described in the chapter. Although no U.S. Supreme Court cases to date involve the issue of separation of church and state in charter schools specifically, the findings of Supreme Court cases involving traditional public schools also apply to charter schools because laws related to the establishment of religion apply to all public schools.

Despite the fact that charter schools generally increase segregation, they may also have the potential to encourage integration. Ayscue and Frankenberg write in their chapter:

> Choice can support desegregation because it breaks the link between school and residential segregation, allowing students and families to choose schools outside of their neighborhoods and allowing schools to draw from a more diverse set of students than those typically residing in close proximity to one another. . . . In most cases, charter schools are not bound by school catchment zones, nor are they bound by district boundary lines. In 36 of the 43 states where charters currently exist, some charter schools do not have a required preference for in-district students. . . . Therefore, the potential for interdistrict or regional charter schools exists in these 36 states. However, there are only a very few examples . . . of intentionally creating regional charter schools. (pp. 177, 185)

The authors give examples of magnet and charter schools that have successfully created integrated environments but note that the charter school sector generally has not focused on desegregation, and charter schools more often are designed to serve specific population groups rather than integrate diverse ones. However, there is a potential for policy to build on the large body of available information about the impact of school choice on segregation "by examining research on a variety of forms of choice—those that have had some success in achieving desegregation, such as magnet schools and controlled choice, and those that have more often furthered segregation, such as freedom-of-choice plans, vouchers, and open enrollment" (p. 187).

The chapter by Adam Gamoran and Cristina M. Fernandez returns to the question of the benefits that charter schools offer individual students by exploring whether charter schools have been effective in raising student achievement (generally measured by test scores) in high-poverty urban districts. They find that although studies of charter schools nationwide show as many negative effects as positive ones, the effects of some charter schools in high-poverty urban districts are more consistently positive and, in some cases, substantively meaningful. The authors attribute that advantage to a "combination of the weaknesses of traditional public schools in these areas and the ability of urban charters to adopt long-recognized elements of effective schools" (p. 144). They conclude:

> At a minimum, findings about the achievement effects of urban charter schools present a challenge to advocates for traditional public schools. . . . Charter schools remain a highly contentious policy, and many states and districts have elected to restrain their

expansion to avoid the collateral consequences for segregation and public sector funding. These steps, however, must be paired with the development of effective schools
in the traditional public sector if they are to meet the challenge . . . to provide equal
educational opportunities to urban disadvantaged students. (p. 148)

The chapters by Jeffrey Henig and by James Harvey consider charter schools
in a broader political and social context. As the chapter by Henig describes, the
rapid development of charter schools was, at least in part, encouraged by critiques
of the public education system. Their growth coincided with other developments
that similarly showed a loss of faith in public education: an expanded federal role
in school choice and testing policies, increased high-stakes accountability requirements, more private-sector involvement in education, and increased numbers of
education leadership positions held by people outside the field of education. Henig
notes that charter schools expanded rapidly, in part because they were aligned
with the broader reform movement.

The political constituencies backing the charter and overall education reform movements . . . substantially overlapped. They included free market advocates, private education service providers, foundations, so-called New Democrats, some civil rights
organizations, elements of the business community, many charter school families, and
deep-pocketed individual donors. (p. 19)

He points out, however, the tenuous nature of a coalition comprising diverse
groups with widely differing agendas and viewpoints:

While this movement could hold together when framed in opposition to a resistant
status quo, its constituent groups held quite different visions of the alternative they
favored—different in the commitment to funding, to democratically controlled institutions, and to emphasizing public versus private aspects of education. . . . Deciphering
what this might mean for the future of charters is made especially difficult by the unusual degree of uncertainty that currently marks the political landscape. (p. 19)

The contextual issues discussed by Harvey begin with relative poverty rates
in the United States, which are among the highest in the industrialized world. He
begins his chapter by asking:

Is it possible that the conditions of poverty under which some children live so diminish
their life prospects that schools face major obstacles in responding to their educational
needs? . . . Do [charter schools], as charter advocates claim, represent a viable response
to the needs of students? Or, as critics contend, are charters a bromide, one that leaves
unattended the underlying issues interfering with students' academic growth? (p. 24)

The effects of high poverty rates are compounded by high levels of segregation
and extreme concentrations of poverty in some school systems. More than 50% of
the students in U.S. public schools are eligible for free and reduced-priced meals,

with much higher rates in urban schools in some states. A wide array of research conducted over many years shows the strong relationship between poverty and achievement. Harvey cites an analysis by the Organization for Economic Co-operation and Development (OECD):

> On average among OECD nations, the combined socioeconomic status of families and schools accounts for about 60% of the variation in tested achievement. In Finland, the combined measure accounts for some 30% of variation in tested achievement, while in the United States it accounts for about 80% (OECD, 2009). In short, socioeconomic status is the majority factor explaining student achievement in all countries; in the United States, it is an overwhelming factor (Harvey, 2014, pp. 37–38). (p. 25)

He continues:

> The conditions in which many children in the United States live are a moral rebuke to the nation. . . . The problem is not one of "fixing" schools by creating novel administrative arrangements for them; it is one of addressing poverty and disinvestment in the neighborhoods in which these schools are located. (p. 30)

The chapters by Henry Levin and by Janelle Scott consider the role of charter schools in a pluralistic society. Levin focuses on the public and private purposes of education. He describes the problem this way:

> Public education stands at the intersection of two legitimate rights (Levin, 1987). The first is the right of a democratic society to assure its reproduction and continuous democratic functioning through preparation of all of its members to understand and accept a common set of values and knowledge required for societal equity and cohesion. The second involves the rights of families to decide the manner in which their children will be guided and molded and the types of influences to which their children will be exposed. To the degree that families have different personal, political, social, philosophical, and religious beliefs and values, a basic incompatibility might exist between their private concerns and the public functions of schooling. (p. 196)

Levin argues that the autonomy afforded to charter schools has shifted the public–private balance in two ways. First, while charter schools may adopt educational approaches that reflect the personal values of the families they serve, in doing so they are less likely to prepare students to participate in a common set of societal institutions. Second, charter schools have led to increased stratification of the student population and, therefore, to less exposure to diverse school environments. In both cases, the potential for a shared democratic experience is weakened. "The risk," Levin notes, "is that if charter schools are designed to affirm the specific beliefs of the families they serve, their educational programs are unlikely to reflect the diverse views of a pluralistic society" (p. 199). He suggests, however, that under certain circumstances it might be possible to strengthen that experience in charter schools, but notes that "no simple solution can resolve this conflict" (p. 201).

Scott's chapter analyzes the popular assertion that "education is the last remaining civil right to be secured and that charter schools and school choice policies are the most powerful manifestation of that right." Her analysis is presented in the context of the Trump administration's policies to expand school choice. She writes:

> The claims that educational policies are generating empowerment for otherwise powerless parents are being articulated against a contemporary and historical backdrop of racial segregation and income inequality, where the state has been a regulator and enforcer of efforts to make schools more equitable and has also been complicit in maintaining inequality through a range of policy levers that have kept many urban, suburban, and rural schools segregated and under-resourced. (p. 208)

Scott goes on to note that many education policies accept existing segregation and assume we can make schools more equitable with an approach that she terms "neo-Plessyism."

> In the last two decades, through the advocacy for and the adoption of market-oriented school choice policies, advocates from multiple ideological standpoints have come to embrace a form of neo-Plessyism, harkening to the logic that held that racial segregation was permissible, provided the separate spaces were equal. (p. 209)

Not surprisingly, these policies have exacerbated segregation. She notes:

> Researchers have found that without regulations or incentives, a negative relationship exists between school choice policies and racial diversity, and that school choice policies tend to further sort and segregate students by race, socioeconomic status, language, and academic performance unless these policies provide clear frameworks, regulations, and incentives for ensuring that they produce diverse and equitable schooling (Scott & Wells, 2013). (p. 208)

Scott concludes, however, that "future patterns of neo-Plessyism in the context of charter schools need not be foreordained":

> While the federal climate might be hostile to these efforts, there is a role for state and local officials to provide incentives and support for diverse, truly integrated charter schools, much in the way that they have provided support for many successful inter- and intradistrict school choice plans. . . . The long-term evidence on desegregated schooling yoked with advancements in broader civil rights is strong and positive for all racial and ethnic groups. . . . The evidence is clear, however, that expanding choice without a commitment to equity, desegregation, and diversity is almost certain to create more segregated and unequal schooling, just as it did in the nearly 60 years between *Plessy* and *Brown* (Mickelson, 2001). (p. 217)

SUMMING UP

The authors of this book describe the various ways that segregation plays out and draw implications for a pluralistic society. They also show the compounding effects of the multiple forms of segregation. Students are often in schools that are separated by race, ethnicity, income, disability, language, culture, or religion—or a combination of these variables. In some schools, students are not afforded the civil rights and other legal protections required under federal laws. Large numbers of students attend schools in districts where the competition among multiple charter and traditional schools has led to resource constraints and inequalities over and above those already existing in the districts. These resource constraints are compounded by the fact that charter schools have more leverage than traditional public schools in determining which students enroll and which are permitted to remain in the school. Education in traditional schools is weakened as the schools become responsible for educating higher proportions of students with the greatest needs at the same time financial resources are declining.

Some charter school students in high-poverty urban districts attend schools that use behavioral practices or instructional techniques very different from those used in districts that serve the rest of the student population. Or they attend schools in diverse districts where charter schools serve as a disincentive to implementing desegregation plans because of a concern that students might then leave the traditional schools for less integrated charter schools. In some districts, transfers to charter schools have become the current iteration of transfers to private schools, but with an important difference—charter schools are a tuition-free option.

In an education system as complex and varied as the U.S. system, there are exceptions. Some charter schools are more diverse than traditional schools in their districts or offer educational opportunities and services comparable to those offered in more affluent districts. Currently, these charter schools are the exception, but they do not need to continue to be. We know enough to devise policies that mitigate the most troublesome social costs of charter schools. The question is whether we have the political will.

REFERENCES

Gilbert, J. (2009, September 26). Liberalism does not imply democracy. *Open Democracy UK*. Retrieved from www.opendemocracy.net/blog/ourkingdom/jeremy-gilbert/2009/09/26/liberalism-does-not-imply-democracy

Labaree, D. F. (2010). *Someone has to fail: The zero-sum game of public schooling*. Cambridge, MA: Harvard University Press.

About the Editors and Contributors

Iris C. Rotberg is a research professor of education policy at the Graduate School of Education and Human Development at The George Washington University, Washington, DC. After beginning her career as a research psychologist, she entered the field of public policy research, holding positions at the National Science Foundation, RAND, the National Institute of Education, and the U.S. House of Representatives Committee on Science, Space, and Technology. Her publications address issues of school reform, school choice, testing and accountability, international education, science education, welfare reform, and federal policy in financing education. She has conducted research for the U.S. Congress on policy options for improving the education of low-income students, technology and human resources, and the outcomes of federal education policy. Her articles and commentaries appear in a range of professional journals and other publications, and she is the editor of *Balancing Change and Tradition in Global Education Reform*, published by Rowman & Littlefield Education (2004, 2010). Dr. Rotberg received her PhD from The Johns Hopkins University and her MA and BA from the University of Pennsylvania.

Joshua L. Glazer is an associate professor of education policy at The George Washington University, Washington, DC. His research and teaching examine multiple approaches to improving underperforming schools in high-poverty, urban environments. He is currently directing two multiyear studies into school turnaround. The first examines the Tennessee Achievement School District, in which the state removes underperforming schools from local control and authorizes charter schools to develop and implement designs for improvement. The second study investigates the efforts of Shelby County Schools, which includes Memphis, to devise and direct its own initiative to improve low-performing schools using district resources. In addition, Dr. Glazer is principal investigator for a study of research-practice partnerships in Baltimore and New York City. Prior to coming to The George Washington University, he was the program director for education at the Rothschild Foundation in Jerusalem, Israel. He received his PhD from the University of Michigan and his BA from Brandeis University.

Jennifer B. Ayscue is a research associate at The Civil Rights Project/Proyecto Derechos Civiles at the University of California, Los Angeles. Her research interests focus on desegregation in K–12 schools and the role of policy in shaping students' access to diverse and equitable educational opportunities. She earned a PhD from UCLA, an MA from Stanford University, and a BA from the University of North Carolina at Chapel Hill.

Martha Cecilia Bottia is a research assistant professor of sociology at the University of North Carolina at Charlotte. Her research interests include the effects of school racial and socioeconomic demographic composition on various educational outcomes, the unequal impact of the curriculum on diverse students, and the role of structural characteristics of K–12 schools on the decision of college students to major in and graduate with a STEM degree.

Nina K. Buchanan, professor emerita of the University of Hawaii, is a founder of the first public chartered high school in Hawaii. As an educational psychologist, she has conducted research on school choice, project-based learning, and gifted and talented education. Her research and writing is founded on 40 years of teaching in preschool through graduate classrooms in diverse settings ranging from a one-room schoolhouse on the Montana prairie to traditional elementary and secondary schools and universities in Indiana, California, and Hawaii.

Suzanne Eckes is a professor in the Educational Leadership and Policy Studies Department at Indiana University. Dr. Eckes has published over 150 education law–related articles and book chapters. Much of her research focuses on civil rights laws and equity issues in public schools. Prior to joining the faculty at Indiana University, Dr. Eckes was a public high school French teacher and an attorney at a national law firm.

Cristina M. Fernandez is a research assistant at the William T. Grant Foundation. Her interests include international development, ways to address the marginalization of immigrants in the United States and Europe, and educational equity in classrooms and schools. She received her BA in political science from Queens College, City University of New York, and her MA in international affairs, with a concentration in comparative and regional studies, from American University.

Robert A. Fox, professor emeritus at the University of Hawaii, conducts research on the politics and policy of school choice from an international perspective and has published extensively in major educational journals. His recent book, *Proud to be Different: Ethnocentric Niche Charter Schools in America*, was published in 2014 by Rowman & Littlefield, and the *Handbook of School Choice* was published by Wiley-Blackwell in 2017. Both books were coedited with Dr. Nina K. Buchanan.

Erica Frankenberg is an associate professor of education and demography and co-director of the Center for Education and Civil Rights at the Pennsylvania State University. Her research interests focus on racial desegregation and inequality in

K–12 schools, school choice and racial stratification, and the connections between school segregation and other metropolitan policies. She has published five books, including *Educational Delusions? Why Choice Can Deepen Inequality and How to Make It Fair* (from University of California Press, with Gary Orfield), and more than 50 articles in a range of professional journals. She received her doctorate from Harvard University and her bachelor's degree from Dartmouth College.

Adam Gamoran is president of the William T. Grant Foundation, a charitable organization that supports research to improve the lives of young people. Formerly he held the John D. MacArthur Chair in sociology and educational policy studies at the University of Wisconsin–Madison. His research focused on educational inequality and school reform. At the foundation, he leads efforts to support research on reducing inequality in youth outcomes and on improving the use of research evidence in policies and practices that affect young people.

Jason Giersch is an assistant professor in political science and public administration at the University of North Carolina at Charlotte. His research addresses issues of school segregation, school choice, and school accountability. A former social studies teacher in Charlotte-Mecklenburg Schools, Dr. Giersch has children attending one of the district's most racially balanced elementary schools.

James Harvey has served as director of the National Superintendents Roundtable for 10 years. He is the author or coauthor of five books and dozens of articles on education, including *The Superintendent's Fieldbook* (Corwin, 2014) and *A Legacy of Learning* (Brookings, 2000). A former staff member of the Committee on Education and Labor in the U.S. House of Representatives and legislative liaison on education for the Carter White House, he helped write *A Nation at Risk* for the National Commission on Excellence in Education (1983).

Jeffrey R. Henig is professor of political science and education at Teachers College and professor of political science at Columbia University. He is a fellow of the American Educational Research Association and a member of the National Academy of Education. Dr. Henig is the author, coauthor, or coeditor of 11 books— including the award-winning *The Color of School Reform: Race, Politics and the Challenge of Urban Education*; *Building Civic Capacity: The Politics of Reforming Urban Schools*; and *Spin Cycle: How Research Gets Used in Policy Debates—The Case of Charter Schools*. His most recent book, coedited with Frederick Hess, is *The New Education Philanthropy: Politics, Policy, and Reform* (2015). In addition to his scholarly publications, Dr. Henig's writing on contemporary policy issues has appeared in newspapers and education policy blogs.

Gordon Lafer is a professor at the University of Oregon's Labor Education and Research Center and a research associate with the Economic Policy Institute in Washington, DC. In 2009–2010 he served as senior policy advisor for the U.S.

House of Representatives' Committee on Education and Labor. Dr. Lafer's most recent book is *The One Percent Solution: How Corporations Are Remaking America, One State at a Time* (Cornell University Press, 2017).

Henry M. Levin is the William Heard Kilpatrick Professor of Economics and Education at Teachers College, Columbia University, and the David Jacks Professor of Education and Economics, Emeritus, at Stanford University. He is a specialist in the economics of education and educational policy. He has published 22 books and about 300 articles in scholarly journals.

Matthew Malone is a doctoral student in educational administration and policy studies at The George Washington University. His research focuses on charter schools operating in turnaround environments. He has experience as a teacher and instructional coach in Philadelphia and Washington, DC, and is currently a school leadership coach. He earned his MEd from Arcadia University and a BA from the University of Pennsylvania.

Diane Massell's research career has focused on approaches to developing effective schooling opportunities for high-poverty, underachieving students. She has conducted over a dozen major investigations into the design and impact of strategies to leverage school improvement and turnaround by districts and states as well as nongovernmental organizations. In 2013, Dr. Massell started Massell Education Consulting, LLC, based in Ann Arbor, Michigan. She earned her master's and PhD degrees from Stanford University's School of Education and a bachelor's degree in political science from Kenyon College in Ohio.

Roslyn Arlin Mickelson is Chancellor's Professor and professor of sociology, public policy, and women and gender studies at the University of North Carolina at Charlotte. A former California high school teacher, she received her PhD from the University of California, Los Angeles. Her coedited book, *Yesterday, Today, and Tomorrow: School Desegregation and Resegregation in Charlotte*, was published by Harvard Education Press in February 2015. Dr. Mickelson's children graduated from Charlotte-Mecklenburg Schools.

Wagma Mommandi is a doctoral candidate at the School of Education, University of Colorado Boulder. She holds a bachelor's degree in biology from Colorado College and an MEd in curriculum and instruction from American University. She is interested in the impacts of market-based education reform on teachers and teacher education, urban school districts, and communities of color. Prior to graduate school, she taught high school in the District of Columbia Public Schools.

Amy Hawn Nelson is the director of training and technical assistance at the School of Social Policy and Practice, University of Pennsylvania. She was formerly the director of the Institute for Social Capital, Inc., at the University of

North Carolina at Charlotte. A community-engaged researcher largely focused on education and housing-related issues, she is a coeditor of *Yesterday, Today, and Tomorrow: School Desegregation and Resegregation in Charlotte* (Harvard Education Press, 2015). Prior to joining the University of North Carolina, she served as a teacher and school leader for 11 years. She is a Charlotte native and graduate of Charlotte-Mecklenburg Schools.

Janelle Scott is a Chancellor's Associate Professor in the Graduate School of Education, African American Studies Department, and Goldman School of Public Policy at the University of California at Berkeley. Her research explores the relationships among education, policy, and equality of opportunity, with a focus on the racial politics of public education, the politics of school choice, marketization, and privatization, and the role of elite and community-based advocacy in shaping public education policies and research evidence utilization. She was a Spencer Foundation Dissertation Year Fellow and a National Academy of Education/Spencer Foundation Postdoctoral Fellow and is the editor of *School Choice and Diversity: What the Evidence Says* (2005, Teachers College Press).

Brenda Shum is the director of the Educational Opportunities Project at the Lawyers' Committee for Civil Rights Under Law where she oversees litigation, public policy initiatives, and programs designed to ensure that all students have equal access to quality educational opportunities in K–12 schools and institutions of higher learning. Her practice focuses on a variety of issues related to education equity including discrimination and segregation, the rights of students with disabilities and English-language learners, and ending the school-to-prison pipeline. She also oversees the Parental Readiness and Empowerment Program, which promotes parental involvement in education as a means to narrow the achievement gap.

Kevin Welner is a professor at the University of Colorado Boulder School of Education and director of the National Education Policy Center. He has authored or edited 12 books and written more than 100 articles and book chapters. His recent books include *Education and the Law* (coauthored with Stuart Biegel and Bob Kim, 2016) and *Closing the Opportunity Gap* (coedited with Prudence Carter, 2013). Dr. Welner's present research examines the use and misuse of research in policymaking and explores various issues concerning the intersection between education rights litigation and educational opportunity scholarship. Dr. Welner has JD and PhD degrees from the University of California, Los Angeles.

Index